OUR HOPE

Fr. DMITRII DUDKO

OUR HOPE

Translated by
PAUL D. GARRETT

Foreword by
JOHN MEYENDORFF

ST. VLADIMIR'S SEMINARY PRESS
CRESTWOOD, NEW YORK 10707
1977

First published under the title
O NASHEM UPOVANII
by YMCA-Press, Paris, 1975

Library of Congress Cataloging in Publication Data:

Dudko, Dmitrii.
Our hope.

Translation of O nashem upovanii.
1. Orthodox Eastern Church, Russian—Dostrinal and
controversial works—Miscellanea.   2.   Theology—Miscellanea.   I.   Title.
BX512.D8213   230'.1'9   77-11051
ISBN 0-913836-35-4

ISBN 0-913836-35-4

© 1975 YMCA-Press
Trans. © 1977 St. Vladimir's Seminary Press

PRINTED IN THE UNITED STATES OF AMERICA
BY
ATHENS PRINTING COMPANY

Contents

Foreword

"Woe to me," wrote St. Paul, "if I do not preach the Gospel (1 Cor. 9:16). The task of any priest is to recognize that he is always placed in the same position as the Apostle and that the same curse hangs over him if he does not preach. However it is relatively easy to fulfill that obligation formally: just to give a sermon at the Sunday Liturgy and to believe—even if that sermon was an irrelevant improvisation which did not reach anyone in the audience—that one's duty has been fulfilled. Preaching is an act of witness, which can and must be carried on not only in words but through one's actions, through one's love for neighbors, through one's ability to be in real communion with those who listen.

In contemporary Russia, the whole issue of the Christian witness through preaching is so central that the very survival of the Church depends on it. State law prohibits schools, publications, discussion groups, social service by Christians and any other forms of Church activity except liturgical worship and the preaching which is part of it. This prohibition, formally codified by the law of 1929 and recently re-enacted in the framework of a more centralized system of State control over the Church (Decree of July 3, 1975), results in a situation in which the vast majority of Soviet people are deprived of the most elementary means of receiving basic information about religion. The results of this situation can be clearly seen in the questions asked in the course of Fr. Dudko's "discussions."

According to the law, the Church is restricted to cultic worship inside the walls of the church building. But the State—officially inspired by the ideology of the Communist Party—employs additional measures to limit the impact of religion upon the people: State presses publish millions of copies of antireligious publications; State authorities exercise constant pressure upon the believers to make them abandon the faith;

State officials assume the right to control appointments to parishes (by granting or refusing the "registration" necessary for employment as a priest) and the election of church committee officers, and to grant (or refuse) permission to open new religious communities. The Patriarch and the bishops have no legal power over the management of parishes, and they themselves are under constant pressure to exercise what moral authority they may still have in a direction favorable to the government's interests. Under such conditions, the survival of the Orthodox Church in Russia and the recent revival of interest in the Church on the part of more and more young people is truly a miracle of the grace of God.

In the past years, an abundance of information has reached the West concerning the legal status of religion in the USSR and concerning various dramatic events, such as the closing of churches, protests by believers and persecution of dissidents. Fr. Dudko's *Our Hope,* however, is unique. For the first time a document on the daily activities of a parish priest—Church life in its very nucleus—has become available. What is most remarkable is that its content is not simply an image of the "Russian situation," but the sort of Christian witness which applies to our own life in a free Western society as well.

Fr. Dmitrii Dudko is a man in his middle fifties, married and the father of three young children. He presently lives in a "communal" apartment in Moscow, from which he commutes to his parish in Grevnevo, in the capital's suburbs. A veteran of World War II, he was accepted in the re-established Theological School of the Trinity-St. Sergius Monastery in Zagorsk. However, in 1948, when he was a first-year student at the Academy (Graduate School), he was arrested and sent to a labor camp in Siberia, where he spent eight and a half years. Reminiscences of his stay in the "Gulag Archipelago" appear occasionally in his sermons.

In 1956 Dudko benefited from the partial dismantlement of the labor camps system during the "thaw" which followed Stalin's death. He was rehabilitated and allowed to finish his theological education at Zagorsk. He then married, was ordained a priest in 1960, and, eventually, was assigned as an assistant pastor to St. Nicholas parish in Moscow.

Until 1972, not much seemed to distinguish him from the many other Orthodox priests serving and preaching in Moscow parishes. Anyone familiar with Church life in the Soviet capital—the situation in the provinces is much more difficult to ascertain—knows that one, or frequently two sermons are given at every service. Sometimes preaching is of high quality and very well adapted to the audience. Antireligious writers often complain of the effectiveness of Christian preaching. But it is also a fact that many priests limit themselves to standard "eternal" subjects without direct connection with everyday life: they play it "safe" with the government representatives, who are always listening and watching. Fr. Dmitrii's preaching was different. Already in 1972 there was an attempt by the authorities to have him fired by his church council. (Legally, the priest is considered only as an employee of the parish.) The attempt failed because of public uproar, which was also supported from abroad, where the quality of Fr. Dudko's preaching was already known.

Late in 1973 Fr. Dmitrii deliberately decided to give to his sermons, preached every Saturday night, the character of a dialogue with the faithful. He suggested that questions be submitted to him in writing, so that answers might be given in the following sermon. Soon, however, he also began to answer direct questions presented by members of the congregation. Inevitably the questions touched upon antireligious propaganda, upon repression of religion, upon government control of the Church. Fr. Dudko did not ask for such provocative questions, but he did not avoid them either. He mainly insisted upon basic religious truths, upon Orthodoxy as the living content of life, upon the hopelessness of atheism. At times critical of bishops and priests who follow the easy path of submission to government pressure, he also took to the Patriarch's defense against those who criticized him for passivity.

The character and content of the sermons was so unusual that the small church of St. Nicholas was soon full beyond capacity on Saturday night. Young people, intellectuals, believers and non-believers—and also foreign journalists—flocked to hear Fr. Dmitrii. The sermons published here are what they heard. The text of the sermons was soon reproduced through notes scribbled on the spot and circulated in "samizdat" (type-written literature distributed clandestinely).

Fr. Dudko was clearly making every effort not to transgress Soviet law, which forbids religious "discussions." He limited his dialogues to the church building, except for discussions 10 and 11, which were delivered at a private home after the measures taken to prevent Fr. Dudko from preaching in Church had succeeded. But clearly he was doing exactly what the authorities are most afraid of. He was making the Church a living center for thought and discussion on contemporary issues.

On May 15, 1974, Fr. Dudko was transferred for service beyond the limits of the city of Moscow by the Patriarch. On May 20, because he refused to comply with what was presented as "ecclesiastical discipline," he was suspended. However the immediate support received from innumerable faithful and also from public opinion abroad saved him from banishment and oblivion. In a letter to his superior, Metropolitan Seraphim of Krutitsa, Fr. Dmitrii also recognized that "he made a mistake and involuntarily transgressed Church discipline." In the summer of 1974, he accepted an assignment to the parish of St. Nikita the Martyr, in Kabanovo, 50 miles away from Moscow. After serving and preaching there (many Moscovites made the trip to listen to him), he was again—"by order from Moscow"—fired by his parish council on December 21, 1975. This time, however, the ecclesiastical authorities of the Patriarchate abstained from any measure against Fr. Dudko. By Easter 1976, he was appointed pastor of the parish in Grevnevo, 20 miles away from Moscow. Always on the very brink of what is "possible" and "permissible," using every opportunity offered to him, Fr. Dmitrii, through his courage, honesty and humility has won a substantial moral victory for the Gospel of Christ and for the Orthodox Church in Russia.

More than any other document coming to us from Russia, Fr. Dudko's sermons represent the religious life of the rank and file of Russian believers. They reflect what simple, direct Christian preaching does for the souls of ordinary, mostly unsophisticated people of various social and professional backgrounds. Here we have no profound theological investigations. Especially in the first few discussions, Fr. Dudko often simply reads long passages from elementary theological text-books—textbooks which his questioners nevertheless would have a difficult time finding in Russia today. Yet in his blunt but always charitable replies, Fr. Dmitrii shows not only human understanding but also a great sense of faithfulness to the Church. He always builds bridges between the simple old woman whose religious life is expressed in the ritual practices, and the intellectual who dreams of "non-institutional" religion; between the loyal churchman who justifies anything coming from ecclesiastical authorities, and the potential dissident who demands social and political leadership from the bishops; between the Orthodox "integrist" and the Christian believer who is tempted by the active proselytization of the Baptists. Characteristically for the contemporary Russian religious scene, Fr. Dudko is rather sympathetic to Roman Catholics (although he recognizes "differences"): in the Communist world today, where Roman Catholic activities are strictly curtailed (while those of the Baptists are relatively free), traditional Western Christianity is often seen as an ally and not a competitor.

At all times, Fr. Dmitrii attempts to maintain a truly ecclesial sense of contemporary Russian Orthodoxy. Both servility and the myth of a "pure church" hidden in catacombs are foreign to him. "The Orthodox Church is the largest religious community in our country, but in a large society there are always great diversities. There are always people who come out very actively against untruth and crimes, and there are always people who endure in silence and pray that the number of criminals would be smaller. Which of these does more? Once again, God will judge."

Fr. Dmitrii, we are with you in your struggle, and we thank you also for communicating to us—to our priests, to our lay leaders and to all the ordinary people who will read your discussions —so much inspiration, so many ideas and so much courage to face a contemporary human society which is in fact, in the West no less than in the Soviet Union, ignorant of the saving message of Christ and so desperately foreign to the life of His Church.

Fr. John Meyendorff

walls)
of catacombs may not be visible, but the catacombs are no less real

An Introductory Word

Spoken in Church on December 8, 1973

I'd like to say a word to you.

A lot of people who come to church don't understand the service, the prayers, the Scriptures. And I'm not just speaking about the young people who have been completely torn away from religious education. People often come asking me to explain something, to tell them about something they don't know or understand fully. Unfortunately, there are still superstitions among the faithful. Our purely Christian ideas are mixed with non-Christian ones.

Books on religion are either non-existent or hard to find. Thus, in order to meet the desires of the faithful half-way, as they say, I've decided to initiate discussions concerning our faith. Write me about what you'd most like us to talk about, about the questions you have, about your doubts, about the things that puzzle you ... Maybe in your meetings with atheists they have asked questions you couldn't answer. I know that happens a lot. All you've got to write down is the questions—not your names, first *or* last.

I think these discussions will be interesting for everyone, and with God's help, they'll be useful for us all—for me as well as for you.

this is the source of the Romanian mythology, e.g.

13

The First Discussion

QUESTION: Often the old ladies interfere with the young people coming to church. They come down on them in irritation; they lecture them, they check them out. Can't anything be done to keep them from interfering?

ANSWER: This criticism applies to anyone who interferes in any way with the young people coming to church. We should *rejoice* when a young person comes and not plague him with explanations. The church itself, the worship service itself will teach the young believers. Now if they come with mischief in mind, that's another matter ... but for the most part they're beginning to come to church because something draws them here.

QUESTION: How should "Here are two swords"[1] be understood? Just figuratively?

ANSWER: Here's how this question is answered in the commentary that Lopukhin edited[2] (and as we know, it's not Lopukhin's personal opinion, but the consensus of the holy fathers). We read:

> The disciples understood the word "sword" as though Christ were indeed advising them to arm themselves with swords in view of the approaching danger. They had already armed themselves

---

[1] Lk. 22:38.
[2] *Tolkovaia Bibliia, ili Kommentarii na vse knigi Sviashchennogo Pisaniia Vetkbogo i Novogo Zaveta* (St. Petersburg, 1904), vol. 10, p. 261.

with two swords, probably during their trip to
Jerusalem, since they had had to travel through
areas which were not without danger. The Lord,
seeing that they did not understand His perfection,
said sadly, "Enough. Let us end this discussion."

As we see, He couldn't have been speaking about swords
in the literal sense, for "all who take the sword will perish
by the sword."[3] This means that He had in mind a spiritual
sword.

QUESTION: I came to the faith only recently, and my faith
is not yet strong. Things often trouble me. Even this troubles
me: They've flown in spaceships but didn't see God. Where
is God, and how are we to understand Him?

ANSWER: This question is sincere, but a bit naive. What
can I say? Strong faith comes not just from knowledge, but
from a life of good. This is what I can advise you to do:
Begin living a Christian life and you'll see if your faith becomes strong. Of course this doesn't mean that knowledge
is unnecessary. Read more. Even reading secular literature
can be of value for your faith. Lack of faith sometimes
occurs because we know so little. As some scholars say: "A
little knowledge removes one from God, a great amount
brings one closer to Him."

Being troubled is nothing to worry about. There will
always be troubles, one must struggle with them. One gains
experience through battle, and as your experience expands,
your troubles will contract. However, as the holy fathers
say, the spirit of evil troubles even the saints, but he is put
all the more to shame by them. His troubles are like the blowing of the wind—it comes and goes. When you are troubled
you have to learn to pray to God.

Being troubled by the spaceships comes from not knowing what God is. After all, God isn't an old man sitting up
in the clouds—that kind of god would be an idol. Idolatry
is when you worship some thing instead of God. First of all,

[3]Mt. 22:52.

we must keep in mind that God is invisible to the physical
eye. So it's natural that they couldn't see Him from the
spaceships. But we shouldn't think that something which
isn't visible to our physical sight therefore doesn't exist. God
can't be placed within the laws of matter. He's above all the
laws which we have in our reach. So, those of us who live
in the physical world needn't even *try* to see God physically,
because the spirit of evil will slip something else in front
of us. Indeed, people even believe in God *because* He's invisible. Only atheists try to imagine God as a material being.
But then they don't know anything but matter, so for them
God *must be* material. Thus, when they refute God, it's not
our God they refute, but *their own*—one they've created in
their own image and likeness. Speaking figuratively, we
could say that they're fighting their own shadow. If we
think about it, it's a ridiculous battle. But we believers
shouldn't laugh at them, but just have compassion on their
lack of understanding, and ask God to forgive them.

God is everywhere. There's no place that He isn't. A
physical body requires a set place to be in, but for a spirit
this is unnecessary.

Let's consider our *thoughts* for a moment. At any given
moment they can be anywhere; they can't be limited. Now,
thoughts aren't even pure spirit, but God is pure Spirit. So
it's not strange at all that God is everywhere. The Russian
poet Derzhavin said something beautiful about this:

> Spirit everywhere yet one,
> For Whom both space and cause are none,
> The One Whom no one can attain,
> Whose Self does all pervade,
> Enfold, uphold, sustain . . .
> The One Whom we call God.

I'd recommend that everyone get acquainted with this poem.
It's called "God." It's not hard to find. It's included in the
collection of Derzhavin's verse published by "Sovietskaia
Rossiia" in Moscow in 1972.

QUESTION: Where can I find a Bible. I'd be willing to pay any amount.

ANSWER: That's a hard question to answer, because *I* don't know where to find one. As everyone knows, Bibles aren't widely published in Russia. But all the same, some people somehow find them. I can only answer: "Seek and ye shall find." If the Bible has become the Book of Life for you, you'll find one. One always finds what is of vital importance in his or her life. If you get access to a Bible for a while, read it and jot down whatever you consider to be especially important for yourself.

What can I recommend for you to read in the literature about God that you can find? The question of religion is of interest to many right now, so there's a lot being written about God in the Soviet press. I'd recommend that you find the last issue of the *Philosophical Encyclopedia.* It contains some interesting articles. There's nothing of direct interest in current literature, although through allusions they give some notions about God. Read the Russian classics; they're religious through and through.

As the Gospel says, when the woman lost the pearl she carefully swept the debris to find it. You've got to learn to read between the lines. Anyone who seeks will always find what he needs. God helps you. A knowledge of God is like the breath of life. A lot of things aren't as they should be because we don't know God. Without God, life is impossible. God is the source of life. So we've got to make our way to this source by whatever paths we may.

QUESTION: We have just one God—all men have just one. So why are there so many faiths? Even among Christians there are various faiths: Orthodox, Catholic, Protestant, etc. So which faith is the most correct?

ANSWER: Yes, all of us have just one God, but we believe in Him in different ways. This is because we are sinful and have gone astray. When people go astray, they seek out their own path in various ways. But there's only one way out: to God. That they seek God is good. It's bad when they don't. Every search of this sort has its own truth, and

happy is the man who finds the surest way out, the truest
faith. This is a great joy.

We can't look down upon those of other faiths. Anyone
who grows conceited about his faith is faithless. The believer who asked this question is respectful and loving towards others.

Atheists often try to reproach believers: "If you have so
many faiths, it means there's no God because everyone understands God in his own way." But they don't take into
account the fact that when people are searching, they always
go in various directions. They come out on the true path
only when they sense the approach of the One Whom they
seek. If we sense God as we should, then we'll confess the
true faith. We have the good fortune of confessing the
Orthodox faith. We must rejoice in this and value our faith.
Anyone who doesn't value his own faith is, in general, weak
in his faith in God. We must value our Orthodox faith.
For us it's the most correct. God will judge the others; we
must think about ourselves. When there's no longer sin and
error among us, we'll have one faith. But until then there
will be many.

All faiths indicate that we seek a way out, that we seek
God, the source of life. Only lack of faith fails to seek a
way out, because in fact lack of faith *is* a way out. But that
means to perish. The atheist doesn't understand that sin is
the major unhappiness, and he perishes in this sin. He seeks
a way out, freedom not from sin, but from secondary causes:
poverty, etc. But just because a person has been freed from
poverty doesn't mean he'll be happy. Today we see that the
most well-to-do people are becoming hooligans, profligates,
drunks. What happiness is there in this? It's perdition! Only
God gives happiness.

Our faith is true when we live correctly. You can confess any faith you want externally and still not know God
as you should. Let's live as Christians should. Then the
faith we confess will be the most correct.

QUESTION: Why go through all the rites, go to church,
know the Church, if you can just believe within your soul?

ANSWER: Faith that is just in your soul is, as they say, just in your head. It's not a living faith. In philosophical language, it's an abstract faith. We know that when a person just *thinks* about God but doesn't live according to God's way, he isn't saved. For faith to become something vital, it must be realized in life—hence the rituals, the church building and all the realizations of our faith in life. Any person who not only thinks about faith but also lives by it will of necessity fulfill the rituals, go to church, and know the Church. Then faith will become life. Only such faith is concrete and capable of saving.

QUESTION: Tell me about the church building as a whole. Also: Why do all church buildings differ from each other in construction, outside and inside? One more question: How should the Psalter be read at home?

ANSWER: The church building is not the Church; it's a house of prayer. But the Church is the essence of our faith. Speaking in figures: the Church is all the very best that mankind attains within the church building. Therefore, while it's possible to create all sorts of scandals inside the church building, this can't be done in the Church. The Church is holy.

We can see the church building and sense it, but of the Church it is said: "I believe in one, holy, catholic..." Christ Himself founded the Church, the apostles and the saints built Her by the spirit of their faith. Thus we say "I believe... in the Church." But we also say "I go to church." And sometimes we see some bad things there, but the Holy Spirit selects only the very best things that people attain and places these in the treasury of the Church. And these best things aren't material goods but spiritual things: love, mercy, holiness, etc. These are the qualities of the Church.

"Why do all church buildings differ in construction?" They don't. They are built according to an established plan, either as a cross or as a ship, the sign of our voyage across the sea of life. Of course, there *are* differences, just as each of us has his own peculiarities even though we are all people.

"How should the Psalter be read at home?" It's useful to read the Psalter. The Psalter is read over the bodies of the dead. From it we pray for health. We read it for instruction. The Psalter is divided into "kathismata."[4] But however it is read, the Psalter is always useful. So whatever sort of Psalter you may have, divided into kathismata or not, read it. Any time, day or night. Read it attentively, prayerfully. It will give a lot to your soul.

QUESTION: I don't understand the Triune Godhead. What is the Trinity?

ANSWER: The Trinity is a mystery. One can't spread it out on the table and explain it—it's an object of faith. Let's use some analogies. The human soul, as we know, is composed of mind, senses and will. But it is still *one*, and it's impossible to imagine one of its parts alone. When the mind is at work, the senses and the will are at work simultaneously. Take another example, from the material world. The sun is one, but simultaneously it gives off light, heat and energy. All of these form one.

It's necessary to understand the Triune Godhead with our whole spiritual being—not just with our minds, but with our senses and will too. Then the Triune Godhead will be clearer to us.

Trinity is the Christian concept of God. Jews and Moslems do not have it. They only understand the *unity* of God. We also recognize that God is one, but He is a God Who has revealed Himself as a Trinity, as a God Who has come into a concrete relationship with mankind: as Creator (God the Father), as Savior (God the Son, Who suffered and saved the human race), and as God the Holy Spirit (Who leads us into all truth). The concept of God's unity is true, but it is an abstract concept, one that's just in your head. But God as Trinity is a *living* concept, linked with our whole human existence.

---

[4]In Orthodox practice the Psalter is divided into twenty sections called "sittings" (Greek: "kathismata"), which are assigned to be read according to prescribed patterns during the daily services.

QUESTION: The people around me are non-believers. I often try to explain to them Who it is that I believe in, and what the content of my faith is. But from their side I encounter mockery. Am I doing the right thing in trying to explain things to them, or is this what our Lord Jesus Christ said: "pearls before swine"?

ANSWER: If your explanations provoke mockery, don't offer explanations. It would be better to pray for these people. The truths of Christianity can't be forced on others; they have to be accepted freely. But if these people ask you questions, you have to answer, but consider why they asked the question. It's important to capture the right moment, when they will listen to you attentively and with a desire to understand.

You also have to take into account the fact that your explanations might really be unconvincing. It wasn't by accident that Christ said: "Don't be teachers." If you yourself would really be a carrier of the truths of Christianity, your explanations would be convincing. To "cast your pearls" means to speak words without confirming them by your life. Whether our words are pearls or the truth depends not on those who hear us, but on us ourselves.

QUESTION: Lately a drop in morality is observable among the people. The family as a "little church" is practically non-existent. Divorces are frequent. How does the Church relate to this state of affairs?

ANSWER: In a *most* negative fashion. The Church has always been up in arms against immorality. She has never shown indulgence for sin of any sort. The family requires ascetic effort,[5] and an immoral person is incapable of such effort. We allow divorce only in the case of adultery, i.e., in the case of immoral behavior on the part of one of the spouses. But in *no* other case. Today it occurs for any old reason, and at the base of this lies egotism—man's sin. Often people don't think about their families; they don't think about their children. They think only about their own pleas-

---

[5]Russian: *podvig*, an act of ascetic struggle, a "feat" or "exploit."

ures. Without a doubt, difficult characters *are* encountered; sometimes people of quite different spirits come together, but we should think about this ahead of time and not hurry into marriage. By the time people get married, and even more so by the time children appear, they should have displayed some spiritual balance; they should somehow have adjusted their relationships; they should somehow understand each other; they should have become intimate in their souls. Where there's good will one to another this is always possible. To make of one's family a domestic church is the goal of each Christian.

QUESTION: How should one understand the thesis: "Man is created in the image and likeness of God."

ANSWER: The image is the spiritual basis placed in us, given to us as a gift. The likeness is all that we ourselves ought to develop within ourselves, in order to perfect the good and the love which are in us. To put it another way, we could say that we have some material from God and we must develop this material.

QUESTION: I'm bothered by the women who collect money. *Several* times during the service and common prayers three of them come through clattering the money and distracting the attention of the faithful from their prayers. I've been in a Roman Catholic church and paid attention to the fact that in their church there are no counters where they sell candles and the like. And they collect money only once— and then just one man does it. It seems to me that the mood of reverence is thus disturbed less. Am I right? Couldn't we somehow change the way we collect money? I'm sure that every believer considers it his duty to support the church.

ANSWER: This question and these remarks are substantial. Indeed, we sometimes criticize the Catholics for their differences from us, but in some things we could learn from them. The custom of collecting money a number of times during the service has been established among us, and we see no sin in it. But in fact anything which interrupts the order of the service is a sin. If Christ were to enter our church visibly at this moment, He would without a doubt drive a lot of things out of the church. What should we do to make things better? First of all, we must have a living conscience, so that everything we do in church is done not for money but in faith. Then we wouldn't do anything that would upset the service. I'm sure that the faithful would never allow their church to fall into distress; when necessary they would come to its assistance. How we can improve our practices—everyone with a living conscience must think about this.

QUESTION: God knew—and knows—the end of each person. He knows if his end will be good or bad. We could even say present, past, and future are our human categories. There is no past or future in God. So, for Him there is no "this person could have been good, but he became bad." For this eternal God, he is already bad. So why punish him? And what sense does it make that He still sends him to do good? God knows that he won't be saved anyway.

ANSWER: Yes, God knows what will happen with each person. But it's also necessary for the person to know, and so he's given a mind, a soul. Everything that happens to man, punishment or joy, is a lesson to him from God. God even knew everything that would happen to mankind before He had created man. But then, Christ says somewhere in the Gospels that the voice from heaven wasn't for Him, but for the people.[6] Everything that is done in the world is done for man. We live in human history. When we shall live in "divine history" (if we may put it that way), things will be different.

QUESTION: What are the "Hours," and when are they read?

ANSWER: The "Hours" are services consisting of Psalms. They are read before the Divine Liturgy at the time when, according to the canon, the Proskomide,[7] or preparation for

---

[6] Jn. 12:30.
[7] The Proskomide, or Prothesis, is the service of preparation of the bread and wine to be used in the Eucharist.

the liturgy, is to be performed. The reading of the "Hours" should be a prayerful reminder to us of the hours of our life, since hour-by-hour we draw nearer to the Kingdom of God. After all, the Liturgy is, as it were, the gracious kingdom of God.

QUESTION: It seems to me that Christianity is a religion of crying and sorrow, because all Christians do is talk about sin and sufferings. Tell me, am I right? If I am, then it's hard for modern man to be a Christian. There are so many sorrows already in life. It seems to me that religion should be joyous. It should set people free and not enslave them. Answer this question which is upsetting me.

ANSWER: Christianity is precisely a religion of joy. Only, how are we to understand joy? If we understand joy in an earthly manner—let's say the joy of drunkenness or the joy of lust—then Christianity has no need of such joy. Here, indeed, there's need for sorrow, for thinking about how we can be delivered from drunkenness and lust. Christianity is the religion of joy at being delivered from sin. Only when he has been delivered from sin can man really achieve joy: the joy of resurrection from sin and death, the joy of eternity. May God grant us not to be deceived about joy, but to understand it as we should. Then it won't seem to us as though Christianity is a religion of sorrow.

QUESTION: What meaning is there in the suffering of children?

ANSWER: We are all linked one to another. Children suffer for our sins. The purpose of this is to improve us. Seeing the suffering of children, we become more compassionate, more sympathetic.

God doesn't necessarily punish for sin. In general He doesn't punish; He educates. Suffering is one means of education. In order for our children to suffer less, we must sin less. When you've seen a suffering child, you should know that he's suffering for *your* sin. Often people grow so hard that their own sufferings don't correct them. But the sufferings of children do correct them.

The Second Discussion

Apparently because Christmas is approaching there have been a lot of questions about the *person* of Jesus Christ, about Christianity. These questions can be divided into three groups.

The first aren't really questions. People just write about their faith in Christ. I understood this to mean that they want to share the joy which has come to them with faith. These testimonies are very interesting for me.

The second group: Here are real questions which *believers* have asked. Many ask whether there are any scientific data to show that Christ really lived? They need an answer not so much for themselves as for those who have in turn asked them this question. They write that they can't find any literature dealing with these questions. The journal *Science and Religion*[1] doesn't please anyone, believers or non-believers. They write that it has neither science nor religion. The *Journal of the Moscow Patriarchate* likewise provides no answer to these questions, even though it's a religious magazine. And even if it *did* give any answers, you just can't find it because it has a closed circulation. I should immediately note that you should still try to obtain a subscription through "Soiuzpechat'."[2] If they refuse, then turn to the Commissioner for Church Affairs for an ex-

---

[1]*Nauka i religiia*: popular-level, illustrated anti-religious periodical published monthly since 1922.

[2]Soviet subscription agency which centralizes the distribution of over 90% of all periodical titles in the USSR.

planation. But then they say there's no need, because there's no demand for the journal.

The third group of questions apparently comes from those who have doubts about their faith or who are unbelievers, because there are expressions like: "It's strange to talk about Christ as though He were a historical figure when science has shown that He never existed." Or: "The Holy Scriptures are full of contradictions." And they say this for themselves. I'm not disturbed by the categorical way these opinions are stated. Everyone is free to think what he likes. Rather, I'm happy. It means that the non-believers are being drawn to the Church and are seeking explanations, even if indirectly. They're beginning to do some thinking, and this strengthens me all the more in my belief that I was right to undertake these discussions. It would be good if other priests took up this undertaking. After all, the antireligious propagandists *like* religious ignorance—their own journal aggravates it! And we priests don't try to dispel it. "For religious enlightenment!" That should be the heading for a whole series of lectures. If no one listened to them, I think they'd disappear. I'll tell you in secret—they've already warned me: "Watch, nothing will come of it." How brash—"Nothing will come of it!" How this paralyzes our activities! I ignore this kind of warning from the beginning. "Nothing will come of it!" Such a warning puts the priest to shame. The priest has to be daring. He's got to be a shepherd who's willing to give up his life for his sheep. By the cross the priest demonstrates what word or deed can't demonstrate. To suffer for one's convictions, for the faith, for God's work—what could be higher? And what could provide a more convincing argument? There's no need to fear.

That's to begin with.

In the second place, I'm doing what's necessary for all, since I see that without Christianity many people, especially the youth, have wandered into blind alleys. What do you get? Drunkenness and hooliganism. My activities are directed toward helping people find their way out of these blind alleys. It seems to me that the activity of priests is

one of those most absolutely necessary today. And so, I've
decided to be daring. God is my helper and I will not be
afraid of what man can do to me. This is my faith, and in
it is the meaning of my activities.

But this has all been an aside.

Let's turn to the questions. As you see there are great,
urgent questions. A couple of three-hour lectures should be
devoted to them if they are to be answered in full, but I'll
limit myself to very short answers. First, let me just read
excerpts from several notes:

1. "My husband died recently. If I hadn't turned to the
Church, to Christ, I probably would have lost my mind.
Thank you, Church!"

What is this?—A tremendous document! Here they say
that in our day the Church is unnecessary, but this woman
who has met with grief and who earlier might have re-
nounced the Church has now found comfort there and an
answer for herself. Probably her whole life will continue to
confirm the Church's usefulness.

On behalf of the whole Church, I say thank you, ma'am,
for these words.

2. "I have a son. I brought him up in an atheistic spirit.
Then he began drinking and acting like a hooligan. I
didn't know what to do. Everyone knows that women are
weak, and my husband left me for someone else. He was
an atheist too, like me.

"Then suddenly there was a miracle. My son somehow
came to believe in God. He began going to church. At
first I didn't know it. I just wondered, why such a change?
To tell you the truth, I was afraid to talk to my son about
the subject because we didn't agree on anything. I just rejoiced over him in secret and was always afraid he'd begin
drinking again, become a hooligan again. But every day
he became better and better. He even changed on the outside—sort of a glow. Finally I just couldn't hold back any
more, and I asked him: 'Son, tell me, what's with you?
You've become so good...' And he said, 'Mom, I believe

in God and am going to church.' That answer shook me.
It was like I'd been struck by lightning. I didn't know
what to say. Then it turned out that my son had been having some trouble at work, at first connected with his drinking, then with something else. They even demoted him. He
got less money. But he didn't despair. I thought a lot, looking at the change in my son, and I began thinking about
myself, too. I came to the conclusion that I should be baptized. Unfortunately, my atheist parents hadn't done it
earlier. At forty I was to be baptized! And I was baptized,
not long ago. Now I go to church and boldly proclaim:
'Faith in Christ is all that we need!' It's more necessary in
our day than ever before. This is my firm conviction."

3.   "For a long time depression had a real hold on me.
Such depression that I didn't know what to do. No matter
whom I turned to, no one gave me any advice about where
this depression came from. I tried drinking. I got drunk
til I passed out—so I could forget. But once I'd sober up,
the depression would be back, only stronger. I tried im-
mersing myself in my work; I tried being civic-minded. I'll
tell you, for a while I almost even managed to forget, but
the depression would tease me: 'What? Are you trying to
hide? Forget it, I'm here.' The harder I tried, the more
I'd be all thumbs. I really got mad and gave up on work.
I wouldn't go to the plant for weeks on end. I'd just lie
around and think—why this depression? I was gnawing
away at myself. I tried to do away with myself. I don't
know why I didn't succeed. I went to a psychiatrist. At first he
gave me sleeping pills (I had been sleeping badly), but
when I'd wake up after the pills I'd feel really worn out,
and the depression would be stronger than ever. I'll tell
you the straight truth—I was on the edge of insanity. But,
of course, I wasn't insane. I was lucid, as they say. I was
fully aware of all I did. I could give myself an account of
everything. I must admit, unfortunately, that I would have
been glad to go crazy, so that I wouldn't know the depression that was devouring me. I could have told stories about
myself so they'd lock me up in a mental institution. For-

tunately, that didn't happen. Fortunately, something better
happened. A small book fell into my hands. (It was a lot
smaller than the books they publish today.) *The New
Testament of our Lord Jesus Christ*. I began reading it, and
it opened a whole new world to me. A joyous, happy world.
I read it and couldn't read it enough. Each word of that
holy little book lay on my soul, and the greatest of all joys
took place—the depression passed! Only one who has suffered from some degree of depression could understand me
properly. The depression passed entirely! I believed in
Christ and was baptized. Now I go to church, and sometimes even try to sing from the kleros.[3] And even though I
have more problems than before—I was laid off in a cut-
back at work and my father is trying to get me committed
because my faith is a reproach to his convictions—still, I'm
happy. I automatically dropped out of Komsomol.[4] They
tried to offer me something, some kind of interesting work,
but I refused. I'm afraid of getting depressed again, but
with Christ everything is good and joyous for me. I tried
to enter theological seminary, but so far nothing has come
of it for reasons which have nothing to do with me. I'm
willing to do any work—even the most insignificant, the
most unskilled. I'll even clean or stand guard in church, just
so that I can be closer to Christ."

4. "Several years in a row I was tormented by a horrible question: What's all of this about? What do we live
for? Sooner or later all our earthly delights are sealed when
the lid of the coffin is slammed shut. If this is so, then we
must really be ridiculous people. Our optimism is ridiculous.
Our activities are ridiculous, the way we try to deceive ourselves. If we know ahead of time that everything will end
in nothing, then why do we somehow keep our spirits up?
As they say, 'everything's in order—we're sinking.' If death

---

[3]The choir areas located on either side of the church from which responses to
the services are sung.

[4]*Kommunisticheskii Soiuz Molodezhi* (Young Communist League), the official Soviet organization for young people between the ages of 14 and 26.

exists, everything is meaningless. Once I sensed the meaningless of everything. I sensed it sharply, to the point of a
consuming depression, and I decided to kill myself. I don't
know who saved me, whether it was my guardian angel or
the prayers of my dead mother, but somehow I began to
think about what religion is. Maybe *it* could answer my horrible question. But who could explain it to me? 'I should
read the Bible,' I thought. But where would I find one?
Once I happened into a second-hand bookstore, and I was
overjoyed—there was *A Bible for Believers and Non-Believers.* I asked the saleswoman to show me one. She did,
but it turned out that the explanations there were just ironic.
I felt awful. How could anyone laugh about the greatest
of human feelings? Religious feelings then seemed to me
to be the very greatest of all feelings. And I felt at that
moment as though someone had just spit on my soul. My
temper flared. In anger I wanted to say something to the
saleswoman, but I restrained myself and said softly, 'If you
have any respect for people, don't offer this book to anyone.'
She looked at me sadly. She didn't ask anything or say anything, but she probably understood. She put it under the
counter. From that moment I wanted more than ever to
know what religion is. For some reason I thought that religion would answer my questions for sure.

"An elderly lady lived next to me. I didn't know if she
was a believer or not, but since she was old, I figured she
must have been a believer, so I asked her cautiously. I
finished university, I told her, and I know historical and
dialectical materialism, but it seems to me there's something lacking there. But what it is, I don't know. The
woman gave me a searching look. I sensed that she wanted
to say something, but I think she was probably afraid. Then
I asked her if she knew a priest.

" 'Wait, I'll tell you . . . '

"A few days later she introduced me to a priest. It was
the first time I'd ever seen a real, live priest. I say 'live' because we'd always imagined priests as dead, superstitious,
ignorant, fraudulent, money-hungry, etc. But here was a
young man, 30 or 35 years old. We talked, and I felt it

was interesting to talk with him. I'd finished university, but in front of him I seemed illiterate. He knew materialism as well as I did, and had his bearings in some other science, but his religious convictions had gotten him expelled from the institute, and he hadn't graduated. We talked a while, and he gave me my first opportunity to read the New Testament. Then we parted. I walked along and thought: 'I have a wife, who is also university-educated. I have a child whom we've been raising in an antireligious spirit, and what's more she's in the Institute for Marxism-Leninism. What if she sees me with the book? Oh well, so what,' I thought, 'I *have* to read it.' I arrived home and hid it. And as it would happen, she found the book and began to read it in secret from me. I read it secretly from her, and she read it secretly from me; we both hid it in a secret place. Later, I found out that my wife had been baptized and had baptized our child. What else was there for me to do? I not only became interested in this book, but I even began to believe. It only remained for me to be baptized openly. I came to church like I should and said, 'I want to be baptized.' For some reason they asked for my internal passport. They record it somewhere. 'What's this?' I think. 'Is the church into denunciations?' (I didn't know yet that the Soviet authorities had established this procedure.) 'Well, whatever,' I thought, 'I'm *going* to be baptized.' I was, and they found out at work. They set up a community court. There they finally dotted all the i's. 'If we'd known,' they said, 'we never would have given you an apartment.' (I'd just then received an apartment.) 'That's it,' I thought. 'You don't have any convictions. Everything comes down to the question of an apartment.' Then it all became clear to me. Atheism is the question of an apartment in our time. Now I believe deeply. The thought of suicide is long past. I work at my old job, but more honestly and correctly. If before I could allow a little waste and evasion, now my Christian conscience says, 'No!' "

I've just read a tiny portion of such letters. Judge for yourselves how eloquent they are.

Now let's talk about the scientific data concerning the life of Christ. Perhaps first we should talk about the historic witnesses to Christ's not being a myth, not a figment of the imagination, but indeed a real historical figure.

As we know, right up until today atheistic literature has maintained that it has not been historically proven that Christ existed, although (rarely) there have been other voices. Thus we read, for example, in *Novyi Mir*[5] (No. 9, 1969) a review of M. M. Kublanov's book *The New Testament: Investigations and Discoveries* (published in Moscow in 1968 by Nauka press). The review is written by Prof. A. Nemirovskii and entitled, "New Data on an Old Argument."

> The absence of archaeological remains contemporary with the New Testament and relevant to the sphere of events described in it has given full range to the creation of scholarly myths and legends which are no less fantastic than they are ancient. These methods can be termed "hypercritical." But the hour of the New Testament has come. In the late 1940's appeared the first announcements of the discovery of literary remains in the regions where Christianity appeared. In our day an entire branch of science already exists for the study of these documents, which either are contemporary with Christianity or somewhat antedate it, but which, in either case, arose in the same social milieu. The findings in the Dead Sea region have dealt a fatal blow to the fabrications of the hypercritics, who have found in the New Testament whatsoever they desired. M. Kublanov's book in a lively, clever, yet substantial way familiarizes us with the theories which, thanks to archaeology, overnight have become a science.
>
> A special impression is left by the analysis of im-

---

[5] *The New World*: the official journal of the Soviet Writers' Union, published monthly since 1925; subtitled a "literary, artistic and socio-political journal."

portant testimonies to Christ which had been declared to be interpolations, insertions by later Christian scribes. The partisans of mythological theories were undaunted by the fact that in reporting Nero's persecution of the Christians in 64 A.D., Tacitus gives to the Christians and to Christianity a character which would be unthinkable for a pious scribe. In his passage on Christianity, Tacitus mentions the Procurator Pontius Pilate under whom the founder of a new religion was executed in Jerusalem. The higher critics considered this mention as a positive witness to the spuriousness of the entire passage. Tacitus (they reason) could hardly have known the name of such an inconsequential official, one unknown to other Roman authors. Therefore, Pontius Pilate must be a mythical person, and mention of him was made only by the sly hand of a Christian scribe. Then in 1961 in the administrative center of the Roman province of Caesarea in Judea, a Latin inscription was found bearing the name of Pontius Pilate, thereby removing all doubt concerning the identity of this Roman. One of the arguments against the historicity of Jesus was the silence regarding Him among the Roman writers of the first century. But as M. M. Kublanov has demonstrated conclusively, this silence is itself a myth. Tacitus, Josephus Flavius, Suetonius, Pliny the Younger—are these not enough references to a person and movement which were insignificant from the point of view of Nero's contemporaries?

I've read this excerpt from an article by a contemporary scholar. As we see, Christ's historicity is acknowledged, although some will still continue to scream that Christ is a myth. But the fact that there are only a few historical witnesses speaks not against Christ, but *for* Him. For Christ outgrows history. He can't be contained within its limits. Who more than Christ attracts the attention of all nations and minds? As the Russian philosopher Berdiaev says, all of history revolves around Christ. Christ is the center of everything. Isn't that enough for Christ to be *more real* than any other historical figure? They haven't stopped talking about Christ for some twenty centuries now. Many of the kings and politicians who lived in the eighteenth, nineteenth and twentieth centuries have been forgotten, but Christ, Who was born almost two thousand years ago, hasn't been forgotten. Now *that's* convincing proof!

Judge for yourselves. Isn't Christianity itself a witness to Christ's existence? What then? Christianity exists, but Christ didn't? Only fools could now claim that Christ never existed. After the recent scientific discoveries, those who would reject Christ must turn not to science, but to their own ignorance.

It would be interesting to look at the debate between the poets Sel'vinskii and Ozerov.[6] The first writes, "I live after Einstein, Tsiolkovskii, Viner.[7] Therefore, don't you dare say anything. What if I do believe? If you don't believe, return to the nineteenth century." He calls the science of the nineteenth century "sober, ruthless, void of romanticism . . . the science of Bazarovs."[8] (The debate was published in *Literaturnaia Rossiia*,[9] Friday, September 23, 1966.)

But such defenders of Christianity, while admitting that Christ was a historical figure, still won't admit that God was in Him. So what? It's completely understandable that such superstition should exist—it's scientific. The first symptom of such superstition is blind faith in science, which (they say) explains everything. Now science does have its sphere of competency. But that Christ is God can only be said by someone who believes, one who has religious ex-

---

[6]Il'ia L'vovich Sel'vinskii (b. 1899) and Lev Ozerov (pseud.: Lev Adol'fovich Gol'dberg, b. 1914): Soviet poets.

[7]Albert Einstein (1879-1955): physicist and discoverer of the theory of relativity. Konstantin Eduardovich Tsiolkovskii (1857-1935): pioneer in Russian aviation and astronautics. Vladimir Vladimirovich Viner (1872-1930): Russian agronomist.

[8]Bazarov: ironic young provincial doctor who is the main character in Turgenev's novel *Fathers and Sons*.

[9]*Literary Russia.*

perience. Many of you here—people brought up in atheistic families but who have become believers—*you* are the best proof that Christ is God. And only we can know this. Science can't. Science can tell us about Christ's historicity, but it can't tell us that Christ is God. Only one who believes in Him can say that, and then only on the basis of his own religious experience. This, of course, does not mean that people in science can't believe. There are a lot of such believers even today. Many scholars write about Christ. Probably some of you here have read manuscripts which, unfortunately, haven't been published. Christ is God. All of us can say this—scholars and nonscholars—all of us who have believed and found Him. To believe in Christ is (to use the scientific phrase) "progressive." But the atheists are satisfied with "scientific data" which are (to put it mildly) a mere two hundred years out-of-date.

I'd like to offer just one more interesting excerpt, from the article "Science—the Source of Knowledge and Superstitions," published in *Novyi Mir*, No. 10, 1969:

> A typical superstition is the conviction that science is infallible, that scientific truths are inerrant. Every scholar has felt, on the basis of his own experience, in his own being, how difficult it is to be convinced of truth, how many errors he himself has committed before arriving at a grain of truth. But this inner kitchen is known but to a very few. For the mass of readers the conclusions of science cannot be disputed, inasmuch as they are illumined (and at the same time somehow canonized) in the mass medium of the press. The dangerous paradox in this consists in the fact that science can easily be transformed from an instrument of critical analysis, a method for utilizing reason in order to verify a fact and to come to understand it, into a source for current opinion.

Not badly put. Thus, if we stop believing this "current opinion" and begin judging for ourselves, we'll come to an acknowledgment of Christ not only as a historical person, but as God. This is a great joy—to find faith in God!

What can I recommend that you read about Christ?

Renan's *The Life of Jesus Christ*.[10] This book was written a long time ago, and perhaps some will find it in some ways obsolete, but it's very interesting to read.

A. Bogoliubov's *Son of Man*.[11] It was written in our day, taking account of the latest scientific data. The author is young, full of strength, and lives in Russia.

The Son of God, by Karl Adam, a professor at Tübingen University.[12] It will probably be hard to find, but it can be found. It hasn't been published in Russia.

Now for the third group of questions—those from non-believers. There isn't a whole lot more that needs to be said. Isn't it comical to read that "It's strange to talk about Christ as though He were a historical figure when science has shown that He never existed." What science? The science of past centuries? Or: "The Holy Scriptures are full of contradictions." I'd say that it's precisely these contradictions which serve as proof of the authenticity of the Gospels, as confirmation that they were written by living witnesses. After all, only those who've arranged everything in advance and who copy from each other will repeat everything the other has written. It's the same in life: witnesses to one and the same event will all say the same thing about the major things, but will differ in details. Atheists often stress

---

[10]Ernest Renan (1823-1892): French philosopher, historian and scholar of religion. His *Vie de Jésus* (1863) was denounced by the Roman Catholic Church for its "mythical" approach to Christian origins. After being published in abridged editions in Western Europe, a full Russian translation appeared in St. Petersburg in 1906.

[11]Andrei Bogoliubov, *Syn chelovecheskii* (Brussels, "Zhizn's Bogom," 1968). The author's preface places this work in the tradition of Renan, as an aid to understanding the Evangelists—from whom we are separated in time, culture, and experience.

[12]Karl Adam (1876-1966): Roman Catholic priest and theologian. His *The Son of God* (New York, 1934) is an attempt at presenting Christology in a language suitable for his contemporaries. The Russian edition, *Iisus Khristos* was published by the Roman Catholic Russian-language publishing house "Zhizn' s Bogom" in 1961.

these divergencies in secondary matters and confuse people. About them Christ said: "They strain out a fly but swallow a camel."[13]

We'll end here today.

May Christ Who is born preserve you all. Greetings at the approaching feast!

---

[13]Mt. 23:24.

The Third Discussion

Before I answer any questions, I'd like to say a few introductory words. What brought about this form of contact with the believers? First of all, as I said in the earlier discussions, many people came to me with questions which I tried to answer privately, but soon I saw that the questions were being repeated and, furthermore, that quick, short answers aren't always satisfying. Therefore I decided to answer publicly, and more or less to prepare my answers. As experience has shown, even if this hasn't been completely satisfactory, it has at any rate excited a lively interest. And this, in my opinion, is necessary. After all, the atheists maintain that questions of religion are already obsolete, of interest only to the elderly. Now here's proof to them that religion is not something obsolete, but something always new, something vitally necessary for everyone—both young and old alike. And I'm very glad that it's also enlivened me, as a priest, and has given greater meaning to my ministry.

But why (they ask) can't everything just be said in sermons? Why do you need questions and answers? It's just not a churchly form. They say.

In the first place, every age creates its own forms, and, inasmuch as today many questions are arising, "questions and answers" will acquire their own churchliness. In the second place, we can refer to the Holy Scriptures: "Always be prepared to make a defense to any one who calls you to account for the hope that is in you, yet do it with gentleness and reverence" (1 Pet. 3:15).

As the earlier discussions have shown, the questions are often quite pointed, so pointed that some have warned me that the conversation might unwittingly take on a political tone. I'd first of all like to assure you that religion and politics are two different realms. I'm fully aware of what I say, and I consider that politics is something completely out-of-place in religion. I'll answer any questions, then, in the field of religion. If the answers are pointed, it's not intended as criticism of anything. The fact is that our defects are my pain. As we know, anyone who conceals a friend's defects isn't really a friend, while someone who points them out in good will is. And if in society it might be politics to point out someone's defects, for us in the Church to point out defects is an invitation to overcome them through faith. And if we do point out some defects it's not with irritation or for reproach, but with pain and with love. We consider defects to be weaknesses, as the Apostle said: "Bear one another's weaknesses." Thus I want to "bear the weaknesses" of my parish and carry them on my shoulders. May God help me!

But in this case some try to warn me that "*they* might misunderstand you." "Look out," they say, "for what might happen." Perhaps they *will* misunderstand me. I try to do things so they'll understand correctly. But the priest can't worry about "what might happen." First of all the priest should care not about his own well-being, but about being of use to others. And if he must suffer, then that will be his greatest joy and the most convincing answer to all questions.

It's with great sadness that I look at other priests who've turned their ministry into a machine for servicing religious needs, and they themselves have become simple hired servants. This isn't ministry; it's speculation[1] on the ministry. Jesus Christ didn't know where to lay His head, yet we

---

[1]Speculation: "the buying up or reselling for profit of agricultural products or commodity staples" is strictly forbidden in Soviet law. Its "bourgeois" nature makes speculation an especially heinous crime, subject to five years imprisonment in jail or concentration camp plus confiscation of property.

transform the priestly ministry into the building up of our
own personal affairs. What will we answer when Christ
demands of us an account of our activities? This is what
I wanted to say before beginning with the questions and
answers.

Now for the questions. As I said at the last discussion,
I was able to answer only an insignificant portion of the
questions, and a great number of them remained unanswered. Now a number of new questions have been added
for today's discussion, so I must apologize that I won't be
able to answer them all today. I'll try to give brief answers.

I've arranged the questions by topic. First our "internal"
ones, the ones which touch upon the faithful *per se*. Then
the "external" ones, those from people with doubts, perhaps even from non-believers. They too are interested in
questions of a religious nature, and this shows that the soul
of each man, as the ancient apostle said, is Christian by
nature. There are questions about all of our defects, our
sins—and this is painful for us all. What's needed is pity
and a search for a way of overcoming these weaknesses.

QUESTION: What is religious fanaticism?

ANSWER: Religious fanaticism is a narrowness of vision,
a blind confidence that you're right, an unwillingness to
listen to someone else's opinion, impatience with others. If
we don't fight religious fanaticism it will grow into such a
defect that it becomes a delusion,[2] and this is a terrible thing.
At the base of delusion lies inordinate pride, and (as we
know), God opposes those who are proud.[3] Deliverance from
delusion requires means which not all people possess. We
must fight religious fanaticism, and our battle will be successful only when we depend not only on our own powers, but
turn to humility and to the help of God. This will put us on
guard against delusion.

But I'd like to mention that sometimes non-believers label

---

[2]Delusion: *prelest'*, a technical term in ascetic theology which means literally "wandering" or "going astray." It is the state of accepting illusion as reality.
[3]Jas. 4:6.

anyone who believes a fanatic. This just goes to show that in this case it's the *non*-believer who's the fanatic, because he cannot tolerate any of the believers' arguments. Then sometimes they call any person with convictions a fanatic. Convictions aren't the same thing as fanaticism. Convictions are a person's confidence in what he does. Without this confidence a person has (as they say) no sense of direction. He's like a weather-vane that turns whichever way the wind is blowing. Thus, there are two extremes—religious fanaticism and lack of principle. Sometimes the latter is called broad-mindedness or patience by mistake.

QUESTION: Something's not quite clear to us. Last time you said that any faith can save, so then why do we say that the Orthodox faith is the most correct? Were the holy fathers wrong when they called the Orthodox faith the most correct?

ANSWER: This question has a certain ring of fanaticism and dogmatism about it. Speaking of the salvic nature of any faith I in no way intended to degrade the Orthodox faith. I only meant to warn against self-confidence which says, "Look, I'm Orthodox. That means I'm on the right path, and anyone who isn't Orthodox is headed for perdition." One can be Orthodox formally and yet perish faster than someone who belongs to another faith. Orthodoxy is joy at having found the truth, and the real Orthodox always looks at others with love. But if belonging to the Orthodox Church is accompanied by irritation at those who think otherwise, then one ought to doubt one's belonging to Orthodoxy. Rejoice that you're Orthodox, but don't look upon others as if they'd all gone astray. God will judge us all, and we should leave such judgment to Him. The holy fathers weren't wrong, but they didn't make Orthodoxy into their own exclusive privilege.

QUESTION: What is the Church's judgment? Is it God's judgment or man's?

ANSWER: The Church's judgment is directed towards correcting defects, and not at a person's eternal condemnation.

God's judgment is precisely God's judgment. But in the Church, *people* pass judgments, and like all people, they can make mistakes. Furthermore, we must distinguish between the church in history and the Church as a divine institution. The Church as a divine institution is called not to judge, but to save. In the historical church there are defects, such as the inquisition, which the atheists lean on especially, and the persecution of the Old Believers. But God's Church doesn't persecute. She saves. The persecution of heretics and schismatics must become our pain, our sin, things *we* must overcome. But this charge can't be brought against the Church as a divine institution. The Church which Christ created is always holy. She is the very best of everything which the best of people have placed in her as a treasury. And against this Church the gates of hell cannot prevail.[4] Her holiness cannot be conquered either by human sin or by human persecution.

QUESTION: How are we to understand the saying, "Whoever does not have the Church as his mother has not God as his Father"?[5]

ANSWER: This is how it should be understood. Anyone for whom the Church is not his mother in holy things does not, of course, have God as his Father. However, one can call the Church his mother formally and at the same time be far from God. The Church is all that Christ taught, all that the apostles taught, and all that the holy fathers later realized.

But here we must make a small note. Often people like to cite the letter, produce all sorts of citations. And it's possible to pile up so many references that you just kill all meaning. Literal coincidence isn't the same thing as truth. The letter kills, as the apostle said, but the spirit gives life.[6] Spiritual meaning is what's important, and if one goes by the letter, then the holy fathers often contradict each other—

---

[4] Mt. 16:18.
[5] Cyprian of Carthage, *On the Unity of the Church*, 6.
[6] 2 Cor. 3:6.

by the letter, but not according to sense. Contradiction doesn't indicate the defect, but rather the *vitality* of a phenomenon. Philosophy has the concept of antimony. Truth is understood in antimonies. We have a so-called "negative theology." For instance, in it we say that God is nothing. Atheists immediately jump on the "letter" and say, "Right, God is nothing." They think they've said something intelligent, but they've really only proved the poverty of their minds. God is nothing in the sense that in Him there is nothing which exists in everyday life; everything in Him is greater than this. God is higher than everything, higher than our concepts. We're even caused to believe in Him by the fact that under our earthly conditions we can't find anything to compare with God. What the atheists call god and fight against is their own invention and not our God.

QUESTION: How should we Orthodox relate to Catholics, heretics, and the various sectarians?

ANSWER: With love. This doesn't mean that we shouldn't differentiate between them. The Catholics also form a church, and we don't call them heretics. But there are differences between us and them, some substantial, others less so. Heretics are those who resist the truth. The established confessional groups understand the truth in varying degrees and can't be called heretics in the sense that the holy fathers understood this word.

A "sect" in the Orthodox understanding of the word represents a narrow view of truth. But we shouldn't be hostile to them; on the contrary, we should respect them for their faith. We can learn something from them—their boldness, for example, and the way they help each other.

QUESTION: What is the Ecumenical Movement?

ANSWER: It is a search for a common language among all believers. Often while believing in one God, Jesus Christ, we speak various languages and don't understand each other. The search for mutual understanding often takes shape at various conferences and meetings, but this often leads to indifference in matters of faith. Ecumenism is a demand of our time and it cannot be ignored. Neither can we reduce it only to conferences. Ecumenism should become a universal phenomenon. It makes many things incumbent upon us: we must know our own faith very well, and be patient with others. We must remember that we are all brothers in Christ.

QUESTION: Why must one know a lot? After all, scholars are often heretics. Isn't it better to be simple?

ANSWER: A scholar or a non-scholar—even a simple person—can become a heretic. Heresy comes from pride of mind (and those with little intelligence can be proud), from a sinful life, when they think that faith can be just a matter of words. Many of our bishops were highly educated, but this didn't lead them into heresy. As they say, "the place doesn't paint the person, but the person the place." Education doesn't make a heretic; man *becomes* one himself.

QUESTION: Can an Orthodox attend Catholic or Protestant churches? Can he go to the Baptists?

ANSWER: To answer in a single word, I'd say, "Yes." But here we have to ask, "For what reason?" If it's to find out more and to understand, it's all right. But if it shows indifference to one's own Orthodox Church ("it's all the same no matter where I go"), then in this case, "No." Here the person isn't firm in his faith and must first of all understand his own church as he should.

QUESTION: What is schism? Why are some people called heretics and others schismatics?

ANSWER: Heresy is dogmatic error. Schism is canonical (primarily ritual) error.

QUESTION: What is dogma? Why are people sometimes scornful of dogmas as if they bind a man rather than giving full range to his mind?

ANSWER: From not understanding dogma. A dogma is a manifestation of truth, and in this case it doesn't bind the mind, but rather helps it to find the truth. We must remember that the definition of truth isn't simply a verbal definition. The person who hopes to exhaust the truth in verbal definitions ends in drying up the truth. In order to understand the truth we must have our mind correctly developed. Our life must be righteous and our heart pure. Then dogma won't be something dead, but alive. A dry dogmatician is someone who understands with just his mind, but whose heart and righteousness are only external. Love should be in everything, and the law of love is vast.

QUESTION: What is confession? Why has "general confession" been instituted? Why do so few priests conduct private confession?

ANSWER: Confession is an account of what's going on in your soul. To go to confession means to tell about your sins. The so-called "general confession" is a result of a formal approach to the matter. In essence it's not even really confession at all. General confession existed in ancient times when everyone confessed his sins openly. But since this became a temptation to others, private confession was established. Today's general confession, if one were to examine it strictly, isn't confession at all. It has done us terrible harm, because people have stopped watching their consciences; there's no spiritual growth. Disregard for one's own salvation has appeared. Only the *form* is fulfilled, and formalism is a horrible danger. We must fight formalism. We must teach sincerely, with great care, to cleanse the soul from sin through confession.

QUESTION: What is a confessor? Is it possible to change one's confessor? Are people right in confessing this time to one priest and the next time to another?

ANSWER: Your confessor is someone who worries about your salvation. He becomes your father in relation to your salvation. A good confessor doesn't coerce your will, but takes your freedom into account. Coercion brings injury rather than benefit. There should be love between a confessor and his son. When one changes his confessor it is the same thing as changing his natural father—it means there is no real contact between the confessor and his son. One should try to go to confession to his own confessor and confess to another only under extraordinary circumstances. They say that a person can't be healed by several doctors at once (or, as they put it, you'll get over-treated). It's the same with going to confession to a number of priests, because you can get messed up in the business of your salvation.

QUESTION: What is the main church service? What is the eucharistic canon?

ANSWER: One must show reverence at any service. Our lack of reverence comes from indifference towards the service.

The eucharistic canon is the principle moment in the service, its center. In order to come to it reverently, we must preserve reverence throughout the entire service. During the eucharistic canon the greatest thing occurs mystically: God suffers for man; He nourishes us with His Body and Blood; the Holy Gifts are transubstantiated. The bread and wine become the true Body and Blood of Christ.

The canon begins with the words, "Depart catechumens..." At that time we should drive out all extraneous thoughts and concentrate especially. We should lay aside all earthly thoughts and cares, and direct ourselves towards God alone. Conversations and any walking about in church become especially sinful at this time. The mystery which is performed is such that the angels try only to penetrate its meaning, while we are called upon to take part in it. The canon ends with a glorification of the Mother of God, who ministered to the mystery of God's incarnation. Many people today fail to understand the service very well, and therefore sometimes the individual prayer services on-demand become for us the main feature of the whole service. This means that the service has become for us something like ordering clothing for ourselves, buying bread, etc. We must fight this within ourselves. We must enter into the service deeply, with all our thoughts and feelings, and then it will lead to our salvation.

Now let's turn to questions from outside.

QUESTION: What is atheism?

ANSWER: In order to answer this objectively, let's consult two philosophical dictionaries, the one published in 1904 (St. Petersburg, edited by E. Radlov) and the other in 1963 (by Politliteratura Publishers, Moscow, edited by M. Rozental and P. Iudin).

We read from the first edition (1904), written when the "majority position" was still faith:

> Atheism is the denial of divinity; a highly indefinite term, receiving greater definition when positive content is counterposed to negation. If by "God" one means what the religious dogma of Christianity has understood by that term, then most philosophical systems will contain a greater or lesser quantity of atheistic elements. Thus, all pantheism, a religious concept which in some degree identifies God with the world, thereby rejects a religious concept of God, and is, consequently, atheistic. Materialism very often has an atheistic tone, but the same can occur with idealism, if, for example, it is cast in the form of subjective idealism or solipsism. Materialism does not of necessity lead to atheism, as has been shown by history (Epicurius, Tertullian, Hobbs), and as is clear from the fact that a causal mechanistic explanation of phenomena need not introduce God as an active principle on every occasion and yet is in no wise required of necessity to reject the concept of a Creator-God. In precisely this way, scepticism denies only the comprehensibility of divinity and consequently reacts with equal hostility towards the affirmation of God's existence as it does to His denial. Only mysticism rests wholly upon the concept of divinity and therefore encounters fewer elements of atheism. Atheism as a system is rather an impossibility because nothing can be built upon

bare negation. No matter how carefully a given writer (e.g., Nietzche) might attempt to avoid reference to the divinity, nevertheless certain of its attributes were of necessity transferred to the concepts which substituted (or were intended to substitute) for the concept of God.

As we see, the answer is rather thorough. Now let us open the 1963 edition, when atheism is in control. We read:

Atheism (Greek: "denial of God"). A system of views which deny faith in the supernatural (spirits, gods, life after death, etc.). The object of atheism is the explanation of the sources of and reasons behind the appearance and existence of religion, the criticism of religious beliefs from the point of view of the scientific picture of the world, the explanation of religion's social role in society, the determination of paths towards the overcoming of religious prejudices. The appearance and development of atheism are connected with the development of scientific knowledge. In every historical era, atheism has reflected the peak of knowledge and interest of those classes for whom it formed an intellectual weapon. The philosophical basis of atheism is materialism. The positive content and the defects of any given form of atheism are dependent upon concrete social conditions, the level of the development of science and materialistic philosophy. Atheism's battle with religion is connected with class warfare. As a system of views atheism arose in slave-holding society. Significant elements of atheism were held by Thales, Anaximenes, Heraclitus, Democritus, Epicurus and Xenophanes. Characteristic of their atheism was the explanation of all phenomena by natural causes, a naiveté, speculation, a contradictory combination of the denial of religious faith with a recognition of the gods. During the Middle Ages, when the Church and religion were dominant, atheism enjoyed no real development. Of prime importance in the undermining of religion was bourgeois atheism, Spinoza, French materialism, Feuerbach, etc. Bourgeois atheism's unmasking of the Church as reactionary played a historic role in the battle with feudalism and aided in its downfall. However, bourgeois atheism was inconsequential and limited. It had an instructive character; it was directed towards a narrow circle of people, not towards the masses. The Russian revolutionary democrats were militant, consistent atheists. Atheism in its most consistent form is found in Marxism-Leninism. The interests of the proletariat, its position and role in society all coincide with the objective tendencies of the development of society, on the strength of which Marxist atheism is free from the limitations of class characteristic of non-Marxist forms of atheism. The philosophical basis of Marxist atheism is dialectical and historical materialism. Marxist atheism has a militant character. Throughout history it criticises religion from all sides, indicating by what paths and means it can be completely overcome. Marxist atheism has established that religion can be completely overcome only as a result of the destruction of its social roots through the process of building communism. The experience of the USSR, where atheism has become a mass phenomenon, provides practical confirmation for the correctness of these theses. The process of building communism results in the formation of a new man, free from religious and other relics of the past, a man armed with a scientifico-atheistic outlook.

I haven't abused your attention in order to pick these long excerpts apart—let that be on their authors' consciences. These are speculative presentations. The truth of any given doctrine can be proven by real-life experience, as the Marxists themselves admit. Let's turn to the practical.

If atheism is really a negation, then it should lose its significance as religion disappears. But today it's still around, a parasite living off religion. We're willing to admit a relative usefulness to atheism; when religion is perverted, when it is propagated by false means, then atheism is *relatively* progressive. There have been martyrs for atheism, and I bow my head before them. But now, in our day, the absolute uselessness of atheism is obvious. Indeed, even its harmfulness is obvious. Science has so advanced as to leave atheism far behind, some scholars think by as much as up to two hundred years.

Let's look at life. It doesn't take much to become an atheist today. Master a few prepared phrases, swim with the current, and you're an atheist! On the other hand, to be a believer you have to know a lot. You have to bear a lot of difficulties. You have to swim against the current. It takes a heroic spirit. It's not an accident that believers today are heroic people.

One can only be an atheist today by misunderstanding; that is, either by having no conception of God, or a distorted one. There are a lot of so-called "honest atheists" who could easily become believers if only they were illumined. But most atheists show only their negative side. They drive a wedge of mutual misunderstanding between people. Atheism is like an atom of evil undergoing fission. Moral, domestic and social disintegration results. People not only don't believe in God; they don't believe each other either. A father doesn't believe his children, or children their father. A husband doesn't believe his wife, or a wife her husband. Having undermined faith in God, atheism has undermined all bases of social life. The destruction of churches in our country (which even have some secular value), immorality, the collapse of the family, criminality and hooliganism—these are the fruits of atheism.

Atheism has developed enmity, suspiciousness, grovelling, self-seeking. Let's take a few examples from life. Let's begin with school. A believing child is badgered and mocked.

There have been cases in which teachers have torn crosses from around children's necks. (Fortunately, these cases are becoming less frequent now.) In some cases confused schoolchildren beat up their believing comrades. There have been cases in which believing parents have been deprived of their parental rights (incidentally, in defiance of civil law, which guarantees parents the full right to bring up their children in a religious way). At work believers are held in suspicion. They are either demoted or not allowed to advance in their jobs. Such situations are frequent, and many believers have experienced this for themselves. The atheists' hooliganism is especially bad during religious feasts, such as Pascha, for example.[7] We don't have to look very far for examples; we can just recall Pascha last year in our church. What a mob of them there was, in and out of uniform, and all gathered just to prevent people from entering the church. When I personally went to ask them why they wouldn't let people into church, they answered with a grin, "We let *everyone* in," and right away restrained someone, twisting the arm of any who might resist and throwing them into a car. When I asked a policeman[8] to put an end to this lawlessness he turned away from me and said that he'd just arrived, that he didn't know anything. Several people even insulted me. Why is there such bitterness against others? After all, these people *normally* carry out their duties—defending our nation and battling hooliganism. They're friendly enough. I remember that one policeman was very friendly to me personally and offered me paschal greetings. Why does atheism try so to embitter people, to make them rise up against each other? Atheism can rehabilitate itself only by lifting up its own voice against such abnormalities and lawless acts done in its name. I haven't said all of this from any desire to "nag." It's painful for me, sad. But as a priest, I must defend the faithful when they undergo persecutions of any sort. I, the shepherd, must defend my

---

[7]Pascha: the term usually used in Orthodox literature to denote Easter.

[8]Policeman: *militsioner* or traffic policeman, as opposed to a member of the secret police.

sheep from the wolves. As long as the atheists act like wolves, I'll come out against them.

But I don't think this will go on much longer. Thanks to God the number of believers is increasing more and more, and soon the atmosphere will clear. There are believers everywhere—among the simple and the scholars, in learned institutions, in workers' organizations, among party members and non-party people. During my priestly ministry, I'm sure I've baptized at least five thousand adults. Now *there's* an indication of the growth of the faithful. The atheists will have to take this into account.

Today faith is becoming the *only* means for saving people. As an example, let me read a letter from a spiritual son of mine:

I was a wasted individual. Alcohol had destroyed me. There was no light, no joy, no rest. My soul was destroyed. My eyes saw nothing— people, the sky. Nothing. Death had arrived. Though I still moved my legs and was able to speak, already I was a corpse, a vile creature, and not a man. There was no way out, no hope. A profound darkness fell. My intimates turned away from me because I brought them so much evil that they couldn't bear it. Only one person bore everything and endured everything without abandoning me. That was my mother. She deserves all attention, concern, and love. After all sorts of terrible experiences, vile deeds, great bouts of drunkenness, debauchery and decay, a bit of sunshine peeped through. I met a priest. He baptized me. (I was already 35 years old!) Little by little, day by day my abominations died out. My soul resurrected! The first signs of Christianity in me—"resurrection from the dead"! I believed, having experienced resurrection from the dead—here in this life, in this world. Everything cleared up, and joy began to abide in me, a serene joy, the joy of the resurrection of the soul. And this power continues in

me still. Now I have a family of my own, a wife
and daughter. I am an artist, and my work has
become more perfect and significant.

This is just one example. There are a great number
of them. The atheists scare people by saying that believers
are poor workers, that they don't fight their own defects,
that the lives they construct for themselves on this earth
aren't very brilliant. These are just atheistic fables. On the
contrary, faith awakens a person to honest work, to refusal
to accept his own defects, and to a way of life which will
improve his relationships with all people. He is a believer
who does evil to no one.

QUESTION: How can we explain the situation we're in,
that the family is disintegrating, fewer children are being
born, and they aren't being educated. Often children don't
know their father or mother. What a difficult life they
have! What can we do to help?

ANSWER: The disintegration of the family can only be
explained by the absence of religious upbringing. When
there is no religion, there are no traditions, and each person
lives as best he can, meeting his own egotistic demands. By
all means try to give your children a religious upbringing.
Don't be afraid of the difficulties that will stand in that
path. The unhappiness which results from lack of religion
can't be compared with any others. Bring your children to
church, accustom them to the holy things, and they'll re-
deem your sins. Only in such a case will the family be
restored.

QUESTION: I know that abortion is a sin, but I'm afraid
with my drunk of a husband—what kind of children will I
have? Do we allow abortions in such cases?

ANSWER: Abortions are *never* allowable, just as murder
is never allowable. Abortion is *murder*. Look at it this
way. But I understand your position as the wife of an
alcoholic. I understand and commiserate with you. May
God help you bear your cross. It is a heavy cross indeed.

QUESTION: Father, I'm a drunk. My family is gone, my life is shot, and yet I can't stop drinking. I'm afraid, but I drink. Tell me, what should I do?

ANSWER: No one can help you in your position, because the disease you have is fatal. But don't despair. If you turn to God sincerely, He can do what's impossible. Only God can help you. I ask all of you in church right now to pray every day for such unfortunate people. Surround them with your attention and warmth. Remember that saving such a person is the greatest of deeds!

QUESTION: Today relations between men and women have become too free and are often impure. Right now this turns me off, but I'm still too young. What will happen later? How can I preserve my purity in such a filthy world?

ANSWER: You'll preserve it if you believe in God. Remember, faith is a miracle, and in your position only a miracle can help. For my part, I hope you find yourself a husband with the same desire for purity that you yourself have.

QUESTION: What should we do if we can't get along, if we fight all the time? Should we go on living together even when we are complete strangers to each other?

ANSWER: I'd like to ask *you* a question. Where were you earlier? If you used to get along, you still can, but it takes mutual understanding and compromises. Do everything you can to preserve your family. Christianity allows divorce in just one case—adultery. If there's no adultery, then you've got to overcome your strife. You've got to understand each other and love each other. Remember—you're both fine people, the image and likeness of God. So build your domestic church—the family—together. This is the great ascetic feat of Christianity. Divorce has reached plague proportions among us, breaking up the family. Fear divorce.

QUESTION: What should I do if my husband has changed,

but I don't want to abandon him for the children's sake? Should I endure this graceless cross?[9]

ANSWER: If you don't want to abandon your husband, don't. Fight for him with all the means at your command, even if this means being on good terms with him. It's a good intention to bear this graceless cross for the children's sake. I'm amazed at a mother's selflessness! May God help you!

QUESTION: What does it mean to say that the family is a "domestic church"?[10] How is this achieved? Can it be realized in our times?

ANSWER: "Domestic church" sounds a bit naive today, because it often happens that the husband is a believer but the wife isn't, or vice versa. The domestic church is the realization of your faith in the family. It means that you live according to the laws of Christianity, that you remain faithful to each other, that you love each other, and that you raise good children. But if you're the only believer in the family this can't be attained. Remember that for the believer there's no such thing as impossibility. "I can do all things by the Lord Who strengthens me," says the apostle.[11]

QUESTION: How does the Church relate to the phenomenon of concubinage? We remember that in the twelfth century the Roman Catholics authorized theological students and others to keep concubines. Today, when morals are falling everywhere, it's very important to know this.

ANSWER: We don't allow concubines. If looking at a woman with adulterous intentions is condemned, how much greater the condemnation for living with someone. There's only one way—marriage. Anyone who would consecrate his life to God should give up everything freely. One must look upon this as sin, because only such an attitude can lead

---

[9]Lit.: *bezblagodatnyi krest.*

[10]"Domestic church": Russian piety traditionally has stressed home and family as constituting a little church, and has seen in passages like Rom. 16:5 ("the church in their house") references to this "domestic church."

[11]Phil. 4:13.

to repentance. To allow concubinage as something legal would be to condone fornication, and fornicators will not inherit the Kingdom of God.[12] The decline in morals comes precisely from such phenomena. Morals can be raised only by raising the people's chastity.

QUESTION: What is blasphemy against the Holy Spirit? It says in the Scriptures that all sins are forgiven but blasphemy against the Holy Spirit will not be forgiven in this world or in the future.[13]

ANSWER: Blasphemy against the Holy Spirit is conscious opposition to truth. So taught the holy fathers. For the most part people oppose the truth unconsciously, often through misunderstanding or delusions. We should feel sorry for such people and pray to God for them that He will give them an understanding of the truth and the power to live according to that truth.

QUESTION: Why are believers so boring? All they think about is death. They don't understand earthly joys. Imagine for a moment that there's nothing *there*, so why do they deprive themselves of everything *here*? In my opinion religion—especially Christianity—is suicide.

ANSWER: Now if that isn't a cloud in the bright blue sky! Where did you deduce that believers are boring? Joy doesn't come from sinning. On the contrary it comes when you don't sin. Believers think about death precisely in order *not* to sin. Does sin give real joy? Hardly. There's boredom and satiety in sin. Sin's joy is artificial—just artificial bursts of joy. People truly rejoice when they're sure that everything they do is necessary, that life exists but death doesn't. Forgive me, but we believers can *never* imagine that there's nothing *there*—not even for a moment! Therefore, earthly joys are more joyful for us than for atheists.

"Everything is lawful for me," said the apostle, "but

----

[12]1 Cor. 6:9-10.
[13]Mt. 12:31.

nothing should control me.''[14] When earthly joy overwhelms me and becomes the only thing I have, then man becomes most unfortunate. The worst boredom comes from being satiated with earthly joy. The worst possible crimes grow in such soil. Earthly joys should become the beginning of heavenly, eternal joy. Man is created for joy, for bliss. The kingdom of God begins while the believer is still here, and physical death doesn't hinder this joy. For the atheist death is the end of joy, but for the believer it's the beginning of even greater joy. Now consider in which state it's more joyous to live, and you'll understand that Christianity is precisely the religion of joy!

I think I'll stop here for today. As a conclusion, I'll tell about two incidents.

An old lady rides by a church and crosses herself. An atheist sitting there, in order to make fun of the ignorant old lady, says, "Grant this, O Lord." She wasn't upset a bit, but said, "Grant him, Lord, enough brains not to laugh at a mother's prayers."

A second incident. An old priest gets on the bus. One of the passengers says in an overly friendly way, "Hey, pop, ain't you afraid of riding on a bus? You think they're driven by demons, don't you?" The priest didn't think long before answering: "I'm not afraid. It's good when you saddle a demon and jump on his back. It's bad when one saddles *you* and takes you for a ride."

But these are just jokes. We have no desire to laugh at unbelievers and atheists. Lack of faith is a terrible disease. May God help all of us, every one, to be delivered from it.

However, lack of faith can occur in so-called believers. Therefore the apostle says: "Now you stand. Beware lest you fall."[15] Let's remain steadfast in our faith, so that our faith, like a candle, will illumine everyone in our Russian house, and today's unbeliever may tomorrow become the greatest of believers.

---

[14] 1 Cor. 6:12.
[15] Lk. 6:8.

Faith is a process of good forces overcoming everything else in our organism, and faith abides: the best, the greatest, the most marvelous thing in life. And with faith life becomes meaningful, purposeful, fearless and joyful: a life which will have no end.

...I just received a note which must be answered right away.

QUESTION: What are you doing? These interviews are propaganda and agitation, and they're forbidden. They can get you for that.

ANSWER: What can I say? "They'll get you..." So what? Should I stop doing God's work out of fear? So why did I become a priest? Why is it written in the Gospel, "The good shepherd lays down his life for the sheep"? Why did Christ say, "Go and preach"? People are saved by preaching. Should I then be afraid? For whom is it said, "Be insistent both in season and out, convince, rebuke"? Let's also recall the *Acts of the Apostles*. When they were forbidden to speak about Christ, how did they answer? "Obey God first, then man."[16] That's how. God sent me to preach, and just because someone doesn't like it, am I supposed to *quit?*...

Propaganda and agitation are for atheists. We use sermons. A sermon can take any form, including questions and answers. It won't do any good to threaten me. I'm ready for anything. By the way, a sermon acquires even greater power when people suffer for it. I'm ready to suffer. The atheists would probably like us to read an article from *Notebook of an Agitator and Propagandist*[17] in church, but I *will not* do so. Preaching is needed now more than ever, and if the question-and-answer format attracts people, it has to be used. I rejoice that people are coming to these discussions. I'm doing God's work. I'm trying to save people. I'm pursuing *no* other goal! Atheism has corrupted

---

[16]Jn. 10:1; 2 Tim. 4:2; Acts 4:18-20.
[17]*Bloknot agitatora i propagandista*: popular-level atheistic title.

people. Drunkenness, debauchery, the breakdown of the family have all appeared. There are many traitors betraying each other and our country. Atheism can't hold this back. Faith is what's needed. I'm convinced on the basis of experience that when a person believes he stops drinking and indulging in lust. He becomes honest, and, finally, he becomes a patriot. If this is so, then I *must* preach. If they forbid me to preach from the pulpit, I'll speak from outside the pulpit. If they throw me in jail, I'll preach even there. Preaching's my main job. Everyone who thinks only of his own security is threatened with destruction. It's a crime.

I preach so that people will turn away from destruction. I have *no* other goal. I'm saying this so that everyone can hear. If the thugs who'd try to intimidate me by asking this question are in church right now, let *them* hear. I don't go to the Atheists' Club. I don't go out on streetcorners. I speak inside the church. The atheists can speak anywhere—in the papers, in the movies, in all the clubs. But we—can't we even speak in church? Then what kind of freedom of conscience is there? . . .

May God preserve you all.

The Fourth Discussion

First of all, I'd like to thank you for the attention that you've shown me. This convinces me more than ever that my undertaking is necessary and that it is becoming vital. And if this is so, then nothing can stop me. So, even if this is new, even if almost no one is doing it—so what? If it interests people and draws attention, then a priest should be daring. So I'm daring. I'm glad that this is becoming interesting. My whole object was to make it interesting—interesting first of all, that is, alive and vital.

I realize that some questions should be answered more fully, perhaps even differently from the way I have answered them. Again, I repeat: I'm not seeking an exhaustive treatment, and even to answer in a way that will satisfy everyone is impossible. I repeat: I'm trying to arouse interest. Then each person will be able to answer things for himself. At any rate, then no one will be satisfied with a prepared stock answer. That would only dry up religion—the most *interesting* thing in life—to such a degree that (as the atheists say) it would seem boring and obsolete. But every person *needs* religion.

Of course, you can drive religion off into the backyard of your life, live as you may, take from life whatever it gives, consider yourself an unbeliever. But at some moment, you'll come to religion. God is the source of life. After all, we don't receive life from ourselves, but from someone else, and so, sooner or later, we must turn to that source. Lack of faith devastates life's powers. If these aren't filled with

63

faith, then in the end comes death, spiritual and physical. Religion is man's link with God, and upon this link depends our existence.

Last time I answered the question, "What is atheism?" I took definitions by believers and non-believers and then tried to show what atheism leads to in practice, how it destroys material and spiritual values. Naturally I've upset some people and probably even offended others. I ask to be forgiven, because I didn't want to offend anyone personally. I know that there are honest atheists who have no desire to harm others. But atheism itself has resulted in evil, as we see in everyday life. Today our discussion begins with the question, "What is faith?" I'll read the question.

QUESTION: Last time you spoke about what atheism is. Now answer this question: "What is faith?"

ANSWER: If you remember, in answering the question about atheism I first read some definitions by believers, then by non-believers, and then I turned to examples from life. I'll use roughly the same plan to construct today's answer, but I'll let the atheists speak first. After all, we know that you can understand yourself better by listening to your opponent's voice. So we'll let "our enemies" speak first. I put "our enemies" in quotation marks because atheists are our enemies only by misunderstanding. After all, aren't they, too, believing people, who have proved on the basis of some sort of experience that there is no God? How can you prove that something *isn't*? We say that God *is*. They say that He *isn't*. Therefore we're all believers: They just come to faith through the back door. After reading an article by an unofficial antireligious propagandist (in the newspaper *Vecherniaia Moskva*,[1] I believe) I was struck by this phrase: "We do not fight with believers, nor even with the clergy. We fight with God on behalf of believers!" There! He just proved there *is* a God—because he fights with Him. Of course, that was just the propagandist's blunder. (It's prob-

---

[1] *Moscow at Evening*: daily newspaper, organ of the Moscow Municipal Committee, stressing the arts and sports.

ably not an accident that he's unofficial, because an official propagandist wouldn't have allowed that to get by. He would have gone over his expressions extremely carefully.) But for us the opinion of an unofficial antireligious propagandist is more valuable because it's more sincere. An official one (i.e., paid) must not allow any blunders. He must carefully conceal his own personality. Oh, how often the propagandist wants to talk about God, but he's got to hide it! "Keep silent and hide yourself, your feelings and your dreams," as the poet said. The unofficial propagandist can make blunders as he speaks, and these are valuable for us because in them he's more sincere and he expresses his main point more fully.

But it is still too early to talk about that. For now, let's imagine that atheists *are* our enemies. Thus, a word to our enemies: "What is faith?"

Let's take the *Short Dictionary of Philosophy* (Moscow, Politizdat, 1970). There we read: "Faith is a relationship to events, theories and even inventions, in which these are accepted as authentic and true without any proofs. (We make note of this definition for ourselves in order later to set it before the believers for them to disprove.) Faith is the antipode of knowledge." And *we* make note of this for ourselves, because atheists, even the most uneducated of them, number all believers among those who are unfamiliar with science, somehow forgetting that the majority of all scientists are, after all, believers. This is a fact, and facts, as the atheists themselves say, are stubborn things. Try to squeeze them into fixed molds and they just resist.

Let's read further. "The object of faith is, as a rule, to reject science and mankind's practical activity." See what they seize upon: science and practical activity. "Take, for example, such 'facts' as the existence of divinity, the creation of the world from nothing by God, etc. All religions are based upon this sort of faith, and their defenders usually understand religious faith to be incompatible with reason . . ." Again they're on the wrong track. The article claims that even the defenders of religion understand religious faith to be incompatible with reason, but in fact they proceed to demonstrate everything. When a person starts lying, he lies and he congratulates himself: "How very fine!" But we, the defenders of religion, understand religion to be compatible with reason, and we believe. Don't you believe? Probably every believer has at some time heard the atheist's question: "Tell me, do you *really* believe?" Thus it's a fact that atheism isn't only disbelief in God, but also disbelief in man. Atheists just can't believe that it's possible both to believe sincerely and to be a scientist at the same time. So let them examine the facts a bit more closely—today's facts, not those of the past. Then they'll see that many scholars engage in science and at the same time are sincere believers. Here we have one more of the atheists' negative qualities: disbelief in human sincerity.

Let's read on. "This is exceptionally clearly expressed in the aphorism ascribed to the Christian theologian Tertullian: 'I believe, because it is absurd.' That is, that from the rational point of view, the dogmas of religion are absurd, and one can only believe in them." We shall speak about this passage and about the word "absurd" later on. For now we'll read on a bit more:

> Therefore the philosophers who have compromised with religion have denied the general competence of reason. "I have had to limit knowledge," wrote Kant, "in order to free a place for faith." The objects of faith, according to Kant, are the immortality of the soul, God and freedom of will. In the theory of knowledge, faith emerges as something akin to intuition, idealistically understood (in the Slavophile A. Khomiakov, in Vladimir Solov'ev's philosophy of all-unity, in James' pragmatism, etc.). Theories and hypotheses built upon blind faith [*it's amazing how "perceptive" atheists are!*] are considered groundless by materialistic doctrine, since they contradict science and practice. [*I'm not stopping you from considering anything, but don't thrust your considerations on others—let your considerations be on your conscience alone.*]

The term "faith" also means the conviction that scientific conclusions are the truth, the certitude that certain events, social ideals, etc., inescapably exist. For example, an enormous number of people believe that in time communism will conquer the whole world . . .

Now that's interesting. It means that atheists *believe*. Well then, what does our difference of beliefs mean? Atheists speak of their faith in this way: ". . . such faith is based upon knowledge; it is the consequence of varied life experience . . ." We, too, have a book called *Varieties of Religious Experience*.[2] But atheists for some reason believe that their experience *is* experience while ours isn't. If you think about it, this is just blind faith, antireligious fanaticism, when they refuse to take other people's experience into consideration when it differs from their own. Finaly, the dictionary's last lines: "Without such faith"—that is, without the atheists' faith—"a person can neither know nor act at full value."

We have come back to where we began. Everything's come full circle![3] Let's listen carefully to what the atheists say: "Without faith"—in this case we don't distinguish the faith of atheists from that of believers—"a person can neither know nor act at full value." In other words, a life of full value is unthinkable without faith. The atheists themselves have admitted it.

When I was thinking of how to refute the atheists' position I sketched out a few questions for myself. Faith, they maintain, is that which is accepted without proofs; faith is the antipode of knowledge; faith is incompatible with reason, etc. But it seems that they've refuted this all themselves: "Without faith a person can neither know nor act at

---

[2]The reference is to William James' classic work.
[3]The Russian reads: *"Nachali o zdravii i konchili o zdravii, a za upokoi— eto neverie"* (lit.: "We began with 'for health' and ended with 'for health,' but 'for repose'—that's unbelief"). Reference is to the prayers of the Proskomide (see n. 7 to the First Discussion), in which intercession is made first "for the health" of the living, then "for the repose" of the departed, and finally again for "the health" of the living.

full value." So say the atheists, and here we must ask, which faith is better? To this we can say, whoever has ears, let him hear. And (we could add) whoever has eyes, let him see; whoever has a mind, let him examine everything for himself. The atheists want to get us bogged down in their own blind faith. They think we're all fools. But after all, we are all still able to think for ourselves.

I said a long while ago that atheism is faith coming in through the back door. As it says in the Gospel, "The demons also believe and tremble."[4] Let them believe and tremble. We'll believe and rejoice. Faith for us is joy, and we consider atheism sadness, as I said last time.

How does our faith differ from atheistic faith? First of all, atheists believe in relative truths while we believe in an Absolute Truth. Relative truths are found at every turn, but the Absolute Truth isn't so easily known. Now I'd like to read a passage from a work of Christian apologetics: "If there is no Absolute Truth, then life has no meaning and no goal." What sense is there if everything ends in death? A person dies and that's it. One can only really speak of life if life is eternal. When we strive for something and die, often without having attained anything, what meaning or purpose is there in our death? Just one: it destroys us. Then what meaning is there in life? To be destroyed? *Really*? Here we reach the point of utter absurdity.

We'll continue our excerpt from Christian apologetics. There can be various solutions to the problem of religion. Atheists solve it just one way: Bang! You're dead![5] But that won't do. Let's hear how the question of religion is settled in philosophy, in its various approaches.

1. Scepticism. Here there's doubt about everything, including the existence of God. Its answer to the question of God (Absolute Truth) goes like this: "I don't know." Now there's an honest answer. But atheists, although they don't

---

[4] Jas. 2:19.

[5] Russian: *"Raz—i v damkakh"*: "Checkmate!" in chess, but with a rather different shade of meaning.

know either, say definitively: "No such thing." They pass off their ignorance as knowledge.

2. Criticism (Kant). Absolute Truth is unknowable, so God is unknowable. Criticism says: "I can't know accurately; it can't be proved scientifically." For that matter, what proof do we have to show that there is no God? But the atheists want to pass off lack of scientific proof as proof by science. But we don't prove God, we believe in Him.

3. Positivism (Comte). This is an affirmation that mankind in its development passes through three stages: the *theological*, when faith prevails; the *metaphysical*, when speculative philosophizing prevails; and the *positive*, when scientific knowledge prevails. Positivism's answer to the question of God and Absolute Truth is: "I don't want to know."

4. Atheism is the affirmation that there is no God. Atheism is a belief because it's impossible to know this. Atheism is the belief that there is no God, a faith in no-God. But a faith in what then? Atheism keeps quiet about that.

5. Pantheism. This is the belief that God and nature are the same thing. One can't know this. One can only believe it. We might note that pantheism is fraught with godlessness and materialism.

6. Deism is faith in God as simply the First Cause and Creator of the world and its laws, but not as its Provider and Sustainer.

7. Theism is faith in God not only as Creator and First Cause, but also as the Universal Provider. One can enter into communion with God in sacraments and prayers. Christianity is the most perfect type of theism.

Atheists want to convince everyone that only they understand everything correctly and view the world and all things, God and man, correctly. But it seems that atheism is just one type of approach.

We read from apologetics:

Let us examine these outlooks briefly. Scepticism is fruitless. It rests upon its "I don't know," and makes no ethical, determined spiritual attempt at knowing the Absolute Truth—God. Consistent scepticism ought to doubt its own doubt (i.e., to become completely impotent in all questions of whatever sort concerning the knowledge of the world and man). Criticism is ultimately only an acknowledgment of the limited nature of scientific knowledge. Positivism is the combination of a peculiar scepticism (theological and philosophical) with a naive faith in science. Cutting itself off from the principle and vital inquiries of the human soul, positivism in this way emasculates itself as an ideology and is reduced to a conglomerate of separate pieces of "scientific" knowledge fit for satisfying the minor practical inquiries of life. Positivism suffers from the absence of a desire for Truth. Atheism, being faith in the absence of God and Absolute Truth, goes astray in a mass of contradictions and is incapable of building not only a comprehensive ideology but even the sort of more-or-less satisfactory theory of matter which it tries to deify, ascribing to it absolute properties. Pantheism, which identifies God and nature, also goes astray in irreconcilable contradiction, because it can explain neither the first principle, goal, and meaning of the world and man, nor expediency in the universe, nor the source of evil, nor moral law. Deism, which denies Providence and Divine Revelation, cannot give any answers to the most vital questions of human life. Only theism (and especially its most perfect form, the religion of Christian revelation) gives the most harmonious, the deepest, the widest, the best reasoned, the most conclusive, the most convincing, and (at the same time) the most radiant, most joyful outlook on life. At the basis of the Christian religion lies a thirst for the Truth and a will for Truth.

Absolute Truth must exist, and I want to know it, whatever this requires! From this resolute act (will for Truth), the construction of the Christian outlook begins. After this moral, resolute effort and seeking, an honest, critical mind will immediately contend: "But man, being part of the world as a whole, being not the Creator, but a creature of this world, limited by the time of his birth and his death, and by the space of his life, cannot himself independently know the entire limitless world, comprehend the thoughts, the plans, and the goals of his Creator, or understand the sense and goal of the life of the whole world or his own life. For an insignificant part cannot understand the absolute whole!"

Absolute Truth is unreachable for mankind. However, there is one—and only one—way by which the knowledge of this Truth is possible. If an Absolute, All-Perfect, Higher Being exists—God, Who is the Author and the First Principle of all, the Creator and Provider of the world—and if this Absolute Being—God—desires to reveal Absolute Truth to man, then and only then can Truth become accessible to our consciousness. In other words, Absolute Truth either cannot be known (and then life is senseless) or it can be known only through God's revelation to man.

Absolute Truth is revealed by God. But does such revelation exist? Yes, it does. Christ spoke about this clearly, simply, and definitively: "I am the Way, the Truth and the Life." That is, the method or Way of knowing truth is Truth incarnate—"everything I say is Truth, for I reveal God, My Father, to men"—and Life—"Without me, there can be no life." How can we relate to Christ's words? We can believe them or not believe them. But "not to believe" means to believe in "no."

Man has free will, and upon his free will depends a decision—what to believe in. It's extremely important that we understand clearly and definitely that *nothing* stands in the way of faith in God, in Christ, in God's Revelation. When one believes in God, in Christ, in Revelation, *no* contradictions are encountered in the process of constructing a unified ideology. Above all, there opens for us the *only* possibility of knowing the Absolute Truth, a knowledge for which mankind has such a thirst.

Only when one's knowledge is superficial—and as Francis Bacon observes, superficial knowledge often separates man from God—do imaginary contradictions between faith and knowledge, science and religion arise in the mind of man. As knowledge deepens, drawing man—again in the words of Bacon—towards God, these imaginary contradictions disappear without a trace. That's why ninety percent of the world's greatest scholars have believed in God. That's why Socrates, Plato, Aristotle, Plotinus, Descartes, Pascal, Newton, Leibnitz, Pasteur, Roentgen, Lomonosov, Mendeleev, Pavlov, Einstein, Planck and others of the world's greatest scholars of all time have been deeply religious people.

Simple people, those who aren't tempted by science and philosophy, those close to nature and pure in heart, also believe in God. Atheists are for the most part those who have just a smattering of knowledge—the simple and the unskilled. (Many scholars have no more than a smattering of skills and are philosophically illiterate.) Atheists are always defective— either mentally, morally, or in will (bad will).

I just read to you definitions of faith from an atheistic philosophical dictionary and from *Orthodox Christian Apologetics*. The author is Prof. I. M. Andreev; it was published in 1953. It gives an answer for the mind, so to speak. Now let's turn to practical life.

Probably a lot of people know the contemporary author Vladimir Tendriakov. He's written several works on atheistic themes. As a realist he takes his materials from life, from what he has observed from life. I'd like to read now an excerpt from his story, "An Extraordinary Incident."[6]

---

[6]*"Chrezvychainoe proisshestvie."*

[He reads a scene of a teacher's reminiscences about his mother.]

Undoubtedly this is an experience taken from life. We're not interested in the way atheists unmask everything. We ourselves know many such "unmaskers." We know what their "unmaskings" are worth. But here's the truth of life sprinkled about a story. It's convincing and shaking. In earlier discussions I've read to you life situations I knew about. I've read, for example, a letter from a spiritual son of mine concerning how faith lifted his life up out of the mud. I have many such facts, and some time I'll tell you about them. But now I just want to say one thing: Our faith differs from that of the atheist by the fact that it gives meaning to our lives, it lifts a man up and makes him viable. Atheism has laid waste to our life. For life to be full, one must believe. It's easy to be an atheist but more difficult to be a believer, just as it's easy to get sick but difficult to be healed. But those who are sick must be healed.

QUESTION: How does faith differ from atheism? Can you really believe that all atheists are capable only of evil?

ANSWER: I already said today that both faith and atheism are faith, but that we believe in God while atheists believe in an idol. Let's assume that atheists have created an idol of science—or of anything else, for that matter. Here is what distinguishes faith from atheism. An idol is something temporary. God is eternal. So the good that atheists do, believing in their idol, has only a temporary significance. Atheists do good according to their faith, but since it's simply impossible "in our enlightened age" to believe in an idol, atheists soon fizzle out and begin doing evil. There's an interesting story told of a conversation between the late Il'ia Erenburg and a French communist. Erenburg told him that he was tired, and the French communist replied, "How is that possible—fifty years old and tired out? Christians have been going 2,000 years and aren't tired." And we add: We *can't* get tired out, because *our* God is eternal. But the atheists' god is temporary, so they get tired.

I'd like to add a bit more here. If atheism is faith

"through the back door," then the atheist is the menial servant of faith. If it weren't for the kind of atheism we now
have in our country, we'd probably have been stirred to believe long ago. The things they wrote against God here before the Revolution! If atheism had followed the same path
it took *before* the Revolution, perhaps all of us would have
stopped believing! But now we've seen atheism in its fulness and we've been drawn to God. And how! Just one of
today's believers is worth ten pre-revolutionary believers. He
must really take up his cross and follow Christ. Now *that's*
real faith. But when faith is comfortable, it's like it says in
Revelations—lukewarm. That's as dangerous as there is. So
atheism even helps us come to faith.

Let me tell you about two incidents.

A physicist believed. Well, as usual they summoned him
and started on a program of "individual treatment," as they
call it these days. It's easy to give some dummy "individual
treatment," but it's harder with a scientist. They asked him,
"Tell us, how did you, an educated man, come to God?"
"Through atheistic literature," he said. "If it hadn't been
for that, I probably never would have thought about God.
I would have just worked on my experiments. But that
literature gave me a nudge. I began to think, to meditate.
And I came to believe."

A second incident. It was Pascha. As we all know, at
Pascha even the unbelievers come to church. So a teacher at
some institute came—just out of curiosity. When time came
for the procession there weren't enough people to carry
everything,[7] so they grabbed this teacher, put him in a robe
(with his approval), and off he went—just for curiosity's
sake. And what should happen? Some students from his
institute were there. Well, they reported him. He was sum-

---

[7]In the Orthodox Church the services for Pascha are held at midnight Saturday. After a brief Nocturn service the entire congregation leaves the church,
led by the clergy and acolytes bearing the processional cross, banners, icons, and
a special paschal loaf of bread. The procession circles the church three times, re-
assembles before the closed doors, and after the first proclamation that "Christ
is risen!" re-enters the church for the celebration of paschal Matins and the
Divine Liturgy.

moned. They tried to disgrace him. But from that very moment he began thinking about questions of faith. Now he's a believer. So perhaps atheism does have some use in our day. Therefore, I'd be willing to admit that atheism does bring some good in addition to the harm it does.

QUESTION: Just why is it that only a believer can do good?

ANSWER: I didn't say that. Non-believers also can do good. But inasmuch as atheists have no Absolute Truth, their good has only a *relative* significance. And one can live only by Absolute Good.

QUESTION: Why do you consider the atheist to be unfortunate? I'm an atheist, and I don't consider myself unfortunate. When things are difficult, I try to forget my difficulties in my work. Selfless labor for the good of humanity is good medicine against all boredom and emptiness.

ANSWER: The question's a bit demagogic, but I'll answer it. The atheist is unfortunate because in death he knows no comfort. "Take it easy. What's the difference? You'll die, and it's all over." That's no comfort. And furthermore, there's nothing the atheist can offer to a person who's suffering. A flower will grow on his grave and his descendents will remember him . . . What kind of comfort is that to offer the dying? That's why the atheist is unfortunate. Now selfless labor isn't the privilege of the atheist alone. Believers, too, can work, but they have something else in addition. And haven't you heard complaints like: "I'm *so* tired! Work's a bore!" So work is no cure-all medicine. Everyone gets bored and empty, those who work and those who are idle.

QUESTION: Can you really consider the evil in our land to be the work of atheists? It wasn't necessarily atheists who destroyed the monuments of old and the churches. Why are you up in arms with such a fury against the atheists?

ANSWER: So who did cause all the destruction? Can you really think that all of this was done "at the will of the believers"? In that case I wouldn't consider such believers to be believers.

QUESTION: If faith and atheism are the work of internal forces within a human being, how can I determine *when* I become a believer? What signs are there?

ANSWER: When you become a believer, you'll understand this yourself. Only atheists can call for signs. We say that all of this can't be expressed in words. As the poet said, "A thought expressed is a lie."

People come to faith in various ways. In our time it wouldn't be a bad idea to write a book on "The Psychology of Faith." As an example, let me tell of two incidents from my own priestly practice. I baptized a scientist. I asked him what brought him to faith. "That's hard to determine," he said. "When a friend of mine was baptized, I was filled with indignation, and when my daughter was baptized I screamed at her so much that now, when I look back on it, it's as though for that moment I was possessed. But later I felt that I myself should be baptized. So I came . . ."

Another incident. A poet sat on his balcony. It was evening. Silent. The moon was bright. And he felt (as he tells it) that he was an idealist. So he ran out into the corridor and screamed, "I'm an idealist!" A neighbor lady passing by put a damper on him with the cold spirit of her words: "What kind of an idealist are you? We're all materialists." "And such boredom," he says, "fell over me that I began to think about questions of faith, and now I want to be baptized."

How can we indicate the signs of faith here? Apparently everyone determines them for himself. But I'd like to note that however much faith we have, it's never enough. It's always worthwhile to say, "I believe, Lord, help my unbelief." Now for the believer there's no such thing as "impossible," but for *us* a lot of things are impossible. Therefore, though we believe, we have to ask God to help our unbelief.

QUESTION: How can one explain why believers do evil things, if as you say they should only do good? . . . [*I'll in-*

terrupt the question to answer: This can only be explained by weakness of faith. A real believer shouldn't do evil deeds. I continue the question:] ... Read in the papers how believers are led to exhaustion and loss of consciousness by fasts, prostrations and all the rest ... [*Again I interrupt the question to answer this part. Fasting is valuable for everyone. Medicine has come to the opinion that our caloric intake should be less than it is. They are beginning to treat diseases through fasting. Hunger is becoming a medicine. In the army light-meal days have been introduced. I know someone being treated by fasting, by hunger. He told me that only the first six days are difficult. You don't feel too well. Then it gets easier. Your consciousness is cleared. Now you say that fasting leads to unconsciousness, but experience indicates the opposite: clear consciousness. Now, as for prostrations leading to unconsciousness—that's your imagination. They say that Lenin, the atheist, did prostrations in prison to keep from getting flabby. So, you see, prostrations are useful. I continue the question:*] ... now this isn't imagination; it's fact. You probably read about this yourself in the papers ...

ANSWER: Unsubstantiated "facts" in the papers are possible. In know of one incident. At the height of atheistic propaganda they wrote in one newspaper about a certain priest, claiming that he was greedy: He even stationed his wife next to the donation box in order to snatch even more from people. When this "greedy" priest went to the newspaper's editor to ask whether they verify the facts they print, they told him "Of course!" "Then I'll inform you," said the priest, "that my wife died ten years ago, so I really can't set her by the box."

So you see, it does happen that they publish some material which isn't completely accurate. Sometimes they write that believers kill children. Now once I was blessing the people with the cross, and standing next to me was a teenager. When I offered the cross for him to kiss he said hatefully, "I'd *never* kiss it. I saw on T.V. how the believers killed a kid."

So there's no sense in quoting the newspapers. In my

priestly practice I've never seen a believer try to do something evil, much less to kill. A Christian could only kill if
he'd either ceased to believe or had become psychologically
ill. Let's not use unconfirmed reports in order to attempt
to ignite antagonism between believers and non-believers.
I don't criticize the non-believers. I'm sorry for them. So
please, don't come up with cock-and-bull stories about believers. Yes, there is evil among believers, but only because
they don't have enough faith, because their faith is dead.
The apostle says, "Faith without works is dead."[8] When
you read the newspapers, remember: They can deceive. Hence
the saying: "Don't believe your eyes."

QUESTION: Our society is atheistic and therefore education can only be atheistic.
ANSWER: We believers attend church. Doesn't that make
us a society? We consider that atheistic education binds us
against our will.

QUESTION: In your opinion, is it possible for atheistic
education to be useful? After all, atheism also trains people
to be good.
ANSWER: Frankly speaking, I don't know how one could
educate anyone atheistically. Atheism can exist as an ideology, but I can't imagine how it could be a method of education. To educate means to create morals, to train one for
doing good. What morals does atheism create? If there's
no God, will we then do good? If there's no God, it's O.K.
for me to do anything. But with God, that's not so. God
sees everything. You can't deceive Him.

QUESTION: What are morals? Where do they come from?
Can one be a moral atheist?
ANSWER: Morals are from God. "Without Me you can
do nothing," said Christ.[9] Morals are created on the soil of
belief in God, on eternal values. With temporal values peo-

---

[8] Jas. 2:20.
[9] Jn. 15:5.

ple are always at each other's throats, to put it crudely. Look
at life. As a rule the more well-to-do a person is the more
immoral he becomes.

QUESTION: Is any alliance between atheists and believers
possible? If so, on what basis?

ANSWER: Some alliance *is* possible, but there are a lot
of obstacles on the way. When we overcome them we see
that there aren't any atheists, that atheists are believers
through the back door. An alliance is possible on the grounds
that we are all persons and that God created us all. We
shouldn't become embittered or upset, or belittle each other.
We shouldn't dream up fables about each other, but we
should understand that we are all persons, God's creation,
brothers who have one Father—the God of Heaven.

QUESTION: Our State is atheistic. What is your relationship to the State.

ANSWER: This question is about the same as the one they
once asked Christ when they wanted to catch Him in His
words.[10] Maybe someone wants to do the same with me.
Well, my relationship with atheism is well-known. I relate
to the State, to authority, just as it's written in the Gospel:
All authority is from God.[11] Everyone who opposes authority opposes an establishment of God. "Render to Caesar the
things that are Caesar's and to God those that are God's."
But I also have a question for whoever asked me this one:
Is atheism a matter of State or a matter of conscience?

QUESTION: What good is a priest?

ANSWER: It's hard to blow your own horn, as they say.
I *am* a priest after all. I'll just tell what a priest *should* do,
and then you'll understand for yourself what good he is.

In the first place, a priest should be concerned about the
salvation of others, be concerned for their moral condition.
He should relieve others' grief and be able to lay down his

---

[10]Mt. 22:17-22.
[11]Rom. 13:1.

life for the salvation of others. That is, a priest should become a true friend to everyone, regardless of any national,
political or other distinctions. Knowing what moral decay
now reigns, drunkenness, debauchery; knowing how people
have been split on political and national bases; knowing
how much grief of all sorts there is in the world and how
little people understand the grief of their neighbors—knowing all this you'll understand that the priest today is *more*
necessary than anyone else. (I mean, of course, the priest
who's sincere, loving, able to direct everything in a way
that leads people along the path of salvation.) It's impossible to imagine a priest who'd fit the well-known atheistic
caricature: an obscurantist, a deceiver, etc. The priest's task,
incidentally, is also to be able to conquer—by love—the person who is spiteful towards him. He cannot resent those who
have been led astray by atheistic propagandists. I consider
the priest's struggle to be the highest of ascetic feats. But,
unfortunately, there are all sorts of priests. May God grant
that everyone who sets out on this path be a *real* priest.

QUESTION: How do you explain interest in religion among
young people? Could it be the influence of the West?

ANSWER: It's strange. It's as though for someone to believe there must necessarily be someone else "influencing"
him. What *atheistic* influence there is! But now, young
people who, it would seem, have been saturated through
and through with an atheistic spirit are suddenly becoming
interested in religion. So the atheists have sounded the alarm
because such a blaze has broken out. They say that Western
"instigators" have caused it, but in fact it's just a normal
religious process in action. The soul itself has sought after
God. Persecutions and attacks on religious themes only ac-
celerate the religious process. As we know, the center of the
religious process is the Cross. They crucified Christ but the
result was reversed—not death, but resurrection. In Russia
a resurrection from the dead is underway. Young people,
who are always sensitive to contemporary processes of any
sort, are interested in religion, and this can't be halted any
more. It's useless even to try. Everyone must hurry to take

part in this process. Otherwise they might find themselves in the position of those who threw lots to see who'd get Christ's robe. The Mother of God wove the true robe when she ministered in the mystery of the Incarnation of God. Now a robe—that's an earthly matter. But resurrection from the dead—that's heavenly.

QUESTION: Where do people believe better, in Russia or the West?

ANSWER: Everyone wants people to believe better where he himself lives. I'm a Russian, and I'd like to think the best of Russia. I know there are more believers in the West, but remembering Christ's words about the "little flock" upon which He leans, I'd say that if you want to believe in Russia you've got to stand there next to Christ as He's nailed to the Cross. In Russia today that's the only way you can believe. Therefore I think that people believe better in Russia, just like the first Christian martyrs. And one such believer can attract many others to himself. Although there aren't so many believers in Russia, there are enough that they could hoist unbelieving Russia onto their shoulders and place it at the foot of Christ's Cross.

QUESTION: Can a believer emigrate to the West? There are more difficulties for faith here than there, after all.

ANSWER: Precisely because there are more difficulties here, a believer should not emigrate. When you run away from difficulties, you run away from Christ's Cross. It's the same thing as betraying Christ. Anyone who doesn't take up his cross and follow Christ is unworthy of Him. That's what the Gospel says.[12]

QUESTION: There's an idea that is hard for me to grasp. Why was God crucified? God should be all-powerful.

ANSWER: You have a modern understanding of power, so you understand God in a pagan way. To suppress by force, by the thunder of artillery—that's your first witness

---

[12]Mt. 10:38.

to God's power. But then, it's known that physical strength is often equal to weakness, even among human beings. Our God is the God of love, and love condescends to man, and while seeming weak, it brings salvation. Our God chose the Cross as the weapon of our salvation. Therefore we see our God on the Cross, and in this way He seems close and related to us. People follow such a God freely and not like cattle which are driven into their stalls with whips.

QUESTION: Why have measures been introduced into the Church so that faith has been transformed from a matter of conscience into various registrations, i.e., christening, wakes, etc.? I know people who have been baptized, and later this was found out at work and there was trouble. Isn't the Church turned into an informer in this way? She gives away a secret, she tells who was baptized. What confidence can one have that the priest won't tell a secret learned from you in confession?

ANSWER: You know that these "measures" weren't introduced by the Church. This is a provocation by the atheists to split the Church from within. But anyone who gives in to this provocation and tells someone about somebody being baptized or publishes a secret learned in confession becomes a Judas. As we know, Judas was among Christ's disciples, but that didn't interfere with the work of salvation. Christ also had faithful disciples, ready to die for Him and for others and not just prepared to cause them harm.

QUESTION: I've got everything—a job, a house, not a care. Yet there's some kind of depression. Not long ago some guy that lives near me hanged himself. He had everything, too. He didn't even leave a note. Why? I don't really deny God. It's just that the idea is far away from me. And I think, why can't you get along without God?

ANSWER: Because what you have isn't saving you. In your position God is precisely what's needed, and if you don't find Him—well, to tell you the truth, I'm afraid for you. Your neighbor's example is horrible.

QUESTION: What is the Kingdom of God? I think it was dreamed up to distract people from the problems of life, just like the "happy ending." You've got to live for today.

ANSWER: But I think that "today" was dreamed up. What boredom and emptiness and depression! The pleasures that you have don't deliver you. Your soul is depressed in any case. And then you're not so sure about those pleasures. An accident—and that's that, as they say. But the Kingdom of Heaven excludes these accidents. It distracts (you put it correctly) our thoughts from life's problems. It's easier to live if you have the idea of the Kingdom of God. You recognize that yourself. Now if you believe, your life will change completely. The Kingdom of God is within us, as Christ said,[13] and it begins already in this life.

QUESTION: Really, how can I convince myself that I'll live *there*? The idea of the Kingdom is still deceptive. Believers are really sly to have come up with the Kingdom of God. Ha, that's pretty good! Especially when it's so dull living on earth.

ANSWER: It's impossible to think up the Kingdom of God. Try living by your own inventions and you'll deceive yourself. Try calming yourself, knowing ahead of time that nothing exists. You won't get anywhere. The Kingdom of God is the fulfillment of mankind's greatest hopes and desires. It's not just thought up. It's *reality*. But then, you know yourself that the course of life isn't real. It's a shadow, a reflection of something. And, suddenly—nothing! But if there's *nothing*, then life's an absurdity. The Kingdom of God unlocks the meaning even of this life. One must choose either the Kingdom of God or absurdity. There's no other way out. When you meditate on that as you should—and what's more when you begin to *live* by truth and goodness— then the Kingdom of Heaven will become your *only* reality.

I think we'll end our discussion with this. I must once again apologize for not having answered quite a few ques-

---

[13]Lk. 17:21.

tions. But I promise to answer them all. The next discussion will be on Saturday when I serve.

May God preserve you. May God help us, so that all the questions we've raised will ripen into a real answer in our souls. For now, we only scatter such seeds as we have. They must ripen in your souls. May God help!

The
Fifth
Discussion

(February 23, 1974)

Finally it's becoming clear who comes to these discussions. Mostly the young. Even non-believers come, and those who perhaps have never dropped into a church before. Non-Russians come, including many Jews. I'm very happy about this. Last time I spoke with you I happened to look around and was touched and moved by the picture. Some were standing, leaning on something. Some were even sitting.[1] But everyone was listening attentively. There was an air of ancient simplicity. But along with feeling moved, I felt afraid: Here I've attracted these people, they're listening, but what am I giving them? What can I give when I myself am spiritually poor? Many of you here know more than I do and understand everything better than I do. Then I thought: I'm a priest, and that which is deficient in me personally is filled up by the grace I received in the sacrament of ordination.[2] And then, must I necessarily give something special? Or perhaps I myself ought to study. Our main object is to find a common language, to find a language of love and truth, the language through which we should speak with God. And God will give everything that

---

[1]In the Orthodox Church one usually stands throughout the service. Sitting is the exception and is normally reserved for the old and the infirm.

[2]Cf. the Orthodox prayer of ordination: "The grace divine which always fills that which is infirm and supplies that which is wanting ..."

anyone needs. The main thing is to find a common language.

I just happened to talk to a priest who asked me, "You preach all the time and aren't you afraid?" "What!?" I said. "That's our *duty*, our first duty, to preach." He agreed: "Go ahead and preach, but we've lost our common language with our flock. Quick, perform the service—bang! bang! bang!—and home again as fast as possible!" Well, I want to find a common language with my flock.

Not long ago one of my usual flock said, "Don't you see that people are coming who don't even know how to stand in church?" I do see. And I'm happy. "Don't *you* know," I said, "that the shepherd must leave the 99 faithful and seek the one who went astray? And look how many strays we have. Don't we have to seek them?" And you really shouldn't consider yourself a "non-stray." We, too, can learn something from our guests. At least we can learn how to listen attentively. You know, for those of us who come to church all the time it all becomes familiar and we behave as though we were in our own homes. We shouldn't forget that the church is God's house. "Don't get accustomed to holy things," a pious metropolitan who died in 1961 used to repeat. "One must be reverent before the holy." We all need to remember that. And those who come to church for the first time are always reverent in front of holy things. That's what we should learn from them.

Of course, every sincere believer would agree with this, and the person who asked me this question also agreed. We must rejoice—with the joy of the father who met his prodigal son coming from afar, with the joy of the woman who found the pearl in the garbage. Rejoice! For a person is coming to God.

"That's all fine," agreed the person with whom I was exchanging questions, "but look what might happen. Attracting people is called propaganda, you know. Wouldn't it be better just to explain things to our own people? You know, even our own people don't know very much these days. You should think about yourself. You have kids . . ."

Now *that's* what everything often rests on for us. "How

will they view what you're doing?" "Won't things go
worse for you?" We've forgotten that *this* was written for
us: "Whoever will not follow after Christ and take up his
Cross is unworthy of Him. Whoever loves his father or
mother or children more than Christ is unworthy of Him."
If this applies to everyone, how much more to the priest?
We often strike a bargain with our own consciences. Just
be quiet and unobtrusive. But how can we be quiet? A
priest has to *burn*! Christ said to preach: "Go and preach.
Search the by-ways." The house of God must be filled!

God's work can't be compared with anything else. All
other work has a temporary meaning, but God's has an
eternal one. The cosmonauts flew in space, forgetting that
they had children. But our work isn't just to conquer space.
It's to bring people into the kingdom of God. Can't we be
just as daring? One must always be daring in doing God's
work. And I've decided to be daring. I'm happy that more
and more people are coming to my discussions. Let's all
be daring together.

We have quite a flight ahead of us today. A lot of
questions have been collected, various ones from various
people—from those who come to church all the time, from
those who have dropped in accidentally, from unbelievers
and from Jews. Today we'll touch on the "Jewish question."
"But how will you link this with Christian questions? Won't
you be evasive?" No, I won't. Christianity must illuminate
all questions. It can't be confined by any limits. It's especially bad when this limitation comes about by atheistic decree. Let's open the Gospel. There everything is illuminated.
Let's glance at sacred history. There everything is spoken
about. It's a great tragedy when Christianity becomes dried
up, when it's transformed into something common. One
must burn with Christianity. Christianity must be a burning
candle which illuminates everyone in the house. That's how
I want Christianity to shine. All the more since I'm convinced—since I *see*—how much smoke atheism has accumulated in our house. In preaching Christianity I'm at the
same time a patriot. After all, no state wants its citizens to
be made up of criminals, drunkards, people in despair, those

who have lost their faith. It's very sad for me to see how
the young people don't know what to do with themselves.
If they come to church they'll know what to do in life.

First I'll answer a question I was asked today.

QUESTION: Did you get the Patriarch's permission, did
you ask his blessing for what you've undertaken?

ANSWER: I was blessed for this by the very fact of my
ordination. "Go and preach": That's what is said to priests.

QUESTION: What should a priest adhere to in his activities? More precisely, should he adhere to the interests of a
given class or nationality? Also, how should a priest relate
to criminals or (let's say) to political activists? I know that
this question is put rather sharply and might be hard to
answer. But there have been and still are priests who express the ideology of a given class. This bothers me. Please
answer.

ANSWER: That's a serious question: "What should a
priest adhere to in his activities?" To Christ. A priest should
act as Christ did. He should be concerned with the salvation of all people. But since the priest must be concerned
with the salvation of all people, he must look at each person
not as the representative of a certain class or of a certain
nationality or of certain political convictions, but as the
image and likeness of God. And the more that image has
been injured in man, the greater the love with which the
priest must relate to him.

QUESTION: Can one limit his obligations as a Christian
to going to church or to works of mercy? What is a Christian's first obligation?

ANSWER: We modern Christians have an expression:
"Sunday morning Christianity."[3] This includes church attendance, normal charity and the enjoyment of age-old Christian culture. It's bad when Christianity serves only one's
personal goals. You know, you can even give a beggar a

---

[3]*"Bytovoe khristianstvo,"* lit.: "everyday Christianity."

dime in pursuit of your own goals. But Christianity shouldn't be limited by anything. It should illuminate our family life, show concern for society. It should become the content of our whole life. If it's just sort of an "Oh well ..." and not the goal of life, then Christianity's not worth very much. This is what Scripture means when it says that in this way the Name of God is blasphemed.[4] The first obligation of a Christian is to save and to be saved. By saving only yourself, you won't be saved nor will anyone else either.

QUESTION: Pardon me, Father, but you're into a lot of heavy things, as they say. But you haven't thought that many of us who come to church don't know the Gospel or the services. You should explain these to us. A lot of people don't know anything. Just talking on and on about God often turns into a habit.

ANSWER: Pardon *me*! Do you think that if I explain the Gospel and the services to you everything will suddenly improve? Sometime I will speak specifically about the Gospel and the services, but for now I'll just answer briefly. The whole Gospel consists in very little: "Repent, for the Kingdom of Heaven is at hand..." "Seek first the Kingdom of Heaven and its righteousness and everything else will be added to you..." "The Kingdom of God is taken by work..." To love God and neighbor.[5] If we remember this, then everything else in the Gospel will become clear to us. If we look at the matter carefully, we all know this. We just lack the seriousness to apply it to our lives as we should. We play games with ourselves, pretending that we don't know anything.

Now, concerning the services. We all know that the Divine Liturgy is the main service. Everything should be focused on it, especially at the moment of the "Cherubic Hymn" and "We Praise Thee," when the Holy Gifts are transubstantiated. But is this the case with us? Let's think

---

[4]Rom. 2:24.

[5]Mt. 3:2, Mt. 6:23, Lk. 16:16 (with an interesting shift in meaning), and Mt. 22:37-39.

about it. Who among us lays everything else aside during
the Liturgy—and this includes lighting a candle, ordering a
prayer service—and turns completely to God? We look
with mistrust when they say that God's just a lot of empty
words. But how do *we* act? Often we're not justified when
we take refuge in lack of knowledge. Everything is necessary—knowing the Gospel, knowing the services, but also
remembering to talk about God. Who knows at what moment grace will touch our hearts and we'll suddenly be transformed? But I most certainly will talk about the services.

QUESTION: Father Dmitrii, at our last session, in answer
to a question regarding death, you said that a person who
believes should rejoice in life. What does this mean? How
are we to understand "rejoicing in life"? I'd like to hear an
expanded answer.

ANSWER: First of all, we should note right off that when
a Christian thinks about death he doesn't think "Well, we'll
die and everything will be over, so it's worthless to pay attention to earthly things." The Christian who thinks about
death shouldn't think about it in this way. We call death
a "passage" from temporal life to the eternal. We call it
"dormition," that is, falling asleep to everything passing and
corrupt. This world isn't given to us by accident, and we
needn't reject it. We must value every minute of life. If
you examine it very closely, you're not even allowed any
spare or chance minutes. Everything is somehow great and
serious. We have just one goal in thinking about death, and
that's to guard ourselves against sin. "Remember the end
and you'll never sin." Remember that you'll stand before
God and get what you deserve. When death has this kind
of meaning for us, then we'll rejoice even in this earthly
life—for after all it's sin that has obscured earthly joy for
us. We'll rejoice at standing before God—can there be any
greater joy? When we don't know any of this, we don't
know any real joy.

Let's remember the ascetics, how they thanked God.
Let's remember at least the elder Zosima whom Dostoevskii
described, how he rejoiced in everything and summoned

others to rejoice. If you know Christian joy, in general you'll never know sadness. But if you suppose that joy lies in satisfying only something earthly, this joy usually ends in profound boredom. Look at the life that profligates and alcoholics lead. Outwardly it would seem that they're happy, but hell has already begun there. Now look at those who have deep faith. How joyful they are in all situations! Death isn't the ruin of everything but the door to the mansion of eternal joy.

QUESTION: Father Dmitrii, don't you talk too much about things that could be spoken about in the club or at workers' meetings? Aren't you turning the church into some sort of meeting? Doesn't this all have a very unchurchly form?

ANSWER: I don't know whether I *have* spoken about things which can be discussed in the club or at workers' meetings. At least, I don't think that I have. Imagine if what I've said here were said in the Workers' Club. I think they'd listen in the same way that we do to the services in church: they wouldn't. Our people are inquiring about religion. They want to believe. Not long ago—maybe ten or fifteen years ago—you could get sneered at, get ironic looks. But no more. Not long ago I still heard people yelling at me from behind: "Hey, priest-propagandist!" I don't hear that any more. On the contrary, I hear things like "Priests are heroes—everyone and everything is against them." I'd add that even the most mediocre priest today is a hero. What am I talking about? About saying what needs to be said. Everyone should be in church, not just those who have chosen a place for themselves here. The church is expanding its boundaries. As they say, "If the mountain won't come to Mohammed, Mohammed will come to the mountain." And here we've come out to meet each other. The church today should encompass both the club and the workers' meeting. If they'd allow me to speak in the club and at workers' meetings I would, but since they don't, I'll speak here. And our discussions *do* have a churchly form. Their goal is to "church" the life which lies outside the walls of our building. An awful lot depends now on that churching.

QUESTION: Father Dmitrii, doesn't it seem to you that the questions, and consequently the answers, last Saturday came not only from church people but also from those who just happened to be here. (However, if they entered the church, it means it wasn't an accident!) While addressing yourself to them, don't forget those of us who have chosen our way.

ANSWER: Your question reminded me of the parable of the prodigal son who had already returned home when the faithful son came in from the fields and heard joyous shouts. "What's that?" he asked. They told him that his father was giving a banquet because his brother had returned. He'd killed the best calf for the banquet. So the faithful son began to reproach his father: "Look how I've worked for you, but you've never done anything like this for me." "My son, everything I have is yours, but your brother was lost and he's been found. We should rejoice over that." *That* was his father's reply.

I'll answer your question with this parable. We should rejoice. If someone comes into our church for the first time, we should rejoice over it. And if our discussions have attracted a lot of people, let's rejoice together. And if they haven't come here by accident, as you yourself emphasize, then it's probably not by accident that our discussions were begun. Forgive me if perhaps I've offended you by atttracting people who seem to you to be here accidentally. No one is accidental with God. Aren't you sad to see young people hardly able to stand on their own two feet addicted to alcohol and lewdness? To attract them here means to satisfy the needs of their souls. After all, they drink and act as they do because of unsatisfied spiritual needs. They've had something drummed into their heads, they're sick of it and don't see anything else, so they come here. *You* must call them here. A Christian can't hide in a shell. He must suffer the pain of others. The atheists want to make us into scarecrows so that everybody will be afraid of us. And they've succeeded pretty well. We too have begun to be afraid of everything—even of expressing our religious feelings openly. But let's be, as Christ put it, "the salt of the earth," "the light to the world." Then we won't frighten people away, but instead we'll attract them.

QUESTION: Clearly, for anyone who considers himself an Orthodox Christian it is necessary to come to church, and probably the more often the better. But sometimes in the rush you have to miss Sunday services, sometimes even the Twelve Great Feasts. Is this allowable? Do we loose our link with the Church?

ANSWER: It's necessary to come to church. Six days are set aside for work, but the seventh is for the Lord your God. Actually it's not so much for God as for us. When a person has no feasts, his soul is not illumined, and his life becomes so humdrum that you just want to scream. Feasts are necessary. We must be delivered from our rush. Rushing about will swallow you up, as they say. You've got to arrange your time in such a way that without fail you'll be able to lay aside all earthly cares for the feast. When you don't come to church, you lose your link with the Church and hence with God. Then you're caught. Your soul is empty, and in time you get used to it, just as though that's the way things should be. Here atheism catches us in its nets. Don't give up coming to church unless you have a valid reason. And these are valid reasons: sickness, having to go to work against your will, or having to help someone out for a short time. However, in the last case it's the same thing as being in church.

These were our questions from our own people. Now those from outsiders.

QUESTION: It's as though you live outside time and space. No matter how hard you try, your voice is all alone. Even your brothers don't support you. Do you really think you'll turn everything upside down all by yourself?

ANSWER: I'm not alone. God is with me—and thousands, millions of martyrs. What do you think? Was their blood shed for nothing? I'm aware of both time and space. Time and space are in the hands of God and in no one else's. I believe in God. Even if no one were to support me (and that's not true—even you, who asked me the question, are supporting me) I'd still believe in God. You must agree: In the depths of your soul you stand in solidarity with me. Only it's horrible for you to admit this solidarity. You might lose the good thing you've got going. Even if no one supported me, I'd still believe that everything would turn out right. If growth has begun, it will continue. When time comes for spring, no matter what hard frosts there are, spring will come. A religious spring has begun here. It's still weak, but it'll come. Look, no matter how alone I seem, you can't overlook spring. And I don't want to turn anything upside down, but to turn it *around*. However, *I'm* not doing this. God is. When you understand that, you'll agree that I'm not alone. The atheist is alone because except for himself he doesn't know anyone else. As everyone knows, you can be alone in the thick of an enormous crowd. But even in isolation you can be together with everyone. I'm with everyone. There have been a lot of believers since the creation of the world. And we are all alive in God. Don't think that I'm naive or some kind of a fanatic. I can give a full account of what I do. And I do it confidently. When you do something with God, you can believe in your victory. I try to be with God, and I believe in victory. I believe with no doubts at all. If I perish physically because of this, the victory will just come more quickly. Perhaps it *seems* to you (I underline the word *seems*) that this is just a lot of high-sounding words. If so, be baptized. Be baptized and see that these aren't just high-sounding words, but faith in God, which (you've heard of this?) is able to move mountains.

QUESTION: Listen, don't you think your performances have a funny smell to them? You're just using religion as a cover.

ANSWER: You've caught wind of "a funny smell," have you? Let's get things straight. I was released from prison in 1956. It's possible that that peculiar prison smell hasn't worn off yet. But that something *else* smells—you're wrong.

You sure have gotten used to looking at everything from your own high horse, seeing evil in everything! I'm a religious person, and I pursue no other goals...

What I just said in this tone was said in deep pain, and you know yourself that when you're in pain you don't think your words through. They just come from the bottom of your soul. But how can you prove something to someone who doesn't want to believe anything? I'm afraid that with your question you've bitten off more than you can chew. Maybe because I don't respond. Or maybe you wanted to make me lose control of myself, get flustered suddenly and blurt something out so that you could catch me somehow. I sat in a camp for eight and a half years, but I bear no grudges. Don't you know that people who engage in politics don't speak this openly? Politicians are always calculating, but as you see, I don't calculate. I speak, risking my own life and the lives of my family. There are no politics in my words. There's no animosity or slander in my words, no hidden meanings of any sort. Just pain. Pain for everyone and everything. There's nothing else there.

Perhaps some of you in church now are upset by such questions. Who could have asked them? Everyone's looking around. Don't be upset. Perhaps they're not even here today. But still, I'll answer with perfect clarity.

QUESTION: What do you think: Are proofs for the existence of God of any use?

ANSWER: Some are, I think, though to base your faith on proofs alone is the same thing as confirming your unbelief. You've got to believe not just with your mind but also with your whole being, that is, with a virtuous life. As we all know, there are word-jugglers who can *prove* anything but who don't believe. Anyway, let's try to produce some proofs for the existence of God. There are four types in apologetic literature:

1. The *cosmological*, from "kosmos," the visible world. "The cosmological proof," it says in apologetics, "usually rests upon two logical laws: the law of causality and the

law of sufficient reason. The former demands the recognition of a First Cause for the world." If the world exists, that means it must have a creator. The world couldn't just create itself. If we're unable to believe that the church building we are standing in created itself, then how can we believe that the planets, the whole universe could have created themselves?

Let me tell you about a discussion I had with a school girl, a sixth-grader. I asked her, "Who created this little post?" (We were standing next to a post.) She answered, "The workmen." "And the church?" "Also, the workmen." "And this whole planet, the whole universe?" "Also, the workmen," she answered smoothly. "There you are, child," I said. "You're wrong. How could workers construct all the planets if we're only now beginning to reach the very closest of them?" She stood there and thought. It's good that she thought . . . Well, let's go on. "Thus the law of causality requires that we recognize a First Cause to the world. The law of sufficient reason affirms that nothing other than the highest of universal principles can be recognized as a sufficient basis for the true First Cause of the world." And the *true* First Cause (I turn to the same school girl) isn't the workmen (Do you hear me, child?) but God. Let's take another extract from apologetics for greater persuasiveness:

> Everything in the world has its cause. Every cause, in turn, is the result of another cause. Thus everything in the world has the cause of its existence outside itself. Nothing is self-existent. Therefore, neither is the world as a whole self-existent, but rather it must have a cause to its existence, and this cause must be outside this world. Such a cause can only be the superworldly, highest being: God.

2. *The teleological.* Here's what apologetics says concerning it:

> It looks upon the world not as just "something"

which exists and requires an explanation of its appearance, but as something unbroken, harmonious, artistically constructed, expedient, indicative of the wisdom of the one responsible for this expediency ... The teleological proof requires acknowledgment of God as an intelligent being capable of expediting and organizing the created world well.

Of course, there can be objections here: (a) rejection of the expedient construction of nature; (b) explanation of this expediency by chance; and (c) rejection of consciousness and personality in the one who is responsible for the expediency of the world. The first point refers to the frequent phenomena in the world which are inexpedient. To this apologetics answers that often we don't see, we don't understand the goal and meaning of certain common phenomena but this doesn't mean that in general there's no goal or meaning in them. To the second objection apologetics answers that if the expediency of a machine cannot be explained by chance but requires recognition of the presence of consciousness on the part of the expedient machine's creator, then all the more is it impossible to explain the expediency of the consciousness itself and finally the expediency of the entire universe by chance. To the third objection apologetics says:

Only to an intelligent, conscious, and personal Being can the expedient construction of the world be indebted for its origin. Observing the expedient construction of the world we infer a conscious being responsible for the world, one who has a mind to which the idea of the expedient construction of the world occurred in advance, one who has a will which strived to realize this idea, and one who has the power to realize this idea in the real existence of the world.

Critics point to the instinctive, goalless activity of animals, but that is untrue. An animal acts without consciousness of the goal of its activity, but it is not without a goal. It acts in accordance with a goal of which it is not conscious.

3. *The ontological.* This is an internal proof, since it's based upon our internal experience.

The basic idea of this proof consists in the fact that in the idea which is inherent in us of the highest all-perfect and infinite being there is necessarily contained the idea of the reality of this being, for the all-perfect cannot but be real...We cannot conceive a non-existent all-perfect being, just as we cannot conceive a non-triangular triangle.

This can be formulated once and for all as follows:

From the fact that within the human soul there exists the idea of existence which in the fulness of perfection also combines real being, it necessarily follows that this existence must exist not in the mind alone, but in fact as well.

4. *The moral.* The moral proof is practical and theoretical. The practical: Faith in God contributes to the improvement of morality, whereas faith in atheism usually leads to a drop in morals. If serious atheists were to look seriously at their life and see what atheism does, especially in our day, then they would say with Voltaire: "If God did not exist man would have had to invent Him." Otherwise, who will stem the tide of crime? Prisons? They just corrupt people more. Newspapers? People often laugh at them.

There also exists the theoretical or so called "scientific-philosophical" methods of moral proof of the existence of God. Since moral law exists, and since it can't be an invention because it often acts against our will, therefore it has a founder. The voice of one's conscience in the soul often can't be silenced. Apologetics says:

> Close analysis of man's moral consciousness shows us that having freedom of action man experiences spiritual satisfaction from being conscious of having fulfilled a duty. In other words, the freedom of man's will guards against arbitrariness by the presence of a moral law which stands above it and which either approves or censures its actions. Man who has this free will nevertheless perceives this law above himself as a nonconditional commanding power. Hence man himself cannot have created this law and set it above himself.

Here are four famous proofs for you. But why each person comes to God is a personal question. And probably each individual will find his own proofs for the existence of God.

You're probably tired of long discourses, so for a little break I'll tell a religious anecdote. Two students were arguing. "What are you proving to me?" said one. "Tell me, have you seen God? If you haven't seen Him, what are you showing me?" "Any God," said the second, "who'd show Himself to just any fool would be a pretty poor one."

Atheists demand of God: "Show yourself. Send down a miracle!" This world is adulterous and evil, as Christ said. It often seeks signs, but it won't get any. If we *seriously* seek to know God, He'll reveal Himself to us. But to seek God for the fun of it—that's not from religious feelings.

QUESTION: What's the meaning of the words: "How can you believe unless the Father in Heaven draw you"?[6]

ANSWER: This doesn't mean that God is like a thief who'll grab us and take us. We just shouldn't lose a single moment once an inclination towards faith begins in us, be-

---

[6] Jn. 6:44.

cause this means that our Father in Heaven is drawing us. But we must also make an effort on our own part.

Now I'd like to read you a letter from a girl. In it she tells how she came to faith.

January 24, 1974

I was born and brought up in a particularly atheistic family, where not only my parents (party members since 1928) but even my grandmother did not believe in God. Ever since I was a child I learned thoroughly, "There is no God, there never was, and there never will be." I was never interested in questions of religion or iconography or religious tales. I knew nothing about them and didn't think about them.

In 1962 after a bout of 'flu I came down with an inflamation of the pautine membrane of the brain (a post-influenzal arachnoiditis). By spring of 1963 I had almost gotten over this disease, although such residual symptoms as strong mystagmus, speech aberrations, certain lapses in orientation of movement, and on rare occasion a recurrance of violent sieges of headaches to the point of loss of consciousness remained.

On April 12, 1963, I suffered a violent concussion of the brain, after which I was again bedridden. After a while I was cured and began to study again on my own, even though the doctors had forbidden me categorically not only to read, but even to listen to the radio. They spoke about a partial disability. I was 20 years old. Besides my studies in the Institute I was also taking voice lessons, and I attended these regularly.

Then one night (at the end of April, 1963) I was awakened by some sort of a warm light. When I opened my eyes, the room was dark.

The head of the bed faced the window. The door to my room was opposite the window. Suddenly in

the left corner, a bit above eye level, there appeared
a bright point. It shone. The light from it spread
out in waves little by little, enveloping and filling
the whole room. The light was very brilliant, but
not blinding white. Somehow very soft and warm.
Then in this light there appeared not gradually but
suddenly, all at once, a woman with flowing hair,
light colored and with sort of a light blue veil on
her head. She looked at me with her deep, thought-
ful eyes half-turned towards me. She smiled at me
tenderly and lovingly. And I *knew* that this was
the Mother of God! (Let me mention once again,
that I had *never* seen an icon or any other rep-
resentation of the Mother of God prior to that time
and had never had any interest in any sort of religion.) This was all accompanied not so much by
singing or music as we understand it, but by some
kind of an unusual melody (if that word is ap-
propriate here), a soothing sound. Then she disappeared, the sound began to fade, the light again
began to be gathered into a point, and everything
disappeared. I pinched myself to be sure that I
wasn't asleep. It hurt. I hadn't been asleep.

In the morning I said nothing to my family.
I told it all to my voice teacher, a believer. She
recommended that I go to church and light a
candle before an icon of the Mother of God. I
objected: "Why should I go?" (or "jump," as I
actually said). If that's what she wanted so badly,
let her light a candle for me, and I gave her a
commemorative coin ruble. A few lessons later
and she had lit a candle for me.

After that I lived with a feeling of not having
fulfilled some debt and with a feeling of guilt
over this unfulfilled debt.

The arachnoiditis left without a trace. Not a
single neuropathologist has found the slightest trace
of abnormality in me. The headaches have disappeared entirely, the mystagmus is completely gone,

I've regained my orientation—something which is practically never observed in medicine.

Many times since that incident the doctors have declared me terminal (beside the severe arachnoiditis I have undergone six operations and I have a weak heart—a radical coronary insufficiency with a combined mitral defect of the heart), but each time at the moment that these medical diagnoses were spoken I would suddenly become conscious, and an enormous power of protest against the words would fill me: "No, I *will* survive!" And I'm alive. But the feeling of unfulfilled debt and guilt didn't pass. Several years later my landlady said: "You should be baptized. I'll be your godmother. You believe in God, even if you don't want to admit it yourself." I was baptized in 1973, ten and a half years after that incident.

To this day it is difficult for me to call this a vision of the Mother of God, since with my poor reason I cannot conceive (nor do I try to do so) why I was made worthy of such mercy. I can only note that I was never a double-dealer. My errors and sins were sincere. I cannot lie and do not desire to.

(Signature)

P.S. But the feeling of an unfulfilled debt is still alive in me today, perhaps because since 1963 I have wanted to learn the services and sing in church, but I haven't yet done so.

QUESTION: Father Dmitrii, last time you read us an excerpt from a work by Vladimir Tendriakov. Did you know that he also has a work called *The Apostolic Mission*? What can you tell us about it? There are a number of convincing proofs for God's existence in it. You just don't know at the end of the work why the hero loses faith. Meeting the chairman of the collective farm (even though he *was* highly educated) isn't a convincing reason.

ANSWER: Let's open this work and read in the Introduction:

> A strange disease, unknown to doctors. Many people probably carry it within themselves and don't even suspect it. In most people it passes, there's but a bit of discomfort. But once in a while it cruelly maims, producing spiritual invalids and suicides the world over. Time heals a person of this disease, but not in every case.

As you see, even the introduction is guarded in its approach towards us. And all the seriousness of the characters and of the situations are just schemes prepared in advance. It's somehow all predetermined: it has to be unmasked. Now this writer has talent, but when he applies himself to things outside his competence, he betrays his talent. He has invented a believer, though perhaps he took some things from life. I think this writer blasphemes here, not noticing that what he blasphemes is above all his inventions.

In the excerpt we read last time, fact is portrayed as it is, with no tendentious appraisals on the author's part, and it seemed very convincing. I was told that many people were even crying. Now when this writer deals not with someone else's experience but when he himself collides with the fact of faith, then we'll see what he has to say. I think he'll be ashamed of what he wrote in the past, especially since he wrote knowing that no one could take exception with him. Jabber, jabber, jabber.[7] If he'd been serious about protecting his reputation, he would never have done it.

But I repeat: he's a talented writer, and I like a lot of his works. I'd recommend that you read his "Potholes," "Three, Seven and Ace" and "The Court."[8] There he deals with serious problems, and they're better written than the one named above. There are a lot of talented blasphemers.

---

[7]Russian: *"Meli Emelia—tvoia nedelia,"* a nonsense rhyme used to ridicule empty words.

[8]*"Ukhaby"*; *"Troika, semerka, tuz"*; and *"Sud."*

QUESTION: How do you explain not-just-isolated baptizings of Jews lately?

ANSWER: As the apostle said: "The hardening in Israel has been partial."[9] This hardening now is coming to an end. So many things of every sort have happened in the world that more and more people are becoming convinced that Christ Who was crucified on the Cross for us is God Who has revealed Himself to the world in all His fulness. Neither Judaism nor any other religion can tell us how we can get out of the dead-end into which we've gotten ourselves. "An eye for an eye, and a tooth for a tooth"—constant war and enmity, and we're all tired of it. "Love your enemies"—only this can bring us to peace. The Jews are a specially sensitive people, all the more so since they were chosen by God from long ago. So now they're accepting Christianity. And this movement will grow and grow. We must rejoice in this, all the more so since among Christians the opinion exists that before the end of the world all the Jews will be converted to Christ.

QUESTION: Father Dmitrii, I understand and accept Christianity. It's very near to me. But somewhere in my heart there's anxiety. Don't I betray my people by this? My people confess Judaism, and I'm Jewish.

ANSWER: Among the Jews there are atheists. Does that mean that *they* betray their people? Many of them, on the contrary, consider themselves devoted to their people. Now what harm does Christ bring to the Jewish people? What harm do *you* bring to your people by confessing the religion which says you must love all people? Love brings harm to no one. Maybe some would say so, but *not* the Jews. After all, the Old and New Testaments are printed in one book. The Old Testament is a prefiguring of the New. The Messiah for whom they waited has come, and He came only to save—but to save not just one particular people nor just from earthly enslavement. He came to save all peoples from enslavement to the devil. The promises given to Israel are

---

[9] Cf. Rom. 11.

fulfilled in Christ. Abraham's descendents are all of us who've believed in Christ. That's why Christians are called the "New Israel." You can't limit Israel to the little piece of ground that lies somewhere. You can't just think about your own personal affairs today. The world is losing its boundaries, and the Jews must understand this first of all. I look upon the Jews who are now accepting Christianity as the best sons of their people. For today no one understands them, neither Christians nor Jews. But I think that by their heroic example they can convince everyone that their divine election now consists in accepting Christianity and living in love with all.

As we know the Jews are often accused of various special sins, although we are all sinners, both Jews and non-Jews. It wasn't only the ancient Jews who crucified Christ. All of us did. When you look at how Christ is being crucified in *our* land, then you'll be convinced that we're all guilty and must all repent. For this reason the proclamation of the Gospel begins with: "Repent, for the Kingdom of Heaven is at hand!" The Jews who accept Christ will become everyone's favorites. May God just grant that they may hold high the torch which they have received.

QUESTION: Say something about the patriotism of the Orthodox Church. I came to Orthodoxy having felt precisely its deep interest in the unity and strength of Russia, its ennobling influence on the morals of our fellow citizens, its teaching of a love for one's neighbors which is also obviously a love for one's Fatherland. Do you understand this to be one of the goals of contemporary Orthodoxy?

ANSWER: As we know, our Orthodox Church in all periods has been afflicted with the afflictions of her people, and her suffering has been profound at having been numbered among the enemies of our people and our Fatherland. You are correct in writing that it is precisely the Church that has had a deep interest in the unity of Russia, that precisely the Church has had an ennobling effect on the morals of our fellow citizens, that she fosters love within them. And that is precisely love for the Fatherland.

I do indeed understand this to be one of the goals of Orthodoxy. That's why I undertook these discussions, to dispel the misunderstandings that are often encountered. I express my love for my fellow citizens and my Fatherland as well as I can. I think that only the Church can teach us how to love people and our Fatherland and can help us to do so. Only the Church can destroy international disagreements. That's why I've taken up arms against atheism, which sows enmity between people and in particular sets the masses against the faithful. To the honorable atheist I reach out my hand: "Look, our country is in danger. Drinking, the disintegration of the family, debauchery—aren't these a danger?" But atheism doesn't deliver you from them. The Church forgets all offenses. She even cares about the atheists. She is concerned that the light of Christ's truth should be revealed to them. "In Thy light shall we see light."

I had planned on ending here today, but suddenly I ran across some questions which upset me, and I decided not to postpone answering them.

QUESTION: You meet a girl, a young woman. Perhaps she's already been married. You become intimate. You persuade her to get baptized. She agrees. You bring her to Church where she receives the sacrament of baptism. Do you then have a moral duty to marry her? There are a lot of cases in which such marriages don't last long. What should be done?

ANSWER: From the question, you get the feeling that this person isn't yet very familiar with the Christian norms of morality. Let's begin answering point-by-point. "Meet ... intimate ... " Do I understand correctly? But then "you persuade her to get baptized." One *can't* persuade someone to be baptized. What must happen is that, having been with you, she herself requests baptism. In the first place, if you've already been "intimate," that is a sin from the Christian point of view. In ancient Russia, once you'd sinned with her you had to marry her. But in your case, if that didn't happen, but rather (as you say) you succeeded in pursuading the girl to be baptized, you have no moral obligation to marry her. However, you should, as her godfather or elder in the faith, be concerned about her faith, support her Christian attitude and be concerned about *her*. This is your true moral obligation. One needn't confuse Christian concern with the obligation to marry. They are completely different things. In the second place, if you became her godfather, then there is no way you can marry, because the sacrament of baptism established kinship between you, and according to Christian laws relatives don't marry.

Marriages today don't last long for many reasons. In the first place, people come together too quickly. Intimacy begins too early. In the second place, they often look not so much at each other's inner, spiritual qualities as at external features, and what they sometimes consider to be love is *not* love. They're just too hot, as they say. Often marriages have no spiritual basis whatever. People don't feel that they have to stay together for their whole lives. Man differs from the animals in that he keeps one woman in his heart. But these days they get around more, and so, at the very first disagreement, they scream about divorce, forgetting that in Christianity divorce is allowed in just one case, adultery.

We must turn our attention to the problem of the family. How much unhappiness, how many tragedies are brought to the children by divorces! Hooliganism and drunkenness are intensified among young people because the strong, moral family doesn't exist. The family should be a "domestic church." What's sacred is in the Church. So too the domestic church must have its sacredness. Remember, not long ago when most people believed (just read the classics of Russian literature), what morally healthy people there were! What traditions there were in the family! How faithful people were to each other! Faithfulness begins with the family. If there's no understanding of faithfulness in your family, you won't be faithful in life, and if you are such a person, it will be difficult to rely on you.

QUESTION: From childhood you've never known or heard

about religion or God, etc. Behind you lie school, your choice of profession, the institute, five or six years of time spent on the job. Now you're already 27 or 28 years old and suddenly you discover a world that is completely new to you. You start to think. You pose a lot of questions. Finally you make a complete reappraisal of your ideal and actual spiritual, cultural and material values. This reappraisal doesn't make you happy. You've been ignorant too long. If your eyes have now been opened and you see everything in a different light, if your ears hear just like before but now with a new understanding, if everything that happens around you now elicits in your heart an amazing reaction against the very essence of everything you've done before—then it'll become even harder for you to live. Because now you've begun to understand a lot of things. Around you life goes on—the same life *you* used to live while you were blind and deaf to truth and goodness. And you feel, you know, and soon you're convinced that the world around you won't change, that it doesn't plan on changing. Even worse, it constantly insults all the ideals which have become dear and holy to you. What are you to do? Lock yourself up? Suffer? Seek contact with just those who think like you? But there's your family, your concerns, circumstances that don't depend on you. What should be done?

ANSWER: First of all, thanks for asking this question so straightforwardly and sincerely. Your soul, the soul of someone who is suffering and misunderstood, has become very close and dear to me. First of all, I commiserate with you from my whole heart. May God grant you everything you need.

Your question contains not just the confession of your soul alone, but (I'd say) that of your whole generation as well. Your question is addressed to us priests and to the whole of the society in which we live. Let's look at the situation. Indeed, antireligious propaganda tries urgently to mutilate the human soul. In school, in the institute, in the newspapers and in books—everywhere they want to hypnotize man. But sooner or later a re-analysis must occur. At age 27 or 28 such a re-analysis is at times very painful. It has its difficulties. Your re-analysis has been made, but you have very little spiritual strength. If your spiritual strength had been tempered since your childhood, that would be different, but now there's not much to it. What should be done? Lock yourself up? Suffer? Seek contact with just those who think like you do? There's your family and problems which don't depend on you. And then—the loneliness. Even the atheists speculate on that. They say, "The believers are cut off from society. They're alone." So what? They are atheists, and atheists don't want to recognize anyone but themselves. They don't have anything better. There's nothing (atheism *is* nothing) to build on—just bickering over material blessings, and then, that's *the* main unhappiness. A squirrel trapped in a cage. What can you do? If you had greater spiritual strength you could say, "Bring the light of Christianity to the world." Christians came into the world at a time when everything was corrupt, when everyone was up in arms against them. Neither paganism with its age-old foundations nor the Jews—their own people, it would have seemed—understood them. All around there were persecutors, persecutors and more persecutors. For three hundred years Christian blood was shed. But the world *was* illumined by Christianity, and wherever we may be, we have lived by Christian truths for some twenty centuries now. Even atheists live by them, stealing from us. Like: "If anyone will not work, let him not eat." This isn't their invention. It's in St. Paul's letter to the Thessalonians.[10] They accuse us of not wanting to work, of not struggling for a better society, etc. Then you should take up your cross and follow Christ, and undoubtedly there would be a victory. But you're still weak. You need experience and testing. Here's the path for you: Be churched as you should, try to realize Christianity in your life. Believe me, in this case you'll never be alone. As a priest I can say that in the course of my ministry I've come into conflict with many things, and I can say, anyone who hopes on God will never be put to shame. I've been imprisoned. I've been at the front. I've seen that only

---

[10] 2 Thess. 3:10.

believers—of course, only the *real* believers—are viable and can preserve in themselves the image of God and man. May God help you. For now it's hard for you, your cross is loneliness, and you don't yet know how happy you are. You've believed in God . . . Everything will be yours . . . Don't weaken. Joy will come. It's very important to receive reinforcement constantly in the sacraments of confession and communion.

QUESTION: Often you come home tired, morally depressed. You've got a headache. And it's understandable. A believer lives under conditions that are spiritually and morally hostile to his senses and ideas. You have to have great patience in order to stand fast in such situations and to preserve within yourself strength, will-power, a good mood and a good disposition. You're dreaming some vain dreams when finally you cross the threshold of your own house. You're home, surrounded by the utensils of your own spiritual household: the icons, the pictures, the books. But it's terrible. You look at all of this with indifference. It's as though some invisible barrier stood between them and you, and it doesn't allow you to approach, to touch, to commune. You want to pray. You know you have to pray. But the desire is eaten up by indifference, nonchalance, spiritual fatigue. And lots of times many days and weeks may go by in succession. What should be done? What should happen?

ANSWER: Be confirmed in faith. You still haven't understood the main thing: that our earthly life has been given to us for ascetical struggles, that in our earthly life a battle rages. The devil fights against God, and the field of battle is man's heart, as Dostoevskii said. The Christian isn't called a warrior for nothing. His battle ribbons and so forth are in the Kingdom of Heaven. Imagine how conscientious and unselfish we should be. But we're all alienated. Often we no sooner do something good than we demand our reward. We don't do very much serious thinking about the Kingdom of Heaven. You know the Kingdom of Heaven is the realization of *everything*. Without the Kingdom of Heaven everything becomes senseless. That must be understood. Also, the Kingdom of Heaven is attained by work) Only those who use force will attain it. Follow Christ, take up your Cross. Begin even with just a little sigh to God: "Lord, help me!" And watch, after a while you won't recognize yourself. Remember, too, that God listens first to those whose lives are sufficiently pure. If your life doesn't differ from that of the non-believers, that is, if you get drunk and carouse, then deliver yourself from this first of all. (I've said this just as one example.) You must become a light to the world. You shouldn't seek support from others: They should seek it from you. Remember, if you remain with God, then you will be able to do as much all by yourself as thousands, perhaps millions, who don't have God. "For the believer, there's no such thing as impossible"—that's not said without a reason.

QUESTION: Orthodox Christianity has accumulated enormous spiritual experience. This experience is in the lives and sermons of the saints, the venerable fathers, the miracle workers, and righteous people the world over. I've heard that for each believer who sets off on God's way there corresponds (let's put it like this) the spiritual experience of some saint, whose righteousness and life and teachings are especially close to him. This righteous person becomes, as it were, your invisible spiritual pastor and mentor, your teacher. But if that's the case, how do we find out who he is? Isn't it the job of the Church and of the clergy, who know the spiritual condition of their individual parishioners, to set them on the path of salvation along which some holy and righteous person has walked?

ANSWER: Exactly. But you know yourself what position we're in. It'd be good if all priests held discussions like we're doing now. Then it'd be possible to tell the lives of the saints. But what I've undertaken is risky. We still don't know what'll happen. Now I'm looking at all of you here. If we were all armed to do God's work, nothing would be impossible for us. So let's help each other. Communicate Christian knowledge to each other, support each other in misfortune and temptations, and in general manifest an active love for each other. The Church has great experience. So let's make use of that experience and communicate it to each other. In the end we can demand that they take us Christians into consideration. If they can implant atheism in the schools, then let them also teach catechism for young believers ... Christianity demands enormous work—in our time more than ever before. We shouldn't just be contemplative, but rather active warriors. We must remember that *everything* depends upon Christianity: our family life, our social life, and our future life.

May God help us all. May God grant that His grace touch your hearts and that we understand the beauty and power of Christianity.

We'll continue our discussions. We'll find a common language. We'll support and encourage each other by our common efforts. There's an awful lot of work to do. The fields are white, ready for the harvest. How many hungry souls there are, and so few workers. So few workers! Let's *all* be workers. May God help us.

We'll end with that for today. Thanks for your attention.

The Sixth Discussion

Today is our sixth discussion. On the sixth day—the last day of creation—God created man. So today we'll talk about man. A lot of questions have accumulated on this topic. We, created by God and endowed by Him with a free will, are called to participate in His work of creation. "How?" you ask. After all, creation is finished. "Lo, I make all things new," it says in the Gospel. A new man is being made in our day, and that's no less complex than the creation of man on the sixth day. Man created in the beginning was God's creation alone, but now man is created not only by God but by man, too. In the beginning man was created in the image and likeness of God and was supposed to do what God wanted. To create out of good-quality material is simpler than from poor-quality. In our days man, who is subject to sin, has become poor-quality material. This makes the job a lot harder. How can man be created from such material? It's very hard. When God created man in the beginning, He took counsel with Himself: "Let us create." Today when He creates, He takes counsel with man. God cannot create or save man without man's own will. Once the act of creation consisted in this: From a bit of earth He created a body, a physical organism, and breathed into it a living soul, the spiritual substance. But now, before creating a new man, God Himself became incarnate. He became a man Himself. He suffered. He was crucified. He died physically. This new act of creation was much more complex. We may boldly say that our discussion is also participation in God's creation of the new man. His material

113

is the worst, but He must create him. The earth is without
form and void, like the darkness upon the universe . . .

Right away, a question arises. How should we understand
the "days" of creation? Were there 24 hours in each, or
what? In Hebrew "day" (*yom*) means both 24 hours and an
indefinite period of time, a whole era. Therefore, if the Biblical "day" doesn't mean 24 hours, but an era (certain people
breath more easily), this doesn't contradict science. After all,
it's hard to agree that there were 24 hours in the "day" of
creation. Nevertheless, a thousand years with God are like
one day, and one day is like a thousand years. We're more
used to thinking that there weren't 24 hours in each of those
"days" but thousands of years. Well, O.K. Today we've begun to verify everything by science. Science has spoken, so it
must be so . . . But remember, there are scientists who maintain that science itself can be a source of superstition. (We've
already spoken about that in a way . . .) So let's neither be
"throw-backs" nor deify science.

O.K. Some sort of light is already breaking through in our
discussions. Remember what threats there were in the beginning, but now it's becoming clear that these threats were the
result of confusion over our intentions. In fact everything's
calm. Our discussions can continue. According to our constitution the Church is separated from the State. The State
doesn't mess with the internal affairs of the Church. And
what we're doing is the internal affair of the Church. Here
is the light of Christ, and "the light shone in the darkness
and the dark did not comprehend it," as the Gospel according to John says.[1] May this light of Christ be spread abroad.
The light of Christ brings good to all. And people come to
this light. Our audience is varied. Some have very high intellectual inquiries, others have really insignificant ones.
From a question like "What is Jerusalem, a city or something?" it's obvious that the person who wrote it is very ill-
informed. But everyone listens attentively. I even thought,
"If only we could have such attention during the services."
You know, sometimes we are inattentive toward the serv-

---

[1]Jn. 1:5.

ices, which are more successful in creating the new man than any discussions. But discussions, sermons, *are* necessary if people are consciously to create in themselves the new man.

Some say that the discussion form is somewhat unfamiliar. They even worry whether this form is churchly. But, you know, the question-and-answer form is very ancient. It's just been forgotten. As we see, people listen to discussions better than to sermons. So of course we must use it. The question attracts attention in and of itself, and therefore the answer is listened to with great interest. But then, how are we to give each person what he needs? How are we to catch what each person needs? I run to you for help. Let's look at these discussions not as though I were just talking to you, but as though we were talking together, finding a common language by which we can turn directly to God. To find a common language is a vital necessity for modern man. Sooner or later it must happen. And, as we see, it's not just old ladies who are interested in this, as the atheists try to suggest. The young people are interested, too. The question of religion is the question of life. You can't give society a one-sided education. We ourselves are seeing what a one-sided education leads to. Anti-religious literature doesn't interest much of anyone. There are a lot of anti-religious books in the stores but not many buyers.

Our society is interested in originals, not just copies. It needs the real thing, not anyone's commentaries, and especially not illiterate ones. The imposition of anti-religious views leads, however paradoxical this may seem, to the opposite results. It provokes religious interest. Already it's becoming more noticeable how people are renouncing atheism and coming to faith. It's quite a remarkable phenomenon: In families where the parents are atheists, the children are becoming believers. From where? How? The atheists are busting their brains! They can't understand it, and what they don't know is that they themselves are partly to blame. So it's the atheists themselves, however strange it may seem, who are speeding up the process of religion. Interest in religion is now at such a level that it's time for this fact to be reckoned with. But since the atheists *aren't* reckoning, they impose their convictions on people from childhood and get deplorable results.

Let me tell about children, how they react. A child's views are most ingenious. They show us a great deal. Once an eleven-year-old girl came to me for confession. She had a five-year-old boy with her. She pushed him ahead. I turned to her and said that the boy didn't have to go to confession. (As we know, children begin going to confession at the age of seven.) She really stopped me dead in my tracks when she said, just like a grown-up: "You should at least bless him, Father." I blessed the boy and gave him the cross to kiss. The girl came up. I asked, "Are you a sinner, child?" "I'm a sinner," she said with such a deep sigh! I think, "What kind of a sin can it be?" (The main thing is—what a sigh!) "Well, so how are you a sinner, child?" "It's like this," she says. "I believe, but they make me wear a Pioneer's tie.[2] Isn't that a sin?" she asks me very fearfully. I even lifted up my head. If it'd been a grown-up in front of me I'd have thought it was some kind of provocation, but since she was just a child, it couldn't be. At any rate, I kept silent. The girl continues: "Of course, we're powerless. They *make* us do it. So this is what we did. First we blessed it with holy water, and then put it on . . ." "O Lord!" I thought. "How the Lord makes the children wise! O.K., so they make you wear it. We'll wear it, but first we'll bless it."

It's both comical and painful. The question of faith is painful in school. It's no secret that believing parents come into collision with this phenomenon when fanatically-minded teachers tear crosses from children and torment them. There have been cases in which schoolchildren have beaten up believing students really badly. I know of such instances. Everyone admits that the question of faith is a question of conscience for each individual. Even the atheists often repeat this, but they contradict their words by their actions. Take, for example, entering the Pioneers. It would seem there's

---

[2]The red neckerchief emblematic of the "Pioneers," the political organization for children, ages 9-14. The Pioneer movement is one of the main tools for the communist indoctrination of school children.

nothing bad here. It's a children's organization which trains in decency. But there's one catch. After all, it's an *atheistic* organization. What happens with the children of believers, with children who believe? Do you teach them a dual existence from childhood, one thing in school and another at home? Once he's grown up he can choose his own path, but while he's a child, while he's made to do things, he has to be tossed between his parents and the Pioneer organization. And misunderstanding occurs. There are, to be sure, some who pay no special attention to this division. But the question isn't settled so simply. We underestimate children's understanding. They often understand things very well, more perceptively than adults. First they get used to this dual existence, then they lose the distinction between good and evil. People grow up with a dual consciousness, and while continuing to believe they do things which are utterly incompatible with faith. It all begins with something small, with a lack of discernment, with a lack of principle. We forget Christ's words of warning: "You can't serve two lords at once." You have to choose one of them. I look at a principled atheist with more respect than at an unprincipled believer. You probably know the words of the Apocalypse: "Oh if you were either hot or cold!" In other words, "Oh if you were a real atheist or a real believer, but since you're just warm—lukewarm—I'll spit you out." Lukewarmness produces lukewarmness. We must declare war on lukewarmness. One of the goals of our discussions is war on lukewarmness.

Today the introduction was really drawn out. Let's get right to the questions.

QUESTION: Tell me, please, is it true that Balaam's ass began to speak? It seems to say in the Bible that it's true. The ass began to speak. It's interesting why an ass wouldn't suddenly start to speak today—just suddenly get up and speak.

ANSWER: The question, as you see, is ironic. And I'll begin my answer with irony. An ass *did* speak. It asked me this question. But it probably considers itself to be intelligent... But let's not laugh. We shouldn't laugh at ignorance. Now I'll answer for real. Let's turn to the Bible, Chapter 22 of the Book of Numbers. We read:

> And the ass saw the Angel of the Lord standing in the road, with a drawn sword in his hand; and the ass turned aside out of the road, and went into the field; and Balaam struck the ass, to turn her into the road [*i.e., he used force*]. Then the Angel of the Lord stood in a narrow path between the vineyards, with a wall on either side. And when the ass saw the Angel of the Lord, she pushed against the wall and pressed Balaam's foot against the wall; so he struck her again. The Angel of the Lord went ahead, and stood in a narrow place, where there was no way to turn either to the right or to the left. When the ass saw the Angel of the Lord, she lay down under Balaam; and Balaam's anger was kindled, and he struck the ass with his staff. Then the Lord opened the mouth of the ass, and she spoke to Balaam: "What have I done to you, that you have struck me these three times?" (Num. 22:23-28)

As we see, the ass began to speak because it was impossible for her to go either to the right or to the left, and here they were still beating her from above.

Here, I submit, there's a paradox. That the ass could begin to speak all by herself is admitted not by believers but by the non-believers. We believers say the donkey *couldn't* begin to speak by herself. Non-believers confirm that she could. Let me explain what I mean. Let's suppose that a monkey began speaking by itself. Whether difficulty forced it to do so or something else—anyway, the monkey began to speak for itself. We believers say that only if God exists could an ass begin to speak. Thus it is written in the Bible: "*The Lord* opened the mouth of the ass." She didn't begin speaking in and of herself. It's an inconceivable miracle when dumb nature speaks by itself. This miracle becomes conceivable only when there exists a God who does miracles. For atheists, nature or a monkey or a donkey, etc., become

God, and miracles are ascribed to them. It's difficult for us believers to believe in such miracles, particularly in the evolution of man from a monkey. Atheists think that in admitting the evolution of man from a monkey they thereby destroy God. (But note that the creator of the evolutionary theory, Darwin, was himself a believing person.) O.K., let's even allow that man came from a monkey. But where does the monkey come from? Once again, we have to assemble a long chain of causes. Atheists deny the First Cause, but they still want to find causes for everything. But we have to understand what is most important. Then everything else will become clear. One Russian philosopher, Vladimir Solov'ev, joked: We come from a monkey, so let's do good. But what good will that be? A monkeyish good? Atheists want to create man in the image and likeness of a monkey. But we are persons created in the image and likeness of God. We do good because our God is the Source of good. We're intelligent because our God is intelligent. "Be perfect as your Father in heaven is perfect," it says in the Gospel: hence our source of morality. There is a Being who stands above us and who is impartial. He can't be fooled. Morality isn't the invention of a monkey, nor even of man himself. It's the voice of God in our soul. Knowing God, we understand what good is, what intelligence is. And we understand that each person is given freedom. Freedom can be given only by a perfect Being, one like God. An imperfect being can't give freedom. Freedom brings fear to the imperfect being. An ass can't begin to speak by itself, but when God opens its mouth it does begin to speak. God opens our mouths, and we begin to speak.

QUESTION: How ought we to understand the words "God created man from the earth"?

ANSWER: Of course, you don't have to understand it to mean that God takes clay like a potter and fashions a man. But we see for ourselves that the elements in the earth are also in the human body. For this reason in the Scriptures it says: "Thou art earth and unto the earth shalt thou return again." We hold that the human body was formed from the

earth, but a living spirit was breathed into this earth from
God. The earth itself couldn't have done that. "You can't
jump higher than yourself," as they say. Only an intelligent
being could create intelligence. And the Church teaches that
there are two elements in man: matter and spirit. Therefore
man stands above nature. He is the master of nature. As the
Russian poet Tiutchev said in the last century: "It was not
the flesh, but the spirit which has been corrupted in our days,
and man deliberately rebels." We have rebelled, and the human soul has been corrupted. All of our abnormalities come
from the corruption of our soul. We've forgotten that our
origin is in God. Hence all the cataclysms, all the misunderstandings of life. I'd recommend that you read Viktor Nesmelov's book *The Science of Man*.[3] It's an attempt at a psychological history and critique of the basic questions of life.
I think it can be obtained in the Lenin Library.

QUESTION: How can we explain the origin of evil in the
world? Or to put it better: Where is God when a child is
suffering? I can't grasp how the goodness of God and the
suffering of a child can be harmonized. The suffering of an
adult is clear: He sinned, so let him pay for it. But the suffering of a child ... Why? How are we to understand that?

ANSWER: Your question includes a number of questions.
Let's begin with the first one. How do we explain the origin
of evil? The simplest and truest answer: Evil entered the
world through sin. Man sinned and destroyed the divine harmony, and from this came all evil. He sinned because he
possessed free will. Some people are ironic when they interpret the Biblical story of how Eve was deceived by the snake,
how she picked the apple, gave it to her husband, and from
this came the sin. A little apple, seemingly innocent, but so
many consequences! But here it is not the apple, but the test

---

[3]Viktor Ivanovich Nesmelov (1863-1920): professor of philosophy at the
Kazan' Theological Academy. His *Nauka o cheloveke* (2 vols., Kazan', 1897-
1902) is, as Fr. Georges Florovsky writes in the preface to the 1971 reprint edition, "a kind of an apologetic treatise, an attempt to demonstrate the truth, or
rather the *credibility*, of Christian Revelation by rational and 'scientific' arguments."

of will that is important. What else can you expect, if the least temptation was not withstood? A break occurred between man and God. Man didn't trust God but rather he trusted the serpent. Then the question arises: Why should this freedom of will exist if so many sufferings result? Those who talk like this forget that freedom is the supreme gift. It just has to be used correctly. The fact that freedom is the supreme gift can be appreciated only once you've lost it. People risk their lives for one minute of freedom. This is probably especially understandable to those who have been in prison or exile . . .

The second question: "Where is God when a child is suffering?" It's understandable when an adult suffers: He's paying for his sins. But it's incomprehensible when a child suffers. Where is *truth* here? How can we call God good if He's merciless towards a child? That was Ivan Karamazov's question. He was ready to turn in his ticket to the Kingdom of Heaven over a single little tear. Indeed, the suffering of a child *cannot* be understood by the mind alone. When you see an innocent person suffering, everything turns over inside and no mental explanations can help. But how can you explain a child's suffering? Precisely by our common sin, for in Adam we all sinned. Man can't be looked at individually. If you don't want a child to suffer, don't blame God, but try yourself not to sin. Furthermore, you can't look at the suffering of a child only from the point of view of this world. If we try to look at things this way, we'll never understand anything. If there's no eternity, then everything is nonsense, the suffering of a child and everything else. Then everything's a mirage, a continual nightmare. But if there is eternity, if all tears are wiped away there, then the suffering of a child acquires an enormous meaning. As one person's sin spreads to others, so does one person's goodness. The child suffers precisely for our sin, but in eternity his sufferings are turned into joy, both for him and for all of us as well. A little suffering—and eternal joy! Also, the sufferings of a child make us better, kinder. So the suffering of a child isn't meaningless.

If we go further and ask the question, "Where is God

when a child is suffering?" we can say: God is *with* the child.
Our God Jesus Christ cannot be accused of cruelty. After all,
He Himself experienced all suffering. One priest told me
this: God suffers along with the child, and *His* suffering in
this way is greater than the child's own. Remember when
you've suffered for someone, or when a mother suffers for
her child. Well, that's just the way God suffers together
with a child. Our God was crucified for us and cannot be
accused of any cruel inattention.

To sum up: Evil entered into world by sin. Sin is an act
of man's free will. Man was seduced. He then had to understand freely through his own experience—just as freely as he
was seduced—that sin carries no happiness in itself and that
he must be delivered from sin. The creation of the new man
consists in this. In the creation of the new man, both God
and man take part. God and man should become like one
whole: the God-man. Then all accusations of cruelty and
inattention to the suffering of children pass away. We sense
our own responsibility for the suffering of children, and we
understand that only a virtuous life can deliver a child and
all of us from sufferings. Our revolt against God is senseless. But let's assume that there is no God. Then whom will
we blame? Once again, ourselves. In either case the guilt
falls on us. But we shouldn't try to cast the blame. Rather,
we must understand the way of deliverance from all evil.
Christianity speaks about this, and Christianity must be realized in life. Then good will be derived from everything.
Then we'll understand that sin and evil are only a shadow
which just appears for a moment. Furthermore, we can say
that the Kingdom of God, of which we should be worthy by
our work, is greater than the paradise which was given to us
for free in the beginning. If we look at things from this
point of view, then what has happened to us has significance.
God can't be blamed for anything. He can only be thanked,
because everything is for our good.

QUESTION: Draw a comparison between "An eye for an eye
and a tooth for a tooth," and "Love your enemies." What do
these passages mean?

ANSWER: Both passages mean that you have to love. When you fight for what's your own, that's a limited love, but it's still love. When you love *everyone*—and most of all your enemies—that's perfected love. A limited love can't understand that when a person offends someone else, he himself suffers, that he is made even more unhappy than the one he offended. You've got to love him because, no matter what, he's a person and our brother. This level of love couldn't be reached in the Old Testament, and so "an eye for an eye" reigned. It was reached only in the New Testament, after the sufferings which Christ accepted for all had united us. At present most of us still live by Old Testament concepts. Hence enmity and wars and all kinds of offenses. We must live by the New Testament concept: love everyone. Only in this way can we rebuild our life.

QUESTION: What does it mean, "If they strike you on the one cheek, turn the other, too." "If they demand your cloak, give your coat as well." Every passer-by could take unfair advantage of that.

ANSWER: Passers-by can take unfair advantage of anything. Christian values, however, don't loose their meaning because of this. "Turn your other cheek" means do good in return for everything. Let's take an example from life: You answer evil for evil. What do you get? Evil increases. But if you answer by good, the evil stops. Of course, you shouldn't exaggerate these truths and give others occasion for taking advantage of this. One can even use force, but once again not for revenge but in order to stop evil.

QUESTION: Father Dmitrii, have you had a chance to read the Cathoic journal *Logos*?[4] In it all types of questions are dealt with, the church keeps pace with the times. Our poor *Journal of the Moscow Patriarchate* offers no comparison. What do you think? Couldn't *we* undertake something like this? But who'll do it? Who has the means? It seems that the Catholic Church is more active."

---

[4]Published in Brussels.

ANSWER: We have our different paths. The Catholics have theirs and we ours. Whose path is better is hard to say. The Catholics have everything—organization, apologetics, defense of Christianity, theology—everything so finely worked out that you have to marvel. But the result is that they have more non-believers than we do. No matter what they dream up to hold them within the bosom of the church (even jazz has come into use), the people are more interested in comfort than in faith. But we don't have anything—just suffering. Last time, I'm told, there was a foreigner at our discussion, a woman who lives here. She was amazed at how carefully everyone listens here. The discussion lasted more than an hour. In addition there was the service itself. In all we began at six o'clock and ended at ten. Everyone stood the whole time. So what does this say? That many of us, even though externally they're considered unbelievers, are really believers. Today almost everyone has a thirst for faith. But what do we clergy do? Nothing! Our theological journal is worthless. Our priests are weak. But the people come to God. Those of us who live here are in a better position than those who live abroad, and we have nothing to be envious of. Imagine the joy to have been with Christ on Golgotha! They say that some Catholics want especially to end up here in order somehow to draw nearer to the sufferings on Golgotha. Today in Russia a tremendous miracle is taking place—not only Christ's crucifixion but His resurrection from the dead as well. You know, it's unprecedented that the children of declared atheists, with all their atheistic training, have suddenly spoken out in favor of faith. They tell me about a teacher who was deprived of his position because of his faith and who was later thrown in jail as a vagrant. Conditions were difficult. He contracted tuberculosis. Before that he'd been in poor health. But he didn't renounce his faith. He accepted everything bravely in hope of the resurrection from the dead. Now, even if just one such instance occurred, it would be worth it to live here. But there have been so many such instances here! And why should I tell about them? You know all this yourselves. I just want to say that we've happened upon the greatest of joys—to be in the position of the first Christians. Let's be worthy of this joy. Let's be faithful to our God and thank Him for everything.

QUESTION: I can understand the Christian forgiving everything, but I don't understand that business about turning your left cheek if they strike your right one. I can understand, too, that it's all right to give your coat to someone who demands your cloak, but I don't understand why if they hit me I should bow my head submissively. Isn't that the same as being passive in the face of human evil? And isn't this the source of the atheists' accusation that Christianity is a religion of passivity, a capitulation before evil? For modern man this is a very tempting argument.

ANSWER: Temptations can come from anywhere, and especially when you don't know the essence of your faith. Modern man often knows the Christian religion according to the interpretations of atheists, but this is a caricature of religion. In order to understand something, you must know the original sources, but these are closed to us. Therefore modern man's imagination is frightened. Let's hear how the Christian approach is to be understood. To turn your cheek doesn't mean to be passive before evil. It means not to make the truth conform only to your own interests. It means to be above personal insults. Therefore a Christian ought not to remember personal insults and seek revenge for them. He should be able to lay down his life for his friends. If truth is insulted, if falsehood is carried out, if "human dignity"— to use today's language—is insulted, a Christian must forget everything and selflessly battle with evil, not even sparing his own life. To die for one's friends is a Christian's highest accomplishment—and *that's* not passivity. It's worth noting that those who remember insults and take revenge for them are for the most part cowards when *others* are insulted. Because they are afraid for their own well-being. They don't understand how the Christian can forgive all things, because they don't want to forgive anything. In other words, they see and protect only themselves. They answer every insult by insult and revenge and call this activism in the battle with evil, while in reality this is only the manifestation of touchiness, of egotism, of the fact that their self-pride has been wounded.

QUESTION: Father Dmitrii, why engage in polemics with atheists? It's a needless waste of time and energy because no one is interested in their doctrine. It's antiquated and obsolete. Better, tell us about faith.

ANSWER: I agree with you that although atheism appeared after faith it's already quite antiquated and nothing new can be said about it. I don't polemicize with atheists. I just answer the puzzled questions that they ask in the name of atheism. But to shut your eyes completely to the existence of atheism is the same thing as to agree with its deeds, and this I cannot do. When I talk about atheism, I never forget about faith. Of course, it would be a lot better to disclose the truth of the faith positively, which is what I *do* attempt in my sermons. But, you know, the theme of our discussions depends upon the questions which are raised. And here we have to confront atheism, whether we want to or not, and somehow we have to react to it.

QUESTION: I happened upon your discussions by accident. To be honest, although I can't agree with you in everything, my eyes *are* beginning to open to some things. They always told us that religion is something obsolete and uninteresting. But now I'm beginning to understand how uninteresting life is *without* religion. Let me tell you a little about myself. I was born in a family of atheists. But can you really call that a "family"? My mother is my real one, but my father is by adoption. Both are high-up in the Party and highly-cultured, or so they consider themselves. I never hear anything from them except that you should get a prize or you should squeeze out a comrade. The main thing is their frequent bouts of drinking. Or else someone is betraying someone else. Bickering, foul language, quarrels ... As soon as I grew up I left them and lived with my grandmother (my mother's mother). My parents rarely remembered me. I became bitter towards everyone, and, to tell the truth, I jumped into the same pool that they were swimming in. "Where and how do I get out?"

That question arose in me a lot. Communism is a good thing, but with the point of view and the moral level of my parents, you'd never come to communism. Yes, religion is a superlative thing. It's full of strength. Why, then, do they hide it from us?

ANSWER: Essentially you've answered your own question. Religion is indeed (to use your expression) a superlative thing. It is (if it comes to that) a good builder of communism. After all, to distribute good things without a Christian point of view is impossible. Fighting is the result, not distribution. Religion is the preserver of the family and of family tradition. It's the guardian of morals. It's the source of all good. So why do they hide it, when so much good comes from it? That's a good question—a good question for me, too. And just like you, I'd like to get an answer to that question from the atheists.

QUESTION: At present they are writing a lot on moral themes, and one must say that there are some very sensible, correct articles. They write about the preservation of nature and of animals. Recently I read a wonderful article in *Literaturnaia Rossiia*. But morality is getting lower and lower. Treatment of nature is barbaric, and there is much cruelty to animals ... What's going on?

ANSWER: Thanks for the good question. Just like you, I frequently brouse through the newspapers, and I did read the article which you mention: "Players at Goodness," by Yuri Iakovlev, in *Literaturnaia Rossiia*, February 1, 1974. I liked it very much. I'd like to take a few excerpts from it:

> We often speak of the harmonious development of personality. We speak of love for nature. But for some reason we limit ourselves to planting trees and flowers. The world of nature is somehow richer and more complex. The person who plants an apple tree yet lifts his hand against a dog has no love of nature. He accepts nature only inasmuch as it "suits his pleasure" or is "profitable." But nature

is too complex and too wonderful simply to suit one's pleasure . . .

(Not long ago I received a letter from Kirovo-Chepetsk, from a Comrade Glushkov. He told with indignation of the mass shooting of dogs. "Quite often," he writes, "children, schoolkids, try to defend their dogs, but they kill them before their very eyes. What could be more immoral and inhumane than that?")

Another excerpt from the same article:

> Let us recall how, when the birds were breeding rapidly here, the children were taught to look after them, the pigeons in particular. Let us also recall how—gradually, almost imperceptibly—their relationship to them changed. I do not know if the birds began to be secretly destroyed, but in any case their feeding was in many places forbidden. On town squares, previously set aside specifically for this purpose, signs began to appear: *"FEEDING OF PIGEONS PROHIBITED. FINE: 3 RUBLES."* Finally, brandishing the journal *Health,* they began speaking about "ornithosis," and mothers, horrified by medical warnings, would tell their little ones: "The pigeons are sick, child. Infectious. Throw pebbles at them to drive them away. Say: 'Get away! Beat it! Shoo! I'll get you . . . !' "

Even from just these excerpts we see that morality can't be subordinated to some primitive "benefit." Morality is deeper and more complex, as the author has indicated. Nor does morality proceed from the simple contemplation of nature. Not everyone who admires the scenery is a moral person. Morality doesn't come from an abundance of material goods. Morality has a religious basis. It was given to us by a higher Being who sees everything and cannot be deceived. "When God isn't in the soul," as the brilliant Russian author Dostoevskii repeated, "anything goes." You can write on moral themes and still be an immoral person. They tell about an executioner who wrote poems filled with sorrow and yet shot thousands of people. Without God there is no morality and nor can there be. There's just profitable/unprofitable. That is, there are just the calculations of individual egotism. You noted rightly that our moral level is dropping. It's barbaric the way that nature is treated. Here's what one writer told me. She was walking down the street and saw some kids ripping apart a cat's legs. They couldn't care less that the animal was screaming. The writer asked them what they were doing, and they told her: "Get out of here before we rip *your* legs apart!"

While it's still not too late we've got to save people from utter destruction. But only religion can save—only a Savior who'd not only preach, but who'd even be crucified for the salvation of others. From this we get morality and a loving relationship towards nature: love for every blade of grass, love for every little flower. As the Elder Zosima said: "Blessed is the one who shows mercy upon the animals."

QUESTION: Couldn't you arrange to conduct a discussion like this in our institute, for instance? Not everyone knows about these discussions as yet, but when they do find out, your church will be too small.

ANSWER: For the time being your question brings a smile to me and to all those who are here . . . It seems that such arrangements won't be possible, but try to arrange it by all means. I think it'll come to that. Judging by what interest religion is now stirring up, by how morality is falling without it, by how many tragedies occur in life, and finally by how artificially our society is divided into believers and non-believers and what antagonism is created between them—from all this one can assume that religion will soon become not only fashionable, as it is today for some people, but a real and active power capable of solving the greatest questions of life. So be patient for a while, and tell anyone who can't fit into this church (if that should happen) about everything. Discuss things with them. Don't be afraid of what they could do to you because of these discussions. It's less horrible than what is done through ignorance of religion.

QUESTION: I've read a lot of all sorts of literature on Buddhism, on Orthodoxy, etc. . . . Of course, I can no longer consider myself an unbeliever, but to tell the truth, my head's all scrambled up. Why do you think that Christianity is the truest religion?

ANSWER: To read doesn't yet mean to find the truth. In order to understand Christian truth you have to be filled with truth. Then the truth itself will show you that it's the truth. But for now you're just seeking. Seek and you'll find. Truth isn't proved, it's discovered.

QUESTION: There are a whole lot of religious trends today—sects, as you put it. Don't many of them react just as negatively to Orthodoxy as you do to them?"

ANSWER: I don't want simply to judge them . . . I try to understand them and to respect their beliefs. In general I respect *all* beliefs. All of us, religious people included, are too divided. This is the influence of the sinful world on us. Now, in the face of common danger, we must all unite. This doesn't mean that any one person will predominate. Christ is our Head. To unite means to learn to understand each other, with all our peculiarities. When people flaunt their allegience to a given confession too much and don't have love for their neighbor, they turn into "publicans and pharisees," and even a non-believer is closer to God than such an "Orthodox." As we know, the publican was a sinner, but Christ justified him. Certainly the pharisee was more righteous than the publican, but he went away condemned. That's how I'd like to understand the sectarians in their peculiarities. Through Orthodox Christianity, truth was revealed to me, and I value that.

QUESTION: At the present time new religious communities are appearing that reject the Orthodox Church. They say that the Church has linked herself to the State and that therefore the people in her have all sold themselves. The sectarians don't have all the pushing and superstition that we have in our church. Their people are more polite. Why's that? Why are Orthodox people below the sectarians morally?

Perhaps the Orthodox Church is in fact worse than these communities. A person who isn't very familiar with Christianity can't distinguish where the truth is, since there are prayers here and there are prayers there, but otherwise everything's more interesting there. Plus, they have music, which creates such beauty. How can we distinguish where the truth is?

ANSWER: You've asked several questions all at once. In general we can answer them all like this: God will judge us all. Furthermore, don't judge by externals. Now, concretely. If some religious communities reject the Orthodox community, that means that the Christian house is divided against itself, but on this subject Christ said that a kingdom divided against itself cannot stand.[5] The question also claims that "the Church has linked herself to the State and therefore the people in her have all sold themselves." This is just too categorical a judgment. The Church lives within the State, and its pains must be her pains. Therefore the Church is concerned that the people who live in this State be honest and good and that they love their country. Anyone who finds himself in any other relationship to the State will be judged by God. This will lie on their conscience.

The Orthodox Church is the largest religious community in our country, but in a large society there are always great diversities. There are always people who come out very actively against untruth and crimes, and there are always people who endure in silence and pray that the number of criminals would be smaller. Which of these does more? Once again, God will judge. It's important that all of this be done sincerely, from religious convictions. Yes, in our churches we have a lot of superstitions and pushing. Perhaps this is even our specialty. But sometimes these crushing throngs in church perform marvelous deeds and surpass those who externally are more disciplined. And who is moral and who immoral, God judges. But as we know, anyone who boasts of his "righteousness" is incapable of "progressing" in righteousness. But whoever repents of his sins can increase from strength to strength. As for music and the resulting atmos-

---

[5]Mt. 12:25.

phere: this seems to me more a matter of aesthetics than of religion. I don't impose my opinions on anyone. If someone likes music in church, if someone understands religion through music, well, let him come to God that way. To tell the truth, I like simple, sincere singing in church. But, as they say, there's no arguing over tastes.

QUESTION: What is baptism? Is it obligatory? I can accept Christianity, but it seems to me that baptism is a superfluous rite. In particular, I can't understand the baptism of children.

ANSWER: If I can put it briefly, baptism is the washing away of our sins. When sin hangs over a person, Christianity is incomprehensible to him even if he might think that he understands it. So to understand Christianity correctly, you simply *must* be baptised. Only the baptised will be saved, as Christ Himself said. But you mustn't consider only the form in baptism. The physical act of baptism is just the end of a process of repentance already begun within the individual. If there were no such process, baptism would remain without effect. Baptism isn't some sort of magic manipulation but rather a mystical process. Baptism is one of the Christian sacraments.

How should we understand the baptism of children? There are religious communities that don't recognize the baptism of children. They think baptism should be on the basis of faith, and what faith can children have? But let's think a bit. Did only a certain fellow by the name of Adam sin, or did *all* of mankind sin, including children? In some people sin is well-developed, in others it's something potential. But if sin exists you have to be delivered from it. We're delivered from sin in the sacrament of baptism, children included. The Bible clearly says that anyone who isn't baptised can't be saved.[6] The faith and consciousness of children are fulfilled by the godparents since, you know, we must all bear one another's burdens; we're all mutually connected; we fulfill one another. But suppose a child doesn't live to maturity.

---

[6]Cf. Mk. 16:16.

What will happen to it? For we know that without baptism there's no salvation. I think that children should be baptised as early as possible so that the grace of baptism will save them throughout their entire lives. Then, once they've grown up consciousness and faith will appear. But in childhood let there be unconscious faith, so the one may complete the other. And if baptised children go bad (and it *does* happen), well, baptised adults sometimes go bad too. When they refer to the fact that it's never directly stated in the Gospel that children should be baptised, this is a reference to the *letter*. But the *spiritual* sense of the Gospel says that *everyone* must be baptised, for baptism is the way by which people are saved. It opens the door to the Kingdom of Heaven. And it's said in the Gospel that the letter kills, but the spirit makes alive. A literal understanding of the Gospel often distorts its meaning. Furthermore, just as it's not said directly in the Holy Scriptures that you *must* baptise children, so also it is not said directly that you *needn't* baptise them. Healthy Christian reason says that baptism is mandatory for all. And anyone who hinders the baptism of children bears the responsibility. They too should remember Christ's words: "Do not hinder the children from coming to Me."[7]

QUESTION: I don't understand what confession is, its purpose. For modern man it's like (pardon me) digging in crap. I understand confession before God. I can confess my sins before Him. But why should the priest be involved in this? After all, isn't he a sinner, too, like us?

ANSWER: Unfortunately the meaning of the sacrament of confession escapes many Orthodox. Confession is a great sacrament, equal to baptism. We often fulfil just the form. People come without knowing what sin is. And this doesn't happen just with us, but in the West as well. They say that there some people coming to confession show a book which shows they've paid their church dues, and they think that this is enough. We have other curiosities. Here's what one priest told me not long ago. A woman came to him for confession.

---

[7]Mt. 19:14.

He asked: "How did you sin?" She answered: "I didn't."
"Well, then, if you're sinless, you don't need confession. Go
on." said the priest. She didn't leave, but demanded instead
that he hear her out. "Listen," she said, "I have a certificate
of commendation saying that I have *not* sinned." It's a bit
funny, and not a little bit sad. We've lost the distinction between good and evil, and that causes our lack of understanding concerning confession. Look, you think confession is like
digging in crap. But if you're covered all over with crap, you
have to be washed, because it's impossible for you to live
knowingly in crap. Confessing before God alone means denying the *human* side of our salvation. But God doesn't save
without people. The priest is God's witness in confession.
It's also necessary to confess before God. But that's more
difficult. It turns into something abstract. We're always
ready to become emotional. But confession in the presence of
a priest is sometimes concrete, objective. Be strict with yourself. To confess your sins before a witness takes courage.
You blush. You get embarassed. But just to confess before
God—"Well, who sees you?" you say. It's not so embarass-
ing . . . There's great danger of deception here. But perhaps
this is preparation for your confession . . .

   We'll end here for today. In conclusion I'd like to say
that this Monday Great Lent begins for us, when we must
think especially about repentance and confession. Before
Lent everyone asks forgiveness of each other, and so I ask
you for forgiveness. Perhaps I've offended someone during
my discussions through sharpness or hastiness, but I had no
intention of offending anyone. Understand me. I have undertaken all of this for goodness' sake, for the sake of creating the new man. Our old man is too decayed. A new man
is needed, one with a sincere and open soul, one for whom
Christian truths are the matter of life, one who's not afraid
to lay down his life for his friends, one who wants people to
know truth and goodness not just as relative concepts. Truth
and goodness are real only if eternity exists: "Awake, O

sleeper, and arise from the dead and Christ will save you."[8]
If there's no resurrection from the dead, if there's no eternity, then our faith is futile and in vain, as Saint Paul said.[9]

Next time our discussion will be devoted to the resurrection of Christ and will include discussion of *our* resurrection. The resurrection from the dead is *the* basic Christian truth. We've conducted our sixth discussion, a preparatory week of work, as it were. This work must be crowned in the feast of the Lord, the feast of the resurrection from the dead.

---

[8]Eph. 5:14.
[9]1 Cor. 15:14.

The Seventh Discussion

All six of our previous discussions have been a preparation for our basic discussion—the discussion of Christ's resurrection, of our resurrection from the dead. If Christ isn't risen, our faith is futile, useless, vain. If there's no resurrection from the dead, then there's no meaning in religion, there's no difference between the believer and the non-believer. True, they say that there *is* a difference, since in any relationship faith is better than no faith because it gives stability to life. But if there's no resurrection from the dead, this stability doesn't amount to much. There are non-believers whose lives are stable, but what is the significance of this stability?

We've been taught to look at life simply in terms of what is advantageous or beneficial at any given moment. This causes our passions to boil. It causes heroics. But we're heroes only as long as we still have our health and success. When death glances our way, then, as the poet Il'ia Sel'vinskii says, you'll change your tune. Death is the test of all our values. We don't like to talk about death. We're afraid to. We look at it superstitiously. But sooner or later we'll have to see it as it really is, soberly, with none of the intoxication brought on by life's blessings. Even contemporary examples show us how some people change at the end of their lives.

The resurrection from the dead—this is the most important question in life. We'll examine it in today's discussion. We won't narrow the question and just speak exclusively about the resurrection of Christ, though in the resurrection of Christ many other questions are resolved. In particular we'll talk about eternal life beyond the grave, about the immortality of our soul, etc.

Our audience, speaking in secular terms, is pluralistic, ranging from atheists to profound believers, from Orthodox to heterodox. Perhaps some will find this theme naive and even a little boring. But I think there's no topic more relevant than the resurrection from the dead. We've been taught to view religion as a fable—a beautiful and tempting one perhaps—but as soon as someone starts talking seriously about resurrection from the dead, about life after death, they say that he's gone off his rocker. But in fact resurrection from the dead is sanity itself, and everything else is folly and madness. These are the positions from which we'll be analyzing the topic.

The resurrection of Christ, resurrection from the dead. Let us concentrate on these words. Let us ponder them... And now, let us glance at our activities, at everything by which we live and which causes us to reject resurrection from the dead. Let us assume that only that by which we live exists, and nothing else. By what do we live? Well, by our success, by our so-called victories. We live by creativity, by love... and, I might add, sometimes by our drinking bouts. But everyone is already bored with all this. We're bored with fooling ourselves, with having constant "pep-talks," as some people put it. There's a whole lot more that we'd really like, but what is available has become too... too insipid. It doesn't satisfy. Many have begun to protest, but protest is no solution either. As soon as one protest is over, another begins. We keep on condemning each other, but that doesn't settle anything, and a whole lot of unanswered questions remain. It's not by accident that the *best* people, even if there aren't yet very many of them, have begun to resolve many of these questions with the help of religion. But religion without resurrection from the dead is no solution. The labyrinth into which we've fallen urgently demands a resolution of the question of resurrection from the dead.

It's no mere coincidence that these questions are of interest to young people, the children of the unbelievers who ridiculed the religion of their fathers. We also have to resolve this question on behalf of past generations. They lived and died, with

everything apparently in good order. Many of them even believed in a life beyond the grave, but they thought of it only in
terms of themselves. We, on the other hand, are bound to think
of it in terms of everyone. We're forced to ponder this by
those who perished in the past two world wars, by those who
perished in concentration camps and other torture chambers.
They were a countless multitude. Now many of them are being
"rehabilitated." But what is the value of this rehabilitation
if their sufferings—their immeasurable sufferings—are not
crowned by something greater? Do we dare to limit life to the
hope that someone may remember us with a good word or, at
best, write an entire book? Can the full variety of extinguished
human feelings and emotions really be preserved in this way?
The memory of those who have perished in horrible torments
demands an answer to the question of resurrection from the
dead.

Only if Christ is risen, only if there really is a resurrection
from the dead, do we find meaning in all this suffering. Each
person is a unique world, and each one wants a unique life.
We have constricted the human personality into the "common
good," but this common good is real only if each person is truly
alive.

Our own troubled times, plagued by growing fears, require
all of us to resolve the question of resurrection from the dead.
One can think seriously about life only if there is resurrection
from the dead. One can speak seriously about well-being and
goodness only if there is resurrection from the dead. Fearless-
ness is possible only if there is resurrection from the dead.
I know that there are courageous people without this conviction, but, you know, deeds of heroism often take place just on
the spur of the moment, the result of some intoxicant. But
permanent courage requires something to lean on. Resurrection from the dead—this is our fundamental support. Why has
crime increased? Because we don't think about resurrection
from the dead. We've given in to despair because we've forgotten resurrection from the dead. Increasing lewdness is also
a result of our lack of attention to life beyond the grave.

We have been lulled by the persistent propaganda of the
atheists. But atheistic ideas aren't profound. They work like

hypnotism, but only on those who are in spiritual hibernation.

Sometimes we are ashamed of our faith. "What if someone sees us?" "What if someone recognizes us?" Someone might suddenly smile sarcastically, or there might be some sort of trouble ... We have become materialists in the worst sense of the word, by exchanging the eternal for the temporal—and all because the resurrection from the dead has become a secondary question for us, and not a primary one.

You're probably waiting for me to begin a profound lecture. But I simply want to pose this question seriously. We must resolve it together, and not only in a theoretical way. Profound minds have already resolved this question theoretically. Our own philosopher, Vladimir Solov'ev, has a work entitled *Resurrectional Letters*.[1] Anyone who's familiar with it knows how profoundly this philosopher resolved the question of the resurrection. By the way, Solov'ev said that he believed in life after death more than in "real" life, because "real" life deceives us every step of the way. Beginning with today's discussion, we'll begin to resolve this question. So far there have been only a few questions about Christ's resurrection, and these have been mainly of a general nature.

QUESTION: What proofs are there in apologetics of Christ's resurrection? How should we understand *our* resurrection from the dead?

ANSWER: *Proofs?* Nowadays we've begun to *prove* everything. *Prove* that you love. *Prove* there's a sun in the sky, or clouds. *Prove* you're a man, not a camel ... So they ask me to produce *proofs* for Christ's Resurrection. We consider proofs to be an important argument, whereas in fact they're no argument at all. Proofs are the fruit of our weakness and not of our strength, the fruit of unbelief. Forgive me, but I don't want to *know* any proofs, and I wouldn't recommend that you seek them. The fundamental proof is our faith. If we have no faith, no proofs will help.

---

[1] Vladimir Sergeevich Solov'ev (1853-1900): Russian philosopher, mystic, theologian, ecumenist. His training in Western rationalistic philosophies carried him through atheism and materialism to the belief that the essence of Christianity lay in the union of God and man in the incarnate Christ ("Godmanhood").

But then, of course, the question arises: Does this mean that we must believe blindly? "Believe because it's absurd," like Tertullian? I would like to address precisely this: the absurdity and the "blindness" of faith. For in fact, faith is vision. Unbelief is the fruit of a depraved life, while faith is the fruit of virtue. It's not easy to believe, not because believing itself is difficult, but because we've gone astray in our sins. We've got to free ourselves of sin, and then faith will become easy. But to be free of sin means to cleanse our consciousness, our senses. If we accomplish this, our faith will not be blind, but completely radiant and visionary. Faith, as one Russian philosopher said, is profound knowledge. The knowledge we glean from books is shallow, and with its help all we can learn are earthly laws. But knowledge of the resurrection of Christ demands profound knowledge—that is, not merely stuffing your head full of quotations and information, but transfiguring your entire being. This brings profound knowledge: faith. Yes, faith often contradicts the shallow variety of knowledge, and shallow knowledge in turn considers faith to be absurdity. It is for this reason that Tertullian said, "I believe because it is absurd"—not because faith itself is absurd, but because shallow knowledge, the sinful world, considers it to be so. I believe, not because it is absurd in general, but only because from your point of view it is absurd. In this way, we believe in Christ's resurrection, but we don't "prove" it. You have no faith? That is your misfortune. You have to work on yourself. The *fact* of Christ's resurrection is given in the most trustworthy of sources: the Gospel.

Incidentally, about the Gospel: Atheism has slandered this book, consigning it to doubt and demanding other sources. But without the Gospel, all sources would be rendered false. Even death-defeating Life would seem false. It's no accident that all intelligent and polite people hold this book in high regard. From pastoral experience, I also know the wholesome effect this book has on people's hearts. In it are the words of God— what can be loftier or more plausible than this? I know that there are people who doubt the Gospel, who insist that it's not convincing. It is difficult to refute such people. They can only be pitied, for those who say such things are unable to believe;

they have not yet acquired profound knowledge. So, we should ponder our own lives . . .

The person who submitted this question about the resurrection may think that I am not answering it. But I am doing more than answering his question. I am providing proofs that certain proofs prove nothing at all.

And now to the second part of the question: "How should we understand *our* resurrection from the dead?" We will be raised up just as Christ was raised up. Just as all sinned in Adam, so will all arise in Christ. The resurrection of the soul is its deliverance from all sinful obstacles; the resurrection of the body is the restoration of material substances. The apostle Paul spoke very well about this:

> . . . Christ has been raised from the dead, the first fruits of those who have fallen asleep. For as by a man came death, by a man has come also the resurrection of the dead. For as in Adam all die, so also in Christ shall all be made alive. But each in his own order: Christ the first fruits, then at His coming those who belong to Christ. Then comes the end, when He delivers the Kingdom to God the Father after destroying every rule and every authority and power. For He must reign until He has put all His enemies under His feet. (I Cor. 15:20-25)

And one other wonderful passage:

> But some one will ask, "How are the dead raised? With what kind of body do they come?" You foolish man! What you sow does not come to life unless it dies. And what you sow is not the body which is to be, but a bare kernel, perhaps of wheat or of some other grain. But God gives it a body as He has chosen, and to each kind of seed its own body. For not all flesh is alike, but there is one kind for men, another for animals, another for birds, and another for fish. There are celestial bodies and there are terrestrial bodies; but the glory of the celestial is one, and the glory of the terrestrial is anoth-

er. There is one glory of the sun, and another glory of the moon, and another glory of the stars; for star differs from star in glory. So is it with the resurrection of the dead. What is sown is perishable, what is raised is imperishable. It is sown in dishonor, it is raised in glory. It is sown in weakness, it is raised in power. (I Cor. 15:35-43)

Those who were dumped somewhere, with identification tags on their legs, who died with curses and the howling of dogs—with what glory will they be raised! This is the gift of resurrection from the dead: It unmasks all human injustice and restores justice. Only those who are afraid of having their own injustices exposed will not want to believe in resurrection from the dead. But we believers read in our Creed that Christ rose "on the third day, according to the Scriptures" and we all "look for—or expect—the resurrection from the dead, and the life of the world to come. Amen."

By the way, I would like to talk from my own experience. Recently I've baptized many adults. One striking feature is evident: Almost no one doubts the resurrection from the dead. Unread in Christian literature, with atheists for parents—and yet they believe in the resurrection from the dead. How amazing! Why do they believe? Simply because the process of resurrection goes on without our even being aware of it. Especially in our country. We are on Golgotha. And after Golgotha comes the resurrection—of necessity, for such is the law of God.

QUESTION: Do you know of any miraculous occurrences in our day?

ANSWER: Yes, I do, and more than one at that. And I'm not the only one. A lot of people know of them. Some say that with the miracles of science, "real miracles" just don't happen any more. But they do—many of them, so many! Here's one such occurrence.

A woman physician comes to our church. About ten years ago she developed cancer of the stomach. The diagnosis was precise, but even with no diagnosis it was obvious that her last days were upon her. She vomited daily. The stench of death was about her. It was difficult to be near her. She accepted her disease humbly, obediently, as a true Christian. At work she was shunned. She was deprived of her children. Her husband left her. Sensing how close the end was, she decided to receive the sacraments of Unction and Holy Communion. It was then that the miracle occurred.

After she'd been anointed and received communion, the vomiting ended immediately. The stench gradually disappeared, and the doctors declared her cured. She's alive and well today, and works once again as a physician. Had this occurred in earlier times it would have been written up in all the newspapers, but today only her acquaintances know about it, only those who see her all the time. But anyone can meet her and talk to her. She's not afraid of witnessing to this event before anyone. A miracle in person, as they say. I don't think anyone would dare to deny it.

Atheists, however, evaluate such events in a different way, considering them the result of auto-suggestion, self-induced . . . A few weeks ago, *Komsomol'skaia Pravda* printed a story about a boy, his legs paralyzed, who had a dream in which the Mother of God told him to be taken to a certain church and to have a prayer service celebrated, and that then he would be healed. So, what happened? Everything took place precisely as foretold. "Self-inducement," say the atheists. "Auto-suggestion." In other words, one can be healed by "auto-suggestion," but for some reason such events occur exclusively on the religious plane and never on the anti-religious. Of course, the person who believes in God doesn't demand miracles, for his faith is itself the greatest miracle. But we don't reject the miracles which do take place. We consider them to be God's encouragement for good works. And anyone who knows the doctor I told you about knows how she uses the mercy which God has given to her.

I could relate a lot of stories like this one, so many that you'd never be able to count them all. But I think I'll end with just one small incident. A woman had a dream. "Give me two rubles," her dead husband asked. She paid no attention, but the dream recurred. She got upset, but she didn't know what to do. Someone recommended that she go to church and commemorate her husband in a service. They told her what to ask for, what to do. When she asked afterwards as to the amount of the monetary offering, she was told, "Two rubles." The woman was dumbfounded... On a few people, this incident perhaps would leave no impression, but it was enough to make her believe.

QUESTION: Father Dmitrii, you're too strict. If you go on this way, people will stop listening to you. Remember, this is the twentieth century. Certain indulgences are necessary.

ANSWER: We're afraid of strictness. We're afraid of life's difficulties. We consider an easy life to be the height of blessedness. But let's be critical of ourselves. We've already been indulgent with ourselves. We've broken with the Church. But the result is crime, corruption, disappearance of the family, dissatisfaction with life in general. No. In order to renew all things, we've got to become ascetics. Indulgence threatens us with destruction. So far we renounce indulgence only when it is hazardous to our health. So-called "light-meal days" are being introduced so that we can be healed by hunger. But gradually we will come to an ascetic consciousness in all things. Luxury and the pursuit of material goods have depleted our material resources. We have devised so much that is unnecessary that we're afraid our planet's resources will be exhausted. Luxury and extravagance lead to barbaric treatment of nature. Bread, which before was always treasured, now is tossed out with the garbage. Luxury has enslaved us, enthralled us. There's the story about the man who furnished his apartment so luxuriously that when guests come they are told not to sit on the expensive furniture. See to what ridiculous states the passion for luxury leads. Instead we should follow Saint Paul, who says that if we have our daily sustenance we should be content. In this there is greater freedom for both the spirit and the body. But you call upon us to adjust to the twentieth century and to make religion into a comfortable mockery. But we shouldn't tailor religion to our caprices. We should follow *its* demands. Then what often happens won't happen to us: We won't be sorry when we look back.

QUESTION: How do you evaluate what has happened and is happening in Russia? What significance does atheism have in all of this? After all, if there is such a thing as the Providence of God, then atheism must have some meaning.

ANSWER: I can answer this question only from the religious point of view, and I ask you to understand me correctly. Our country is Golgotha. Christ is crucified. On his left and on his right—thieves. One of them is wise and has believed in Christ. Many who found themselves on Golgotha have believed and have asked Christ to remember them in His Kingdom. The wise thief stands for all of them. The other thief is still mocking Christ. But who knows? He too may yet ask Christ to remember him in His Heavenly Kingdom... Golgotha isn't just sufferings, but sufferings that lead to resurrection, enlightening people.

Let us be objective, as they say. What will we see? Many young people are accepting Christianity. In fact, Christianity interests both those who accept it and those who for the time being reject it. They still rebel. They still set up all kinds of barriers. But the person who is really alive cannot continue in this way indefinitely.

Not long ago, I baptized a number of people, ranging in age from 24 to 30 years. "What brought you here," I asked. "What did you read?" They answered: "We don't know what brought us here. We just felt that something was missing." "Have you read anything?" "Nothing in particular." "The Gospels?" I asked. "How could we have done that, since they're impossible to obtain?" I continued my questions: "But you understand that you must believe that Christ is risen from the dead, that we too shall rise, that there is life beyond the grave—something that many people consider a fable. Do you believe all this?" Their answer: "We don't doubt any of this. It's all we can believe in, otherwise life would be meaningless."

Lord! This is what's needed. In Old Russia there was everything—any books you might want, plenty of churches. In short, everything for belief. But at best people simply conformed to tradition. At worst they subtly but cruelly mocked Christ. These atheists come from Old Russia. Many of the older people, in their seventies and eighties, do not believe, while their children do. Why? Simply because this is Golgotha, here and now. Christ has been lifted up on the cross. On both sides, people are crucified. They thought that you could kill everything like that, but they didn't understand that this is precisely how resurrection begins. And now, any reminder of Christ is of interest to us. Icons—monographs on iconography are being published. Some are indignant at this, but their very indignation arouses more interest. Works of the past also are stirring interest—like the Bible, and especially the New Testament. It's curious. Every bookstore offers titles on atheism, but these are of no interest to anyone. But let's imagine the opposite. Suppose some bookstore would offer the Gospels, the Bible and other religious literature. No matter how many copies they had in stock, such a line would form that there would not be enough for everyone. This confirms that after Golgotha, the resurrection begins. Atheism, so to speak, is the manure that has prepared the ground for this resurrection. This is its significance. It is doing the dirty work, the slave labor. Atheism labors with all its might, imagining that its labors are its own. But the slave does not labor for himself, but for the master. And our master is God.

Christ was crucified some 2,000 years ago. But Christ our God accepted our human image. Therefore, in everyone who is crucified, in everyone who suffers, Christ is crucified too. And let's remember how many were crucified in this way. In this regard, our age can be compared only with the first three centuries of Christianity. In fact, maybe it was even easier then, for the refinements of torture were not so developed as they are now. What then? Are these crucifixions simply to be forgotten? Are they to yield no fruit? No! We are seeing their fruit before our very eyes. The resurrection is beginning. "Once the chalice has been drunk to the bottom," writes the Russian philosopher Evgenii Trubetskoi, "then the Church will rise and with her Russia will rise as well."[2] The French writer F. Mauriac says that if he sees light anywhere, it is coming only

---

[2]Sergei Nikolaevich Trubetskoi (1862-1905): Russian philosopher and historian of philosophy, who stressed the "evangelical preparation" for Christianity provided by Greek philosophy.

from Russia.[3] Why? Simply because Russia is Golgotha, and where Golgotha is, there too is resurrection. If we think about it seriously, we'll see that we're now participating in the most interesting process in history. If we compare our religiosity with that of the West, the balance will fall to our side. Why? Simply because Golgotha is here, and not there. Can an abundance of material goods bring about a religious rebirth? They say that the Catholics don't know what to do in order to keep people in church. They have everything: books, churches... But the people, if they believe at all, do so only weakly. We have nothing. But if people believe here, they are ready to die for their faith.

On the basis of letters received from the West, it is evident that they've taken notice of the Russian Church. Some people are even studying the Russian language, in order to participate at least this way in our Golgotha and our resurrection. Such a situation places a great responsibility on us. Whoever believes here, but does not take up Christ's work with greater zeal, earns greater condemnation than if he were in the West. All of us must now become tireless Christian workers: aflame, courageous, fearing nothing. I appeal especially to the young: We must now labor on behalf of our unbelieving fathers, so that they—many of whom died with no faith—may be raised to life in Christ. Our lot is to labor on behalf of all generations. These are not just high-sounding words. This is beginning. Perhaps not everyone notices it. But this will continue, and nothing can stop it.

QUESTION: You said at one time that Golgotha is in our country. That means that there are the persecutors and the persecuted, that there might be hostility and vengeance between them. How should we view this from the Christian point of view?

ANSWER: Naturally hostility can exist. Sinful people are hostile. People who don't know Christ, for whom all is here and not in other worlds, try to get revenge. You can be venge-

---

[3]François Mauriac (1895-1970): French novelist and spiritual writer, winner of the 1952 Nobel Prize for fiction.

ful only if you consider earthly goods to be the only ones. But for those who transpose everything to another world, there should be no vengeance, no offense. The Christian isn't offended. He loves his enemies. He hopes that they'll be enlightened, that they'll understand what they're doing and how harmful it is for them. I recall from my life in the camps one young man, about 16 or 17 years of age. He didn't have much education—just high school, if that—but what great faith he had! He didn't know what it means to be sly, diplomatic, so as not to annoy others. He always did just what Christ commanded, spontaneously. And it was his very spontaneity that infuriated the camp administration. He was placed in a special punishment cell, which was cold enough to begin with, but then they would douse him with cold water. Did he show any bitterness? No. He just prayed for his enemies. Kolia Anufriev they called him, as I now remember. Quiet, good, sincere. He had a friend, Kolia Denisov. He was older, almost illiterate, with a third-grade education. For some reason he had no run-ins with the administration. He always worked on general projects: physical labor, heavy work. But his face always bore a certain smile. It is interesting how a lot of the highly-educated, finding themselves in the camps, were broken to the point of losing all their civility and culture: cursing, cheating, scheming, hating one another. But these two were models in everything. This is what Christianity gives. Christianity, first of all, is love. Love heals any situation. Why do we now suffer terrible calamities? Because of a lack of love. But if love has been crucified, that means such love raises the dead. Resurrection comes only through love.

QUESTION: If, as you say, Golgotha is here, what should we do in order to participate in this mysterious and saving process?

ANSWER: This question reminds me of the one put to Christ by one young man: "What should I do to inherit eternal life?"[4] Christ told him: "Keep the commandments." But when it turned out that the young man did keep all the command-

---

[4]Mt. 19:16-23.

ments, Christ said to him: "You lack just one thing. Sell all
you have, distribute it to the poor, and follow me." The young
man departed dismayed. Christ, turning to those who were
with him, said: "It is hard for those with possessions to enter
the Kingdom of Heaven."

But I won't put it the same way. Our situation is different.
We have broken all the commandments. And we have no possessions to sell. Instead of possessions, we have a multitude of
sins, from which we have to be parted. If we fail to do this,
then our participation in the process that's taking place will not
bring us salvation. As everyone knows, the religious question
is becoming fashionable, and today's writers are taking it up.
But sometimes in raising this question they avoid turning attention to the condition of their own souls. Their talent is what
counts, they say—a writer will be forgiven much. Sometimes
they even cite the classics in justification: Pushkin, Tolstoi,
Dostoevskii. Of course, anyone can be forgiven anything, but
only if he repents. Yes, the classical writers also had their sins.
But they repented of them, they suffered on account of them.
But now, when sins forgive themselves, when they're considered standard equipment for a person of talent, then let that
person not deceive or delude himself. You can create something of value only if your soul has values. If it hasn't, you
produce only the form, which for a time may be appealing, but
eventually its emptiness becomes manifest. While the classic
writers grew in significance after their death, the others—those
who trusted in their talent alone—were fruitless even in their
own lifetimes. We all have to pay attention to the state of our
soul, and first of all to examine our own faith. Faith can't be
just words. It has to be deeds. Only the person who truly believes can truly act. Protests and causes may be heroic and
popular, but they'll come to naught. One falsehood leads to
another. One can labor only in the name of Christ, in the name
of eternity, for the Kingdom of Heaven. Such activity is at the
same time entirely unselfish and sincere and yet completely
objective, for it always keeps everything in proper perspective.

We must also pay attention to how we live. Let's begin with
the family. Family life requires ascetic effort and sacrifice.
But often nowadays people enter into a relationship just for

pleasure, for egotistical goals. Let's imagine the following situation: the very best people, a husband with wife and children, and everything seems to be fine. But that's just on the surface. Their children are not their own. Let's say the father is the real father, the mother not. What's it like for such kids? Why are we surprised that, when they grow up, they abandon their parents? As a priest, I know how much pain such so-called parents can inflict on their children, how they can split their psyches right down the middle so that they end up feeling worse than orphans. But this is a relatively happy example. Now let's take a worse one. Not long ago I met a teen-ager. He relaxed a bit and confided to me that his step-father is a drunkard who beats him. The boy hates this "father" and his own mother along with him, though at times he feels sorry for her, since the father beats her too. The boy already smokes, uses foul language, and is probably psychologically disturbed. What kind of generation is this going to be? The family is our sore spot. And yet it is precisely the condition of the family that determines the condition of all society.

Now, about our relations with each other. Words like "chastity" and "innocence" have become almost incomprehensible for us. We even make fun of them. At times even ten-year-olds lose their virginity, becoming promiscuous at this tender age. What do you think? Can the promiscuous be holy? No. If there is no holiness, then everything is permissible. Without holiness a person cannot really live as a human being. Even the atheists are beginning to understand this. They try to "copy" holiness by seeking out models—holy days minus God, "marriage salons." But all this can be holiness only with God. Without God, you're left at best with something beautiful, which can't make you any better but which perhaps makes you happy. And at worst you've got just an ugly farce.

And what about mutual commitment, honor, fairness, courage? Commitment has become something temporary, all right only while you've got something in common. But later you betray each other in order to get a better deal. Betrayal is the fruit of building friendships not on religious principles, but on all manner of commercial "deals." Parents can thus betray their own children, and children their parents—to say nothing of friends. Honor, fairness, courage—these are spoken of in relative and not absolute terms. That is, we can be relatively honest, relatively fair, or relatively courageous—but only in relation to something else. When nothing compels us—our job, let's say, or material interest—then it's possible to be scoundrels, cheats, cowards. Only on the religious plane can this all be avoided, for there everything is considered in absolute terms. Truth and honor are not temporary and relative categories, but absolute and eternal. So, in order to participate in the mysterious and saving process of Golgotha and resurrection, we must really pay attention to ourselves. God needs not words, but deeds. Whoever teaches this and fulfills it, only he will be called great in the Kingdom of Heaven.

QUESTION: What is eschatology? Give the Christian definition, and touch on eschatology in general.

ANSWER: Eschatology is the doctrine concerning the end of the world. Today eschatology has gained a particular urgency. The means of destruction attained by our age threaten universal annihilation. So in order not to become confused by all these impending events, we must examine the "end of the world" from the viewpoint of Christian eschatology.

What does the end of the world mean for the Christian? The beginning of eternity, the inauguration of a better life. The atheists want to distort our understanding of eschatology. They say that Christians are pessimists, that since Christians consider the next world as the only real one, they do not want to work in this world. This is not so. That world is attained in this one. So for the Christian every minute in this world is precious. The fewer of them that remain, the more effort he must exert. True, we must make one reservation: There can be an unhealthy eschatology, one that fixes the end of the world for a specified year, with people running away and renouncing everything. But this is a distortion. "Of that day and hour no one knows, not the angels nor the Son of Man, but only the Father in Heaven."[5] Now many signs and utterances tell us that the end is near, but just when it will take place is impos-

---

[5]Mt. 24:36.

sible to foretell. But no matter how much time remains, there should be no panic. Panic can exist only on non-religious grounds, because for unbelievers the end of the world means the destruction of everything. But for us eschatology is the expectation of the Kingdom of Heaven, eternity and blessedness. Eschatology can also be individual, for each person. Remember the end of your life and you'll never sin. Remember that the last day is coming, on which you will have to give an account, and you will fear sin.

QUESTION: Does the Church believe in hell and eternal punishments the way it used to, or does hell now have only a symbolic meaning? The presence of hell upsets the whole harmony of eternal bliss. Can you really enjoy bliss when you know that someone else is suffering?

ANSWER: Hell, in fact, is a relative concept. But only in the event that there are no sins. Sin carries hell within itself. Hell exists only as long as there is sin. Therefore, strictly speaking, the Church does not believe in hell. Only non-believers believe in hell. But it would be impossible for sin to remain and hell to cease. Eternity, after all, can be contained in a moment. Therefore the eternity of hell and the eternity of the Kingdom of Heaven must be understood differently. There should be no evil; there should be no sin; there should be no hell. They exist, but only because we are lazy and irresponsible. By our actions we allow hell to exist. Goodness and truth must exist, for these make life possible. But you cannot live by falsehood. By falsehood you can only delude yourself. For us the Kingdom of Heaven must be what is real and vital. Hell, on the other hand, is only a mirage, though for some this mirage is real enough, both real and eternal. God created the Kingdom of Heaven. We create hell. The Church does not believe in hell. We sinful people do, and then we try to harmonize eternal bliss with hell. These cannot be harmonized, but we try. The existence of hell cannot be blamed on God, but on us. God is the one who frees us from hell. We must be vigilant, lest we create a hell for ourselves, for this hell will be everlasting and eternal if we do not free ourselves from sin. But the ultimate goal, of course, is that there be no hell for anyone, but rather the Kingdom of Heaven, resurrection from the dead and eternal life.

QUESTION: God established the Church, and it is said that the gates of hell will not prevail against her. But why is the present-day Church in such a miserable state? Surely you will not say that her clergy are the best people.

ANSWER: God established the Church, that's true. That the gates of hell will not prevail against her is also true. But it is false to say that the Church is in a miserable state. We would be in a miserable state without the Church. The Church cannot be identified with mediocre clergy, for she consists of the best people. All those who realize Christ's commandments in their lives enter into the Church. Those who do not are outside the Church, even though formally they may be numbered among its members. The Church is holiness, goodness and love. The Church is not limited by the walls of the building. She is not limited even by time. The true Church is also invisible. What we see is not necessarily the Church. In our Creed we say: "I believe in One, Holy, Catholic and Apostolic Church." When we say "I believe," this already suggests something not visible, for one does not "believe" in visible things. But we *believe*. We *believe* in the Church. At the same time we should not create simply an abstraction and deduce from this that something visible cannot be "believed" in as well. Christ united the divine and the human in himself. The Church is called the Body of Christ. As the Body of Christ, the Church takes on an invisible form. Christ was seen by men on earth, now He is no longer visible. Anyone who does not confess that Christ has come in the flesh is antichrist, said John the Theologian.[6] Likewise, anyone who conceives of the Church in the abstract alone does not really believe in the Church. And it is not necessary to identify the Church with mediocre laborers. Those who come into the church building also come to the Church, but only when they have sanctity within themselves. If there is no sanctity, then nothing can save us. The Church is holy, and we should be holy, for then the Church becomes a

---

[6] 1 Jn. 4:2-4.

reality for us. The Church is catholic, for all holiness is gathered in her. The Church is apostolic, for she is of the apostles
appointed by Christ. The Church is made up of the divine and
the human: these should not be confused, but neither should
they be separated.

QUESTION: Father Dmitrii, the religious question obviously interests many people today. But you surely understand that
it's one thing to be religious in word and quite another to be so
in deed. Yet we are all so debased that somehow we're embarrassed even to let religion touch us. What can we do? This is
sad but true. And at times even religion is hidden from us. So
don't judge us harshly. Such are the times we're living in.

ANSWER: This question is a question for confession, and I,
as a priest, cannot judge, but only have pity. Yet to feel sorry
for a person doesn't mean to pat him on the head and reassure
him by saying: "Yes, it's difficult for you, so continue living as
you are now." I can say with all seriousness: to live the way
we live is abominable. We have no conscience left, nor even
honor. We have lost the distinction not only between good and
evil, but also between decency and indecency. Yes, it's true
that conditions sometimes seem to compel us to act this way.
Yet if we don't want to, we don't have to. We're not happy
with the atheists, with their coercion. But how do we ourselves
act? They sin one way, we another. Antagonisms often arise
among us believers; we attempt to correct the situation somehow, yet in fact neither the situations nor our lives are corrected. Why? Simply because we have forgotten that our responsibility does not lie before this world, that the food of man
does not consist of material things and privileges. Our responsibility lies before God. Everything earthly is passing away,
and to offend another person for something earthly is the low-
est form of irrationality. Eternity awaits us all, and we must
attain it by all means. But we can attain eternity only by joining
ourselves to Christ and dying to this present sinful world. "As
many as have been baptized into Christ have put on Christ."[7]
We need to be filled with Christian ideas, to change our life-

7Gal. 3:27.

style radically. Otherwise everything will be just a game, both atheism and religion. This pertains to all of us. But the religious process, the process of resurrection from the dead, will continue without us and in spite of us, because Golgotha has taken place on our earth, because the torments of the tortured are gradually beginning to freshen the air. Those who are now being born, and especially those who are yet to be born, will sense this better than we. As everyone knows, bad parents usually produce bad children. Heredity plays its usual big role. Yet we should not forget that hereditary characteristics aren't necessarily transmitted directly from parent to child. At times a generation or more passes before these become evident. Not long ago I baptized a young man whose parents had provided him with nothing pertaining to religion, but as it turned out, his great-grandmother had been very religious. And this was transmitted to him. Also not long ago, I was quite touched by one letter. I'll go ahead and read you a few excerpts from it. The letter tells how children accept Christianity. In the Beatitudes it says: "Blessed are the pure in heart, for they shall see God." And children really are pure of heart. We are the ones who have lost this purity. Here are the excerpts:

> ... The child ran into my room, saw the icons and began asking questions. I was amazed that she didn't fuss about, she wasn't mischievous, but silently she looked wide-eyed at the faces of Jesus and the Theotokos, which she was seeing for the first time in her life. Though hesitant, I nevertheless tried to explain to my little cousin the simple meaning of what she saw on the wall. "You know," she said, "I always knew He exists, and I always talk to Him before going to sleep. I knew that He is everywhere, and I knew that He sees me when I am being mischievous. [*Notice the last word used by the girl, how precise and honest it is!*] Only sometimes I was frightened of Him. How can I speak to Him?" Startled by the child's words, I showed her how to make the sign of the Cross, and I experienced a peculiar awe, watching those little fingers trace the cross on her frail body ...

"And now I probably can kiss Him, can't I?" she continued to my amazement, "but not on the face or cheek, like I kiss my mommy. He is greater and better than mommy. He sees everything I do, and yet He's not angry with me. He is better than anyone else, and He loves me. Please give Him to me. I want to see Him all the time. I'll hang Him by my head, and His mother too. Please!"

Startled even more, I removed the icons of the Savior and the Mother of God from the wall and looked for some paper to wrap them with. The little girl began helping me.

"I want to wrap them in *white* paper," she insisted. Could you get me some?" "I don't want them to see all the handkerchiefs and pencils in my mother's purse. Mommy's purse is always such a mess!"

The conversation was interrupted by the entrance of the girl's mother, my aunt.

"Mommy," she cried, "come quickly! Kiss Him! He loves you too. Finally I've seen His face. I've known Him for a long time. Mommy, why do you look so stern?"

My aunt, her face drawn, began dressing her daughter, having put the icons into her purse, which, by the way, really was packed with articles. The little girl was dismayed: "Mommy, why are you quiet? Tell me about Him. I want to know everything about Him. I need to." [*Let's remember the child's words*: I want to know everything about Him. I need to!]

After my relatives had gone, I was no less dismayed than my little cousin. To see the light of such a little creature, straining towards Goodness and Truth ... almost a particle of the Great God Himself ... And then what? Her mother's cold expression, her furtive glance.

In a few days, my aunt came again, but without her daughter.

"Where is Irishka?" I asked. But my forebodings were correct.

"I didn't bring her. And I ask you never to say anything about God to her. She attacks me with questions, leaving her toys aside. She'll blab about it all, and then I'll be fired from work."

"But I warned her not to talk about it in nursery school," I countered.

"That's beside the point. In fact she doesn't talk about it. But yesterday, in front of all the children and their parents, she fell off her toboggan while they were coasting down the hill. She got up and crossed herself! What if people start asking questions? I'm a teacher. I've got a good position. Futhermore, she keeps asking for her icon. She wants to pray before going to sleep. It's better if she doesn't know anything. I'm tired of all her questions. I'm a teacher, and I am supposed to be disseminating antireligious propaganda."

"But you believe in God, don't you?"

"Of course, there's something there. But I would advise you not to go to church either. Someone might find out, and you'll be thrown out of the Institute and you won't be able to find other work. Life is difficult now."

"But what happened to the icon?" I asked, saddened by such a lack of understanding in someone so close to me and remembering Irishka's radiant little face.

"I didn't give her the icon. Her friends come to visit, and they might see it. As if I didn't have enough troubles. She cries, begs me to hang it up over the bed: 'I want to be able to see Him. I have to talk to Him. Give Him back to me, Mommy.'"

"And where is the icon?"

"In my purse. Let it stay there. But I want you to buy me a couple more of them the next time you're in church. Remember, I sort of asked you to do this for me before?"

Left alone later, I thought about Irishka's tears, about her being forbidden to visit me, about the icons in the purse . . .

What a letter! The cry of this child! "Mommy, give Him back to me! I have to talk to Him!" It sears the soul. Children want to speak with Christ, their Savior, and we forbid them, we don't give Him to them. We don't give Him to them at school or at home. We're afraid that "something might happen." We forget that children who are separated from God, deprived of holiness, will face a fate worse than any external misfortune: They will have nothing holy in their lives.

After Golgotha in our country, the resurrection is taking place. Its rays are extending wider and wider. We must all participate consciously in this resurrection. The more we enter into communion with this resurrection, the more it will become a reality for us. But instead, we still cling to the dust of the earth, seeking something in it.

In our time, faith must be conscious and active. We must not hide our faith, but bring it out onto a candlestand, to give light to all in the house.[8] A person is baptized, he receives a name, he receives a patron saint. Imitate that saint. Do everything to resurrect your soul also. You've experienced faith. Now don't be torn in two between this sinful world and God. You can't serve two masters. You can only serve God. And of course this applies to priests more than to anyone else. Their example is Christ Himself. Accompany Him to the Cross for the salvation of mankind. That's the only way. There is no other.

We'll continue this discussion about Christ's resurrection another time. This has just been the beginning. I have a request to make of everyone. Tell me about the events of your lives. You know, life is our most convincing example. Speak your opinions, share your thoughts. I'll read them out loud. Take an active part in our discussions. Let's work together. Christ's work is the work of life, the work of eternity. Let's not exchange it for temporal fears and privileges. The danger of not knowing God is greater than any other danger. The process of Christ's resurrection is as divine as it is human. Let's be as active as God is. Let's be crucified with Him in order to rise with Him.

---

[8]Mt. 5:15.

The Eighth Discussion

Thank God! Through God's mercy once again we have been enabled to gather and to hold a discussion. I'm told that these discussions are uniting us, that a kind of unwritten brotherhood is forming. Believers and non-believers are coming, Orthodox and non-Orthodox—Roman Catholics and evangelical Christians. Apparently that's what's necessary. I remember when the idea of holding discussions first came to me—I hadn't yet known what format to choose. I couldn't sleep all night. I was excited. But once I'd decided to hold these discussions I became calm. The discussion format—questions and answers—came to me just at the moment that the discussions were to begin. And here we are, holding a discussion.

I want to emphasize that it's not *I* who am holding a discussion, but *we*. More and more people are being included, but more importantly, our activity is growing. In the future I think that the believers themselves will answer the questions, and I'll just read them out loud, perhaps with a short commentary. Good company strengthens morals, as the saying goes, and good discussions strengthen our inner man. And a strengthened inner man then begins to discuss things with God, and discussing things with God is our gradual resurrection. It is said of the Kingdom of God that it doesn't come noticeably. It's within us. Nor does the resurrection from the dead come noticeably, that is, suddenly. It's necessary for this resurrection to begin within us. Then the universal resurrection won't seem something so unexpected and unlikely. It will be natural. Just as it's natural for us to be born into the world, so it's also natu-

161

ral both for our physical death to come and for us all to be
raised up and for there to be life eternal, the Kingdom of
Heaven, marriage with Christ. Man was not created to be born
into the torments which all men experience in this life, to die
and disappear without a trace. Imagine if we were given freedom of choice in the matter. Probably no one would accept
such a fate. But, inasmuch as it's a law of nature, as atheism
suggests, we do accept it—what else can you do? No, this *isn't*
the law of nature. It's the spirit of evil that secures our voluntary consent to death, and we, having lost our faith, agree. But
as free people, endowed with a free will, we must oppose this.
We'll never agree to voluntary death. Man was created for
life. He is free. Only sin has made him subject to death. But
we must freely accept life, and then we'll be alive. This depends upon us, upon our faith in the Risen Christ. And our
discussions are one form of the resurrection from the dead.
We have begun to be resurrected, unnoticeably, in our souls.
Later on we'll be resurrected noticeably. To someone unprepared for the resurrection from the dead, the universal resurrection will seem first of all to be unlikely and secondly to be
some sort of idolatry. Why are miracles of resurrection from
the dead so rare today? Because, unprepared as we are, they
would distract us from faith in the true God. We'd make the
resurrection from the dead into an idol, and this would dimin-
ish the miracle of the resurrection. It would become some sort
of focus, but it wouldn't give anything to our soul. Christianity
is careful in its approach to miracles. Only this sinful and
adulterous world seeks after signs, said Christ.[1] But for us the
main miracle is precisely Christ's crucifixion. An inner light
tells us that Christ's crucifixion is already resurrection. Such a
situation already in and of itself makes us better, more creative.
As free creatures we are called to co-creation with the Lord.
And look! The crucifixion of Christ in Russia today, the persecutions and the mockeries, lead to the resurrection of men's
faith. This is the main miracle. It's natural. It gives us
strength and power. It makes us better then we now are.

While the crucifixion continues, the resurrection is begin-

---

[1]Lk. 11:29.

ning simultaneously. In a Christian light, crucifixion and resurrection become synonyms. We cannot fear crucifixion. Let's take the simplest example. When all goes well with a person, is his soul resurrected? Let's pretend we're rich and glorious. We have reached the pinnacle of earthly successes. What feelings will we have? Not holy ones, of course, not ones which resurrect us. Riches mean greed and concern over not loosing them. Hence cowardliness, hence bargaining with our conscience, hence slavery to sin. And what does glory mean? Glory brings pride and conceit. As a result, a person doesn't see his own faults. He considers himself superhuman. Hence all sorts of crimes: "I can do anything I please," he says. Hence the Hitlers and all the "cults of personality."[2] Earthly success gives birth to an overestimation of your own strengths, and as a result you start worshiping yourself instead of God. You begin to consider yourself rich. Because of all of this, life becomes impossible: gas chambers, concentration camps, trampling on the human personality. The human being becomes simply a thing with which you can do anything you please without fear of punishment. There's just one result: depravity and destruction. Thus, neither riches nor glory nor earthly success can make us better. But something else can ...

Now let's take another example. Let's take sufferings. Let's say, a mother's sufferings over her child. Or the most horrible of all, an execution. What happens? The eyes of a mother who is suffering over her child are almost holy. In her soul she is actively reacting against all sufferings and untruth. The mother who is suffering over her child ceases to sin. Probably only a mother who was insane would, let's say, commit adultery at a moment like that. Naturally I have compassion for a suffering mother. Suffering over one's child is more horrible than one's own sufferings. And may God help her in her sufferings. But forgive me: I would still *rejoice* over such a mother. Many women today have lost their maternal feeling, perhaps because they so rarely suffer over their children. Quite often a woman no sooner gives birth to a child than she tries to separate it from herself, to get it off her hands to that she can

---

[2]Standard reference to Stalin.

more easily abandon herself to her own passions. In turn, when the children grow up they don't love their parents. We've been fooled by the cunning power of the devil. We've forgotten that life isn't pleasure, it isn't freedom for sin. Life on this earth should be selfless. Then and only then will everything become normal and man won't be degraded and transformed into an animal. (The animals would probably protest against such a comparison, if they only knew how man sins. They are better and purer than any man.) Degradation—that's what fear of suffering brings us to. On the other hand, sufferings resurrect man. It's not an accident that Christ chose the Cross of suffering as the weapon of man's salvation.

The highest form of suffering is death. Every death involves torment, but greatest of all is the torment of a martyr's death.[3] Imagine an execution. Dostoevskii was prepared for execution, and with just five minutes left before the sentence was to be carried out, he experienced an entire eternity. Perhaps this accounts for his unique talent. He provided the thinking and reflection of whole generations. Hence also his confidence and his selfless love for Christ.

There have been a lot of executions in our country. Let's imagine the situation of these martyrs. Does the thought of committing a sin enter their minds at such a moment? No matter what sinners they may have been, at that moment they turn into saints. Tortures make people holy. And those who survive also become better. I sure don't envy the executioners who are ordered to shoot. It's hard even to imagine a lower moral level than theirs.

How many martyrs there have been in Russia! And thus, how many holy feelings have there been! Is it possible that these holy feelings bear no fruit? Perhaps we live and will continue to live by the feelings of the holy martyrs, supported by them. It has not yet been revealed whether there were any great saints among these martyrs, but when this is revealed, the whole world will get down on its knees in reverence before the Russian martyrs.

---

[3]The Russian here involves a play on the words "torment" (*muchenie*) and "martyr" (*muchenik*).

Why do I say this? So that we won't be seduced by riches and glory and earthly success—they have very little real use—and so that we won't be afraid of suffering. Of course, we shouldn't invite sufferings, because there's the danger that we'll overestimate our strength. But those that are given to us we must accept as joy sent from God.

Today we've received a lot of questions on the theme of the resurrection, which we've already touched upon. You've sent me whole notebooks with records of your personal lives, and I'm very happy. This means that our discussions are becoming our common project. But before beginning to answer the questions, I'd like to say a few words of introduction.

We are conducting our discussions in an Orthodox church. I'm an Orthodox priest. Therefore I ask that you understand me in an Orthodox spirit. I say this to the heterodox, since a number of questions have come which evidently challenge me to an argument. I'll read certain of these questions today and give an answer, but for the future, I'm asking that you not send in such questions, because my purpose isn't to argue but to seek a common language. There have been periods of controversy in history—the ecumenical councils, for example—that were pleasing to the Providence of God. Today is different. This is a time of ecumenism. We mustn't argue but rather seek a common language, try to understand each other. Of course the ecumenical conferences aren't yet very effective, but the process is underway and we must aid it. The various denominations in existence today are a measure simply of human opinion. I look upon any sincere faith with respect, although as one who believes in the Orthodox way I do not share the views of the heterodox. Only one controversy remains for us: the controversy with atheism, and this not in the sense of rebuking the atheists for their errors but rather in relating to them compassionately and seeing in them a faith in God. After all, they *do* believe, only they come to God through the back door. We must argue with them when their atheism is converted from words into sin and crime, and then we must not just argue but fight with all our strength. One of my listeners once alleged that bitterness creeps into my words. Let me say that it only seems that way. I harbor no bitterness towards atheists.

Rather, I feel a great pity for them. I'm sorry for those who don't know God. But this doesn't at all mean that I should remain silent. We've begun to be lenient towards sin, too patient, to the point, in fact, that we become participants in the sin, unwitting accomplices. You can only be impatient with sin, and the more you love a person, the more impatient you are.

I'd like everyone who comes to my discussions—believers and atheists, Orthodox and heterodox—to feel like those who come by invitation. Many of those who were called didn't come, didn't respond, so we've gathered people in from the highways and byways, from the byways of atheism and sectarianism.[4] Let some of the Orthodox take a lesson from them. The Kingdom of God is prepared for all. Come and inherit it. Just let no one be found to have come in clothing unfit for a wedding.

Now let's turn to our questions.

QUESTION: Concerning asceticism: Throw the icons out of the Church. Just one thing is necessary. Revive simplicity of worship, translate the service into Russian.

ANSWER: Last time I said that asceticism soon will become a real requirement of our times. Even now when health fails, people resort to asceticism, to hunger and fasting. . . . When I spoke about asceticism I meant that things shouldn't enslave man. But now the person who asked the question is going a step further, by suggesting that we throw the icons out of the Church. Judging from the tone of the question, it's either from an evangelical Christian or from someone who lacks an authentically Orthodox consciousness. Of course it's very sad that we Christians are divided, that each has his own point of view and thus the robe of the Church is torn to pieces. We must seek that which unites us. For the sectarians the icon is a thing, at best, a picture. For us Orthodox, the icon is something holy, and to be ascetical with regard to the holy is the same thing as limiting yourself to a single good deed. The more holy things there are, the more good deeds there are, the better! That's how we understand it. Throwing the icons out of the Church

---

[4] Lk. 14:16-24.

is the same thing as destroying the books of the Holy Scriptures and limiting ourselves to just one book of some sort, as ceasing to do good deeds. We don't need such asceticism. That's what the atheists are pushing. After all, that's what they said: Why do you need so many churches in Russia? So they destroyed the churches, and people stopped hearing the Word of God, went astray and declined morally. Icons speak to us about God. As everyone knows, during the first years after the Revolution in Russia a massive restoration of icons took place. Perhaps some of you present remember this. I was just a child, but when I grew up I heard stories about how God spoke miraculously to people through icons. I happened upon a book containing a list of all the miracles worked by icons. This isn't an invention but a miracle of our own days, performed in order that people might be resurrected in soul. If I ever get hold of this book again, I'll read you several of the incidents from it. Now let me ask something of all of you here: If anyone knows of an incident about the restoration of icons, write it down for me or tell me about it. The icons of those years must now begin to talk to *us,* since they are witnesses to a unique history. I've been told that in that era people would suffer for icons. They became martyrs. Where I lived they put priests on trial. And we know from history about the iconoclastic period, when there were many martyrs who defended the icons.[5] Thus, for us Orthodox, icons aren't something which one must give up for the sake of spiritual benefit but something holy which one must cherish and before which one must show reverence. The icon was won by martyrdom, yet you recommend that we throw them out of the Church? Perhaps it never occurred to you that by this very suggestion you offend the feelings of Orthodox people, you enter the ranks of our persecutors. The icon has begun to speak in a special way in our days. There are already numerous cases in which people have come to faith precisely

---

[5]The iconoclastic controversy rocked the Eastern Church from 725-843. The Orthodox defended the veneration of icons as a corollary to a correct understanding of the incarnation—that God having become man is henceforth representable. The Seventh Ecumenical Council (787) upheld this teaching and carefully differentiated between veneration (applicable to the saints, and hence their representations) and worship (applicable to God alone).

through icons—those involved in art restoration, for example.
I personally know many such facts. So try to understand our
approach to the icon, and even if you don't agree with it, let
your understanding remain your own opinion, one which you
don't have to force on others.

Now, concerning the second half of the question, where
it's suggested that we restore simplicity to worship and translate the services into the contemporary language.[6] I agree with
you that we do have great splendor. Sometimes this inheritance
from the past jars me too. But this splendor also can arise
among the sectarians—they have organs, for example. How to
contend with this is a complex question. Even more so as re-
gards the translation of the services. Before the Revolution
there were attempts made at doing so, but they weren't crowned
with success. Perhaps some day they will be. But for the time
being we needn't sigh over what needs to be done or changed.
Instead we should consider how, under actual conditions, we
can do the work of God. It's obvious that God allows us to
have difficulties so that we can become more independent and
develop our creativity. Worship in Church Slavonic is indeed
incomprehensible for some. But Slavonic isn't *that* difficult to
understand. It's still our same Russian language. And it's not
so complex to master. Can we, knowing that our worship is a
centuries-old treasury, be so lazy about learning Slavonic?
Futhermore, it is rather dangerous to make hasty reforms. Reform can accomplish something good, but often it doesn't consider the tradition of centuries. Strictly speaking, any reform
is necessarily one-sided. The second half of your question is
understandable to me, even somehow close to me. But, I repeat, you have to consider the times in which we live and in
which we preserve our tradition. The conditions which our
Church faces are also a manifestation of the Providence of
God, and our goal is to learn to make do under these conditions. It would be nice if our singing were simpler, for ex-

---

[6]Old Church Slavonic is the language in which the services of the Russian
Orthodox Church are celebrated. Considerable lexical, morphological and syn-
tactic differences between Old Church Slavonic and modern Russian make the
former quite difficult to understand for the uninitiated.

ample. I'm tired of the concert style—"Italianate," as some call it. It's unfortunate that not everyone has sufficient taste in these matters, that many strive just for the external effect. It would be nice if priests would explain the liturgy more often. But, then, we're intimidated now. Sometimes we're afraid to do even this. It's good that many believers now are educated, so that they can fill in the gaps in their religious education for themselves. Let's not regret spending time in studying our Orthodox worship, in mastering its riches. Many holy feelings will appear. And how much poetry there is in it, how much beauty! So don't let the initial difficulties scare you off. They'll be repaid with interest.

QUESTION: You speak about miracles as "examples." The doctor didn't die; there was no miracle . . .

ANSWER: This person has in mind the case of the healing of the woman doctor which I told about last time. Just as she was about to die, an authentic miracle *did* take place. Her days were numbered. I repeat: she was exhausted by daily bouts of vomiting, the stench of death was all about her. As it says in the Gospel about Lazarus, she already stank.[7] After the Sacrament of Healing and Communion, her vomiting ceased immediately and the odor disappeared. Now, isn't that a miracle? To this very day she is healthy and goes to work. This didn't happen somewhere overseas, but here in Moscow. This woman often attends our church, and if you'd like, I could introduce you to her. She'll tell you about everything in detail.

Let's read further in the question: " . . . internal necessity (I speak figuratively)—light—can be the only proof . . . "

When I spoke about miraculous healing, I deliberately did not stress that resurrection from the dead consists specifically in this. But this healing does, after all, mean something. Christ's raising of Lazarus after four days means something. This same Lazarus later died, but the miracle with Lazarus, as with any miracle, leaves light in the soul, and this light hastens the universal resurrection. Sure, if there is no internal light,

---

[7] Jn. 11:39.

then a miracle will mean nothing. There are "miracles" among the atheists. Reanimation, for example, the restoration of the vital functions of an organism after clinical death. But the *atheist's* miracle doesn't transform him, it doesn't make him any better or confirm him morally. The person upon whom a *Christian* miracle has been wrought becomes different. He's already on the way to the universal resurrection. And the inner light is supported and expands as the result of a miracle. We don't seek miracles. We don't demand that God strengthen our faith miraculously. But once a miracle does occur, it has some meaning for us. First of all, it means that God has manifested His mercy to us. That's why I try to demonstrate the resurrection from the dead through examples taken from life. In the future I'll tell about miracles, and will do so today. However, I don't mean to say that the resurrection from the dead takes place only in this one particular way. It's just one of the ways, and God has many . . .

Let's read on in the question. It's formulated in a rather confused way. " . . . not choice from among the 'possible' situations—after all, who knows what's possible? . . ."

The second half of the question isn't entirely clear. How is the resurrection a necessity? Is this the point here? If so, I can say that such an understanding is non-Christian. The resurrection isn't forced upon us, and for this very reason we believe in it. It develops naturally and gradually, in concurrence with the human will.

The question continues: " . . . Where is it in the world of events and actions? Where's Christianity's necessity? Where is the necessity of the resurrection from the dead?"

This necessity is in everything. In miracles, in our sufferings. If there's no resurrection, then life loses its meaning. And our faith loses its meaning. If Christ isn't risen, our faith is empty, in vain, as the apostle said.[8]

I'll allow myself to read one letter. It's possible that the instance described in it won't convince the sceptics, but then the world doesn't consist of sceptics alone. It may touch some-

---

[8] 1 Cor. 15:17.

one. He'll be disturbed and begin to be resurrected in his soul, thereby shortening the distance between himself and the universal resurrection. The miracle which occurred to one person will become a universal inheritance and thus a universal miracle. Here's the letter:

> When I finished technical school they made me a supervisor. Then they made me enter the Party, and I did. I forgot the Church. I removed my cross. I began catching all sorts of diseases. I became irritable. I went to a health resort, but to no avail. I did not know why. Previously I had been healthy and did not even know what disease meant. Ten years of my life passed in diseases. I was blacker than the ground. Nothing was pleasant for me, even though I had all I needed. I ate and drank all I wanted. The only thing I lacked was faith in Christ. But the Lord stopped me. He brought me to the truth. I put my cross back on, I believed in the Lord God, and suddenly my superiors began to put me to shame, saying: "You've sunk into the mire. And you're young." I was defeated. I had a dream. Someone brought me a post card, and on it was printed: "Don't believe the false prophets." There were other dreams which strengthened me in the grace of God. The point came when they excluded me from the Party, discussed me at meetings, frightened me, intimidated me. But with God's help nothing and no one frightened me. I answered all their questions fearlessly. Finally I left that factory, since it was impossible to work there. I am now employed as a common laborer. Thanks to God, my soul feels light and happy. What happened with the diseases? The Lord helped me get rid of them. With the Lord God the adventures of men hold no terror. I can't describe everything, my dears. Whoever believes will understand me—even in summary form.

This is a simple human document. I read it just as it was given to me, changing nothing. The document's artlessness is its power. "Whoever believes will understand me," says the author. And for my part, I'll add: "Whoever has ears to hear, let him hear."[9]

As educated people we often strike poses, pass ourselves off as something which we in fact are not. In this is our weakness. We've forgotten simplicity and wear a mask. It wouldn't hurt us to learn sincerity from the simple people. Unfortunately there are fewer and fewer simple people around. The Russian countryside—the source of morality, where there were simple ways and characters—from the earth, as they say—is dying away. The rivers of morality flowed to us from there. The city doesn't have it. The city corrupts. I look upon this with grave alarm. I rejoice somewhat that our best contemporary authors have begun to sound this alarm. Apparently for every action there is a reaction. Thank God!

The second document is a whole notebook. I won't tell you the author's surname. If she wants to, she'll say something herself. It's her own personal matter. Judging by the way she writes, she's a simple woman. Many miraculous incidents are described in the notebook, but today I'll just read about one.

Now I'll tell about how my son was healed by Communion. Until he was fourteen I took him to church and to Communion. Then he didn't want to go, and it got hard to take him to church. After he was fourteen he started jumping out of bed at night and screaming about how someone was catching him. He'd be real upset. More than once I went to the doctor. They thought it was adolescence. It'd pass. They prescribed some powders for him, but that didn't help him. It happened to him more and more often at night. They began to identify it as lunacy. There was no help from doctors. He was healthy, physically strong. He studied well, especially mathematics and physics. He even amazed his teachers. He entered the Moscow Institute of Physics. His nightly attacks tortured him more and more, but nothing happened during the day. Finally, after suffering for about eight years, he had already reached

---

[9]Mt. 11:15; Mt. 13:9, 43; Mk. 4:9, 23; Lk. 8:8.

the third year at the Institute, and he started getting attacks about three times a night, and he got absolutely no better. His grandmother (my mother) talked to a nun in church and told her about him. She asked if it had been a long time since he'd been to Communion. And we remembered—it had started the minute he stopped receiving Communion. The nun recommended that we take him to Communion with faith. He didn't want to hear of it. We lived in a little place in the country about half-way to Zagorsk. My mother and sister drove out to our place to talk him into coming to church, but he said no. He didn't even want to listen. Finally his grandmother and my sister began to cry, saying that he didn't respect them. Finally he let us put a shirt on him, and then he began to get himself together. That was Sunday morning. We just barely caught the train and got to Zagorsk.

To our joy, there were a lot of young men and women there. He did everything we asked. He prayed seriously, with his soul. And we prayed hard. He confessed to a young priest, received Communion, stood through Liturgy, and we went home. My sister and mother went to Moscow, but we went to our place in the country.

Imagine our great joy. From that very day he never so much as raised his head at night. It all ended. The attacks passed. And the last time before Communion it had happened three times a night, and not a single night had passed without any attacks. It was horrible for me, his mother, to watch him during an attack. But now, great glory to God!!! He's married, with two kids. There's nothing like it! . . .

I've read incidents not from long ago but taking place in our own day. I know there'll be sceptics, who'll try to explain all of this in their own way. But no matter what they say, those to whom this happened know how much it meant to them. And not even because it somehow made their lives easier, but because it resurrected their souls and leads them to the universal resurrection.

I'll tell about one more instance. One of our church's parishioners told me this. He was a hopeless alcoholic. He says he happened upon an icon of Saint Nicholas and asked with his whole soul: "Help!" And here's the result. He found the power to stop drinking, although earlier nothing had helped. Everything we find in the Church, all of her holy things—the icons, the holy water, etc.—they're all mysterious signs through which God grants us His mercy. We must make use of all of the Church's means—prayer and holy water. We've forgotten that there is power in the holy water, but that's the way it is. The modern scholar and surgeon Voino-Iasenetskii—they probably still use his textbook on suppurative surgery—that is, Archbishop Luke, said: "Try taking some holy water. Then you'll understand what it means."[10] It's easy to laugh and deny, but be sure you're not laughing at yourself. I know from my own priestly experience how much Communion and holy water and everything else in the Church means.

Many of you probably know the Russian philosopher Vasilii Vasil'evich Rozanov. He was a highly original philosopher.[11] For a long time he received no Christian sacraments. He even ridiculed them. You couldn't say that he didn't believe at all. The man just had an itch to provoke people in everything. Berdiaev even called him the "brilliant provocateur." So this is what happened to him before his death. I'll read an excerpt from Erich Gollerbach's book, *V. V. Rozanov: Life and Work* (Petersburg, 1922):

> V. V.'s final days were a continual "Hosanna" to Christ. His bodily sufferings could not extinguish in him the spiritual joy, the brilliant transfiguration. "Let

---

[10]Abp. Luke: Valentin Feliksovich Voino-Iasenetskii (1877-1961): Soviet surgeon and medical researcher. Ordained to the priesthood after becoming a widower, he served a parish in Tashkent, in Soviet Central Asia, at the same time teaching medicine at the University. In 1923 he was elected Bishop of Tashkent, taking the name of St. Luke, the beloved physician, at the time of his monastic tonsure. His renown in his secular profession is shown by the coverage given him in the Soviet *Great Medical Encyclopedia*.

[11]Vasilii Vasil'evich Rozanov (1856-1919): Russian writer and critic. His negative views on Christian asceticism and his inclinations towards naturalistic religion brought him into conflict with Orthodox teachings.

us all embrace, all," he would say. "Let us kiss each other in the name of the risen Christ. Christ is risen! How joyous! How good! Miracles are indeed occuring with me. What sort of miracles I will tell later, some time."

Just before his death the sufferings lightened. Four times he voluntarily received Communion, and once he received the Sacrament of Healing. Three times they read over him the Prayers at the Parting of the Soul, and he passed away without torment, quietly and nobly.

To die with Christ—what joy! Not only to pass from earthly life, but from death to true life, eternal life. For this reason Communion is so precious for each Christian. For this reason people always try to receive Communion before death. But how painful it becomes when we remember that many people go off into eternity without Communion. In many places there are neither churches nor priests. There are people in places of confinement where they'll be treated with contemptuous mockery if they so much as mention Communion. This seems a bit savage. I remember when I was in confinement, while I was quite young and still had a countryboy's naïveté (I was born in the deep woods), I wrote a message that I wanted a priest to be sent to me, that I wanted Communion. "What?! What?!" said the startled guard. He looked at me incredulously, and I tried to explain to him what Communion is and why I needed it. Finally he shook his hand sullenly at me and said, "The interrogator will give you communion." Such mockery of human feelings still happens frequently even now. Upon whom does this depend? By whose decree is it done? There's a veto imposed on many of the Church's personal ministrations but not on the Sacrament of Healing or on Communion. But *in practice* will they really admit a priest into a hospital, let's say, or into a prison in order to bring Communion to an inmate? You've got to take risks, to break through barriers. There are good, bold people who will help in this. Let me tell you about how once I was able to break through. I went to bring Communion to a woman with cancer. She had a private room. I read the prayers in a half whisper. It seemed as though no one could hear me. I was about to conclude when the door opened and in came patients from other wards. I had no way to give them Communion. I'd brought only enough for one. They began asking me to bless them at least. A line formed for my blessing. But I haven't succeeded in breaking through into prison. The walls of a prison are strong. But then, I know from my own experience how people suffer there without Communion. During the "cruel" days under the czars there were special prison priests, you know, but today you can't even think about such a thing. Why is there such cruelty towards our sick and imprisoned? The Russian man always used to be compassionate towards the unfortunate. During the days of Pascha the czars would even visit the jails and share the paschal joy. Atheism has deprived people of the best feelings of goodness and mercy. It's led to moral dullness. Atheism is incapable of comforting anyone. It's just the pastime of cruel people. But you can amuse yourself too soon. Probably many of you know of startling instances, such as one metropolitan's denial of God, for example. God only knows what happened to his soul. They sounded the trumpets about him in the newspapers. They set him up as an example. But he found nothing in atheism, just emptiness. Who knows what happened with him afterwards? He was sick, on all fours, as they say. He crept up to the Church and died there. Whether God will forgive him, we don't know, but we see how horrible it is to play at atheism and rise up against God.

One woman told me about how such a picture struck her. She saw a person *crawling* out of a subway train through the mud, refusing help from anyone. It turned out that this person was a woman who had once destroyed churches and laughed at her faith. Later she was paralysed, and she understood why. Now she's trying to be worthy of forgiveness from God.

Many have to hide their faith today. Not all are bold. Atheism has deprived us of normal human relations. One woman told me not long ago about how a lieutenant-colonel who was rather friendly toward her family dropped into their house. When he saw the icons he changed immediately. "You know, you and I are enemies!"—that's what he declared. Atheism has made enemies of people. We must battle atheism as an enemy, the destroyer of people.

Almost no one holds to atheism to his death. Many know the Soviet writer Aleksei Nikolaevich Tolstoi.[12] But probably no one knows how he asked Metropolitan Nikolai to give him Communion before his death. The game was over. Death looked him in the eye. And he asked for Communion. But some play the game so long that when they *do* ask, God doesn't listen to them. They remain abandoned by everyone, alone, useless. "Forgive us, O Lord, that we have exchanged eternal spiritual values for earthly things which mean nothing." That's what we should shout from all the housetops, because our silence makes us accessories. You don't light the candle of faith in order to put it under a bowl. You've got to place it on a candlestand so that it can illuminate all.[13] Believers *must* be daring.

QUESTION: Father Dmitrii, listening to you one would think (I speak from my own point of view—I'm a non-believer) that you don't notice anything that's going on in our country. Can you really think that we've lagged behind in everything? Who launched the first sputnik? Did ancient Russia have the same technical abilities we do?

ANSWER: I know that we launched the first sputnik, and as a man, I'm even proud of that. I know we're a great power. But as you know, technical progress is one thing, and spiritual progress is another. With the growth of the technical, the spiritual side of life can be completely degraded. I see this, and as a priest I see great danger here, danger not only for the soul but for progress as well. The best minds come to the conclusion that if things continue as they are, in the end we'll destroy ourselves. We've got to sound the alarm. I've begun to sound it as much as I can. So what if a lot of people don't understand me? In the end they'll understand that I wish evil

---

[12]Aleksei Nikolaevich Tolstoi (1883-1945): Soviet author, "fellow-traveller" who emigrated to the West and then returned to the Soviet Union. An able writer but inconsistent in quality, he is highly popular with Soviet critics.
[13]Mt. 5:15.

on no one, as some claim, but good. I'm aware that I'm just a drop in the ocean, just a mote. But with God, I'm not just a mote. We often measure our strength in human terms. We become horrified—everything's destroyed. But we must orient ourselves towards God, and then everything will fall into place. Christianity has found a place for itself in the deepest of minds. It set the earth on a completely different path. With God everything will become possible. And I believe that a spiritual cure is possible. . . .

Now, *my* question: You're zealous for the honor of your country. You're to be praised for that. But how do you assess instances of this sort: Often several non-believers, when they see a believer, will say that he's abnormal just because he's a believer. Is *that* right? (I'm addressing this especially to any psychiatrists who might be present.)

QUESTION: What difference is there between an atheist who does good and a believer who does so?

ANSWER: The difference lies in the fact that the atheist assigns no eternal significance to doing good. For him both good and bad are temporal, relative. The believer does good and knows that it's eternal. He doesn't place it on the same level with evil. Evil has a temporal significance for the believer, but good doesn't. Thus when the atheist creates something good, he immediately ruins it by believing in the all-victorious power of death. But the believer does not believe in death. Therefore for him good is truly creative.

There's another difference too. Good is limited for atheists. Something is good for a certain class—and often this means simply that it's good for one's own friends. According to believers, good is for all mankind—not just for one's friends, but for one's enemies, too. But in fact the believer has no human enemies. For the believer, *sin* is the only enemy. The believer's goal is to make enemies into friends. Thus, good has a more essential significance for believers.

I bow down before atheists who do good, but I also feel very sorry for them. If there are such, I ask their permission to feel sorry for them. I say to them: May God help you! Listen, you atheists, *may God help to do good!* Don't laugh. Don't fall into doubt. God is no daydream, and we have no source of life and strength within ourselves, if for no other reason than that we didn't create ourselves. *God* is the source of our life.

QUESTION: Father Dmitrii, you confuse atheism with the hooliganism that comes from atheism, and therefore you don't admit anything positive to atheism and don't allow the idea that any good can grow up on atheistic soil.

ANSWER: I don't confuse atheism with the hooliganism that comes from atheism. I only say that there's no such thing as pure atheism. You can't build anything upon bare negation. And the *honorable* atheists are believers. The whole problem lies in what they believe in. I respect such atheists more than the believers who try to make a profit out of faith.

QUESTION: The Catholics foretold, about twenty years ago already, that the atheists would become more subtle, that they wouldn't persecute as they used to. And now they've fixed it so that the higher clergy of the Russian Orthodox Church—the bishops—have become simple bureaucrats, unfit for God's work. Mostly they hinder this work. Perhaps they do more harm to the Church than some atheists do. But the Church is supposed to stand upon the episcopate. Does this mean that the Orthodox Church has fallen?

ANSWER: I don't know whether the person who asked this question is a Catholic or Orthodox, but the question carries great truth in it. Yes, our episcopate doesn't worry too much about the Church, and sometimes it even harms the Church's affairs. But does this mean that the Church has fallen? No! It's impossible that in the Russian Orthodox Church there's not a single good bishop. That's the first point. Secondly, the bishop in the Orthodox Church isn't a master who lords it over the people of the Church. He's bound to the people only by a bond of love, as was stated in the circular epistle of the Eastern Patriarchs.[14] A bishop who doesn't do the will of God is a

---

[14]*Circular Epistle of the Eastern Patriarchs* (1848): declaration by the four ancient patriarchs of Constantinople, Alexandria, Antioch, and Jerusalem, co-

withered branch. Only a green branch has significance for church affairs. And even if there aren't many such good bishops, there *are* some and enough of them for the Church to stand. There are still priests, too, and they now bear the most difficult work. There are still believing people, you know. There's still tremendous power, inaccessible to atheists. Thus the atheists made a mistake in thinking that, if the bishops became their henchmen, all church affairs would perish. In Orthodoxy the lead role is played not by quantity but by quality. There may be only a few of these, but they are the salt of the earth. Christ paid attention to His "little flock." "Fear not, little flock!" He said.[15] Guided by the Holy Spirit, the little flock achieves catholicity. Although the Russian Orthodox Church doesn't embody the whole of Orthodoxy, nevertheless as a part of it, the gates of hell cannot prevail against her.

QUESTION: Father Dmitrii, what you say is frightening. Even before you start to speak, we're afraid for you. They could misunderstand you.

ANSWER: I too am afraid that they might misunderstand me. I'll express my position once more: I wish evil on no one, including the atheists. Nor, moreover, on the authorities or on the government. But if someone *does* misunderstand me, that doesn't mean that I should keep quiet. I'm doing God's work. I've put my hand to the plow, I'm tilling the soil of human hearts, and I mustn't look back. As we know, anyone who looks back is untrustworthy.[16]

But I hope that in the end not only will I be understood correctly by those who have power but also that my brothers will pick up my undertaking. It's not by accident that I've become daring. The time has come for *doing*. The fields are white for the harvest. We need workers.[17] Without workers the fields will perish. And such ruin is useful to no one. Once again I ask

---

signed by twenty-nine metropolitans, which stated that "no patriarch or council has ever been able to introduce any novelty among us [Orthodox] since the Body of the Church, that is, the people themselves, is the guardian of religion."

[15]Lk. 12:32.
[16]Lk. 9:62.
[17]Jn. 4:35.

you to understand me correctly. Scientific development and progress have taken great strides forward. I recognize this. But moral conditions have taken an even greater stride backward, so that progress is threatened with ruin if we keep on living as we have been.

QUESTION: Father Dmitrii, admit that you don't love our country and our people.

ANSWER: If you wanted to say—as you probably did—that I'm just anti-Soviet by nature, it would have been easier just to put it that way in order to frame me and get me locked up. But you're wrong. I love my country and my people and I'm sorry for those who have gone astray. I'm especially sorry for atheists.

QUESTION: Father Dmitrii, you're wrong if you think it's easy to oppose atheism. You don't know what a great ideological army is being prepared. Not just the one in *Science and Religion*[18]—that's just a trifle. This army is scattered throughout all the journals and publishing houses, and it studies theological and other ecclesiastical subjects far better than we do. And don't forget: They won't give you free rein, you know. After all, there's sheer physical force, which will make you keep quiet.

ANSWER: As they say, the devil is threatening, God is merciful. I take this question as the usual warning. The atheists have nothing left but the physical force which forces you to shut up. But physical force shows their impotence. Physical force summons new forces to life. As the ancient apologist said, "The blood of Christians is a seed." By their repressions the atheists help us to sow Christian seeds. There are cases in which people come to faith in God precisely through atheistic literature. Warnings from this direction are effective only with cowards, half-believers and those who are depraved, grabbing for earthly goods. For real believers this isn't terrifying. For them, when they take a stand against atheism, their real field of action is opened to them. As the apostle said, nothing

---

[18]*Nauka i religiia*; see above, n. 1 to the Second Discussion.

is impossible for a believer. The very death of someone who is firmly convinced is converted into a final and most convincing sermon.

Now concerning the ideological side, I doubt whether anything so great has sprung up from atheistic soil. Atheism hasn't produced a single real philosopher, a single real scholar. Those the atheists sieze upon are really believers, or at least idealists.

But let's suppose that some unprecedented atheistic philosopher did appear. He'd be an enormous barren tree, because neither philosophy nor scholarship can attract people today. People are disappointed in these things. They need atheism for a material advantage alone. It's perfectly clear: If there's nothing *there,* why be an ascetic *here?* But every real activity demands asceticism. You can't make a "hero" out of earthly goods, even though everyone these days thinks he knows how.

In any event, I take your question to be a personal warning to me to shut up. But I won't do that, and I won't smooth over our discussions or round off the rough edges. You have to talk straight and make your questions sharp.

QUESTION: What do you think: When is the best moment for the Church?

ANSWER: Right now. The Church is powerful when she's on the Cross, when she's persecuted. When she has a "guardian," she gets weak.

QUESTION: Father Dmitrii, it seems to me that you're deceiving yourself. Listening to you, one would think that all of Russia has nothing better to do than to busy itself with religious questions, whereas in fact the religious movement is still weak, especially in the big cities, Moscow and Leningrad. (It's even weaker in Leningrad than in Moscow.) Here's a second question: You belittle the West, but there the religious movement has taken on a massive character. It's good to be patriotic towards your own country and your Church, but this should be based on something more substantial.

ANSWER: I'll answer your question beginning from the end. My patriotism is based upon the greatest and most solid thing there is—on faith. Faith can move mountains—you know that saying from the Gospel.[19]

But to reason in human terms, I'd say: Yes, I know that the religious movement here is still weak, and that *officially* there are more believers in the West. That's all true. But let's consider some examples. Spring is approaching, but snow still covers the ground, and there are still frosts. But spring *is* approaching—that's both faith and reality. If we didn't look at anything but *today*, we'd think there would be no spring. But if we look to tomorrow, it's clear that spring will come. And we don't doubt this, because that's the law of nature. The time for atheistic revelry in Russia has ended. The snow storms and blizzards have blown away. There will be a religious spring, and *everyone* is working towards it, believers and atheists alike. That's the first point.

Second point: the comparison with the West. Let *me* pose a question: On which soil is faith stronger? My answer: On the soil of sufferings, of the Cross. That's why I feel that faith is stronger with us—because we're on the cross. Faith withers on earthly well-being, and in the West there's well-being, so faith is weaker there. The West's "comfortable" faith must receive strength from our "cross-bearing" faith. In general, wherever it may be found, faith is the inheritance of all mankind. So if I speak about the strength of faith here, I am also thinking about the strength of faith there. Believers must now form a common front.

QUESTION: Father Dmitrii, why do you set up the Church as an example? Open your eyes and look at today's clergy, even at the Patriarch himself—grovelling before the authorities, cowardly. The Church has gotten too stained. The modern intellectual is ashamed to enter the church. There's a lot that needs to be cleaned up in the church, a lot to be renewed and reorganized if she's to become accessible to the modern mind.

ANSWER: That question's a killer, as they say. But if you tell me "open your eyes and look at today's clergy," I say: be objective. You see the inadequacies of today's clergy and point

---

[19]Mt. 17:20.

to the Patriarch himself, but are you aware that you're looking at things too superficially? Who has fewer civil rights than the Patriarch? They say he's surrounded by thousands of informers. He so much as sighs and it's heard in every government department. Everything that he does against his conscience he does under pressure, and, of course, out of weakness, like any man. But you don't want to be compassionate. You sit in the judge's seat and pronounce sentence. Know this: Weapons of all sorts are aimed at us, and it's the greatest of miracles that we still manage to exist. I don't want to justify those who are unworthy among us, nor do I want to accuse the traitors and cowards from among your intellectuals. I only want to say that we must understand each other and not rush to judge.

I bow before the heroic intellectuals. But do you think that *we* are completely fruitless? I'll offer an example from your own sources. I won't name the author, you can guess for yourselves. Women prisoners on a collective farm are defending their small right of not going to work on the first day of Pascha. They are driven out by force. They beg, promising to produce twice their quota the next day. No one listens to them. They are stripped naked in the northern frost. They stand there like the first Christians.... What happens? Their spirit isn't broken. The next day they really produce twice their quota, and that even though—as the author concludes—they caught cold standing barefoot for so long in the snow. Then the author exclaims: Could *we* do the same? The author is a communist by conviction. I won't offer other examples, though there are a lot of them. It's not really necessary. An intelligent person will catch on fast enough, as they say. I'd just like to point out one characteristic of Christians, once again drawing on examples from prison camp—I was there. Among the nonbelievers there were heroes, but there was a lot of bitterness too. Often in protesting injustice they themselves degenerated morally until they were like everyone else. The Christians, though, opposed injustice without bitterness. They prayed for their enemies. And what conviction and courage were needed under those circumstances! In that world of cursing and swearing they didn't let out a single foul word. Perhaps this wasn't a mass phenomenon, but then, heroism never has been. There always has been a "little flock," as Christ said, but that little flock is the salt of the earth, the salt of the Church.

I'm probably being blamed for offering collective farmers —women—as examples, for as we know, the intellectual worships education. Therefore I'll now offer an example from among the "educated." The priest Paul Florenskii,[20] a man of world-renown, perished in Stalin's camps under conditions which we still know nothing about. We are now collecting his works little-by-little, and people who have no relation to the Church are taking part in this, since he was a tremendous mind in various fields of knowledge. Or the philosopher Lev Platonovich Karsavin.[21] Those interested can read about him in the latest edition of the *Philosophical Encyclopedia*. He perished in the camps in Abez, in 1952. Probably few people know the prayer he composed. Permit me to read it. Let's listen to the spiritual purity which it breathes:

> I confess to Thee, O Lord my God, all my sins from my youth up even unto this present day, and I know that for their sake Thou hast suffered me to fall into my present straits, into the hands of those who blaspheme Thy holy Name, and who seek to destroy me . . .

What unbeliever would seek to find the reason behind his sufferings in himself? Don't they often make saints of themselves? As Esenin wrote to Dem'ian Bednyi,[22] "You've only been imprisoned once, yet you've made yourself a hero, you grunt at Christ. But if you had borne *that* much, what would have happened?"

---

[20]Father Pavel Aleksandrovich Florenskii (b. 1882): Russian philosopher, theologian, and scientist. His refusal to renounce the priesthood caused him many persecutions, ending in a ten-year sentence to a concentration camp in 1935. The place, manner and date of his death have never been verified.

[21]Lev Platonovich Karsavin (1882-1952): Russian historian of the Middle Ages in the West and patrologist.

[22]Sergei Aleksandrovich Esenin (1895-1925): Soviet poet. Dem'an Bednyi ("poor Damian"): pseud. for Efim Alekseevich Pridvorov (1883-1945): Soviet poet and fablist.

... But Thou hast created all things by Thy grace ...

Such sufferings, and yet he writes: "Thou hast created all things *by Thy grace.*" Think of it! Yet we grumble so much that in our sufferings we're ready to blame everyone but ourselves.

... My soul doth thirst for repentance; yea, it doth seek Thee, Who alone cleansest and savest ...

But who among us is able to repent? We've all been corrupted and spoiled by our sins, and we've forgotten how to repent. Someone else is always to blame, not us.

Yea, O Lord, Jesus Christ, my Creator, Provider and Savior, grant that I, Thy creature, may not perish with mine iniquities; but create in me a sign for good. Bless the days of my imprisonment; convert it to an image of cleansing repentance, of ceaseless prayer, and make it a living and anxious standing before Thy face. And vouchsafe unto me, O Lord, to love Thee with all my soul and mind ...

In his sufferings he asks for love—that's what faith means! So often we just become bitter.

... and to do Thy will in all things and to walk in the ways of Thy commandments every day. Grant me a spirit of patience, humility, continence, forgiveness, charity and love ...

Let's listen. What tremendous words! Not everyone can rise up to such a spiritual condition.

... Deliver me from a spirit of evil speech, abuse and judgment of my neighbor; from self-exaltation, desire for glory from man. Set a guard over my lips. Moreover, grant me prayerful silence. Cause a spirit of continence in all things with charity to abide in me. Bless

the scarcity of our food, giving it the grace of a fast before Thee.

Accept me in repentance; set me on the path of confession; multiply my faith; establish me; create in me no
doubt. Destroy in me the bonds of lasciviousness, O
most merciful Lord . . .

But today we don't even consider lasciviousness a sin, although
through it the family has fallen apart and children have been
made unhappy, their psyches depressed and their conscious-
nesses split, because often they don't even know where their
father and mother are.

. . . whereby Satan hath bound me a multitude of times
and a multitude of ways from my youth up. Destroy
them, crush them, finally annihilate them; cleanse me,
wash me, lighten me, for Thy Name's sake.

Such a prayer could be written only by a person who has a
deeply Christian consciousness, one who loves and who gives
an account to himself for the reason for all evil.

That's the Church. But *you* point to certain inadequacies
and see nothing beyond them. The Church is the only thing
which can correct our situation in all relationships. The Church
must be supported with all our strength, by all of us and each
of us, even by the atheists if they desire our life to become normal. The Church is the source of the resurrection from the
dead.

I would suggest that we now all sing "Having Beheld the
Resurrection of Christ":[23]

Having beheld the Resurrection of Christ, let us worship the holy Lord Jesus, the only sinless One. We
venerate Thy Cross, O Christ, and we praise and glorify
Thy holy Resurrection. For Thou art our God, and we
know no other than Thee. We call on Thy Name.

---

[23]Hymn sung at Sunday Matins throughout the year, and daily at Matins during the forty days from Pascha to the Ascension.

Come, all you faithful, let us venerate Christ's holy Resurrection, for through the Cross joy has come into all the world. Let us always bless the Lord, singing His Resurrection, for having endured the Cross for us He has destroyed death by death!

May God protect us all!
Until we meet again.

The Ninth Discussion

I've begun to rejoice over every meeting that we have. Last time I said, "Until we meet again," and I waited impatiently. And now we've met again. God has led us to meet again. If we think about it, we should *all* rejoice at meeting together. The meetings we have in this life will be the ones we also share in eternity. Let's take a step towards that today.

What joy to be able to say at today's meeting: "Christ is risen!"[1] It's the music of eternity! How fantastic the paschal hymns are! How the soul rejoices! The paschal joy catches everyone up, even those who don't want it to happen. Remember, for example, the gloomy faces of the atheists who surrounded our church before the procession. They were all frowning about something. Nothing seemed to please them. But when we cried out, "Christ is risen!" smiles appeared on their faces, happy, radiant smiles, and their angry expressions just turned into an amusing grimace.

Remember the paschal troparion:[2]

Christ is risen from the dead,
trampling down death by death,
and upon those in the tombs bestowing life.

That is, Christ, Who arose from the dead, has killed all death by His own death, and has even given life to those who seemed

---

[1] The traditional Orthodox Easter greeting, to which the reply is: "Indeed He is risen!"

[2] The principal hymn or "theme-song" of Easter.

to be dead, who lay in their graves. For the present, this is just our faith and nothing more, while death still exists as a reality. But faith is the beginning of life, and it gives life to everything. Without faith everything is dead. Let's sing the troparion. [*Everyone sings.*]

How shall we begin today's discussion? The first week of Pascha has passed—"Bright Week." Tradition tells us of how Saint Mary Magdalene brought the emperor a decorated egg, saying "Christ is risen!" With this she began her preaching of the risen Christ. During the first years of the Soviet regime they still allowed debate on religious themes. One resourceful metropolitan, instead of answering the claim that "today nobody believes in the resurrection of Christ," turned to those in the hall and proclaimed, "Christ is risen!" The hall, which was overflowing with no one but "atheists," answered with a roar: "Indeed He is risen!" We in the Russian Orthodox Church have a remarkable saint, Seraphim of Sarov, who was canonized just before the Revolution. He lived in the nineteenth century. No matter what time of year it was, he greeted all who came to him with the words: "Christ is risen, my joy!" And the warmth of Christ's resurrection filled the soul of each individual.

Some of you write that this is already our third discussion dealing with Christ's resurrection, yet we haven't even spoken about Christ's resurrection itself. We've always wandered off onto other topics. So now let's talk specifically about Christ's resurrection.

There are some people who need only to open the Gospel and read about Christ's resurrection (a total of eleven pages of Scripture deal with it), and that's enough for them: they believe. Blessed are these people! But there are a lot of people who wish we'd tell them about Christ's resurrection in modern language. Some ask, "If Christ is risen, and if this prefigures the resurrection of each person, then why today do people only *die* and no one is resurrected?" Finally, there are also people who ask us to disprove the atheists' arguments against Christ's resurrection which get in the way of their believing. But what's there to disprove? The ancient fantasy that Christ's body was (supposedly) stolen, thus giving rise to the claim that He was risen? Or the modern atheistic invention that there never *was* a Christ? We *could* disprove either of these, but I don't think it would be worth it. Such polemics would just lead us astray once again into history and philosophy, distracting us from our main topic. And *that* is to explain for ourselves just what Christ's resurrection means for us believers.

Today is Thomas Sunday,[3] the so-called "Sunday of Anti-Pascha." ("Anti" in this case doesn't have its usual meaning of "against." It means "instead of" or "in place of" Pascha.) "Doubting Thomas." This has become the usual term for someone who doesn't believe. But in the Gospel, Thomas is the apostle of the resurrection. This is what the Russian philosopher Vladimir Solov'ev wrote on this subject in his *Resurrectional Letters*:[4]

In times of predominant unbelief it is important that we clarify with which type of unbelief we are dealing. If it is a flagrant lack of faith—material, beastly, incapable of rising to a real understanding of the truth—discussion is pointless. If it is an evil unbelief—a conscious misuse of various half-truths through hostile fear of the full truth—one must pursue such a serpent without anger or fear, disclosing its devices and its wiliness. Finally, if we are dealing with an honest, purely human unbelief, which but hungers for a full and complete certification of the full truth—the type of unbelief which the apostle Thomas had—it enjoys a full right to our moral recognition. And if, unlike Christ, we are unable to give such people the certification of truth which they demand, then under no circumstances ought we to judge or reject them. Without a doubt these seemingly unbelieving people will precede the vast majority of all believers into the Kingdom of God. If Thomas' unbelief had resulted from a profound materialism which reduces all truth to sensory evidence,

---

[3]So-called because the gospel reading for the day is the account of Christ's appearance to the Apostle Thomas (Jn. 20:24-29).

[4]See above, n. 1 to the Second Discussion.

then having been tangibly convinced of the fact of the
resurrection, he might have invented some materialistic
explanation for it. He would hardly have exclaimed,
"My Lord and my God!" From the point of view of
sensory evidence, the wounds from the nails and the
pierced side could in no wise demonstrate Christ's divinity. It is even clearer that Thomas' unbelief was not
due to some moral bankruptcy or hostility to the truth.
The love of truth drew him to Christ and engendered
in him a boundless devotion to the Teacher ... Christ
did not judge Thomas, but utilized the means which he
demanded in order to convince him: that is, He allowed
him to put his fingers into the wounds from the
nails. . . .

The apostle Thomas is a symbol not of doubt but of confirmation. His words, "Unless I see in His hand the wounds
from the nails, and put my hand in His side, I will not believe,"
do not suggest unbelief, much less materialism. Christ's
wounds are the proof of His resurrection. In other words, you
can't understand the essence of Christ's resurrection through
abstract reasonings alone, but only by communing with Christ's
wounds, with His sufferings.

If you want to know what freedom is, you've got to experience captivity. By being in prison, for instance. Anyone who
has ever experienced this knows the feeling with which he
drew that first breath of free air, how the fresh breeze of freedom lifted his depressed spirit, how each free sappling, each
tiny blade of grass, each little worm or mouse filled him with
joy—how everything was sweet, alive. But when we are free,
we often don't place any value on freedom. We trample it
underfoot. Often we offend it. Sometimes prisoners—even
when they know beforehand that they're doomed to perish—
still attempt their escapes. A breath of freedom becomes more
valuable than life in captivity. I remember the first time I left
the detention zone, how the freedom which poured into my
breast seized it. I just stopped. I couldn't take a step because
of the amazing feeling of freedom. It was real blessedness.
But now I no longer experience that amazing feeling.

Some people accuse me of indelicacy—I talk about my imprisonment all the time. But remember how the apostle said that if he could boast in anything, it would be only in his cross and suffering. My imprisonment is my cross, my boasting. I know that a great number of my countrymen share this same boast. I just can't understand why some of them aren't proud of it. It's as though they were *ashamed* of their cross. But I'm proud and will be proud, and I'll thank God for the trials He has sent to me. The memory of them even today gives me strength and enlightens my mind. That's why Christ's resurrection is so close and so dear to me. I just can't understand people who hide the object of their true pride and rather are proud of vain things—success at work, for example, or owning their own car, furniture . . . . I'm sorry for them. In my opinion this is empty pride. I remember the words of one of my former prison friends, who'd spent seventeen years in the camps. He said to me, "We've gotten so much worse, so much more *unfree* since we've been set free. Remember our discussions in camp? Boy, did our minds soar! How aflame we were! But now, we've begun to burn out and to fill up with smoke."

The atheists use our fear of suffering to stifle our spirit, our free thoughts and feelings. And they in turn frighten us. We must overcome our fear of suffering. Only then will we become really free, active and invincible. Only then will we overcome the arguments against Christ's resurrection which the atheists use to coerce our minds—the coercion of "proofs" which at first seem to free our minds but which in fact only fetter them. Faith is the overcoming of all coercion of the mind. It's the smashing of all obstacles and impediments set up by "proofs." It's each person's *free acceptance of Christ* in his heart. To believe in Christ's resurrection means to free your mind of doubts, to cleanse your heart from slavery to sins, to fortify your will against all coercion and weakness. Faith is a breakthrough into eternity. Unbelief is non-freedom in everything: in mind, feelings and will. I recommend that we all now sing the Creed:[5]

---

[5]The Nicene Creed, sung at every Divine Liturgy.

I believe in One God, the Father almighty, maker of heaven and earth, and of all things visible and invisible. And in one Lord Jesus Christ, the Son of God, the only-begotten, begotten of the Father before all ages. Light of light; true God of true God; begotten, not made; of one essence with the Father; by Whom all things were made; Who for us men and for our salvation came down from heaven, and was incarnate of the Holy Spirit and the Virgin Mary, and became man. And He was crucified for us under Pontius Pilate, and suffered, and was buried. And the third day He rose again, according to the Scriptures, and ascended into heaven, and sits at the right hand of the Father; and He shall come again with glory to judge the living and the dead; Whose Kingdom shall have no end. And in the Holy Spirit, the Lord, the Giver of Life, Who proceeds from the Father; Who with the Father and the Son together is worshipped and glorified; Who spoke by the prophets. In One, Holy, Catholic, and Apostolic Church. I acknowledge one baptism for the remission of sins. I look for the resurrection of the dead, and the life of the world to come. Amen.

Let's remain silent for a moment and listen to our hearts and wills—to hear whether they've answered this call from the distant past.... The Creed—the "symbol of faith"—isn't just some abstract words. Each word has been reached only through much suffering, poured out with blood and heart. Each word is the free self-expression of a man who believes in God, in the resurrection from the dead.

"I look for," that is, "I await," "I believe in," "I want," "the resurrection of the dead and the life of the world to come." That's how the Creed ends. We Christians await the resurrection from the dead and eternal life. We *believe* in it. That in particular is why I ignore these "proofs." Faith is stronger than any proofs. In my view, proofs are *non*-freedom, while faith is freedom.

But faith isn't just given to man in an instant—just like that. The gift of freedom is sent through the cross, through sufferings. Only then does freedom become real and understandable for man. Thus, sufferings become the *only* reliable proof. Thus, when Thomas wanted to place his fingers in Christ's wounds, he wanted to accept Christ's resurrection freely. Christ's wounds and sufferings became for the apostle the proof of the Savior's resurrection.

But Christ's sufferings weren't those of just any person of any era. Christ our God became incarnate, He became a man, He was *in* man. Christ stands for each man. "I was sick and you didn't visit Me, I was in prison and you didn't come to Me," said Christ. "Lord, when were you sick or in prison?" they ask Him. "If you did so to this person, you did so to me," He answers. "Depart from Me, workers of iniquity!"

Anyone who hasn't in some way tasted of sufferings has no right to talk about the resurrection. It's blasphemous towards the resurrection for anyone who's afraid of sufferings or who runs away from them to talk about Christ's resurrection. Therefore, I repeat, I now simply *ignore* intellectual proofs. To endure, to experience sufferings—or at least to do so through compassion for your neighbor—*this* is the path of free faith in Christ's resurrection. Let's make use of the apostle Thomas' proof. Let's thrust our fingers into Christ's wounds. This will be the most reliable proof of the resurrection.

Remember that unfortunate Russian czar, that monster of the human race, Ivan the Terrible. How much human blood he spilled! How many executions! What senseless crimes he committed! He was even guilty of the death of the greatest Russian bishop, Philip the Great Martyr. But this monster, who was also a man of the greatest intelligence, would descend into the dungeon during the days of Pascha to visit the prisoners who were languishing in captivity. Aren't we worse than him, when we fail to extend a hand to those who suffer and are persecuted, when we don't cheer them up?

Let's descend. Let's exchange the paschal kiss and proclaim "Christ is risen!" to those whose graves are snow-bound in the northern blizzards, whose bones are spread abroad all across our vast land, whose names people were afraid to mention out loud not long ago. Some people who are especially fearful are still afraid today to commemorate the names of the millions of people who were tortured and shot and suffocated and stuffed away in prisons. "Why open old wounds?" they say. For the atheists, remembering the martyrs is only "opening old wounds." They're afraid of commemorating their names, because these names expose their deeds. But the martyrs are arising. *They* begin the singing of the paschal hymn. *They* are beginning to cause uneasiness in those who would like to forget all the crimes—those who would cancel these crimes through posthumous rehabilitations and write into memoirs the lives which have been destroyed. The martyrs are a source of uneasiness for those who, in denying the resurrection from the dead, are trying to fill the prisons and mental institutions. (I speak not of Russian prisoners alone, but of those, too, in China, in Africa, in Greece—all over the world.) We must descend to them, overcoming all prejudices and slander, and say to them, "Christ is risen!"

We must say, "Christ is risen!" to the students who have been expelled from the institutes because of their religious convictions, to those who have been fired from their jobs, oppressed or persecuted in any way. So what if their faith isn't yet real, or even if they still consider themselves unbelievers? Faith *will* come to them, because Christ is with all those who suffer. Christ's resurrection extends to all people, but those who suffer receive it first of all. If in our love we kiss the clotted wounds of the crucified thief, even while he's still reviling Christ's Name, perhaps we'll be helping him to believe in the risen Christ and be showing him the meaning of existence—in the resurrection from the dead.

We mustn't make Christ's resurrection into anyone's special privilege. Christ suffered for *all*—the righteous and the unrighteous—in order to resurrect *all*. Anyone who knows the truth of Christ's resurrection but hides it, who doesn't take it to people, is a criminal, whatever his faith. The light of Christ's resurrection must illuminate all. Just imagine that we possess the key to eternal happiness and all around us there are unhappy people who are perishing. We could make these unhappy people happy if only we'd use our key. But we hide it—not because we're afraid of losing it, but simply because we've been warned: If you show your key, we'll deprive you of temporal prosperity. And in exchange for this temporal prosperity we give up many persons' eternal happiness, *and our own as well.* What are we after this? Is there any justification for us? Every believer possesses this key to eternal hapiness, but if he hides it, he's the first to be deprived of all this happiness. You don't put a lighted candle under a table. You put it on a candlestand, so that it can illuminate everyone in the house.[6]

Sometimes people justify their faintheartedness by saying it's pride if you exhibit your faith. The holy fathers, they say, went out into the desert and hid themselves from everyone. Yes, we find in the Gospel the words: "When you pray, shut your door and pray in secret, and your Father who sees you in secret will reward you openly."[7] Yes, there are times when you need to shut yourself in and do God's work in silence. But there are also times when you've got to encourage others and lead them to salvation by your own personal example when you see they're perishing. There was a saint who left the desert and walked about the city making the sign of the cross in order to encourage the fainthearted. *Now* is such a time, when you've got to encourage others, when you've got to *scream* about the danger they're in. But often we make Christianity into our own privilege. Moreover, we indulge in godless intrigues, whereas Christianity is the inheritance of all and is necessary for the salvation of all.

People are perishing. Earthly success and glory don't save anyone. Trying to save themselves from the bitter taste of disillusionment, lots of people are becoming addicted to drinking, to lewdness, to crime, thus only hastening their destruction. Everyone who knows the truth of Christ's resurrection, who returns from His empty tomb, the scene of the atheists' crime, should run like the myrrhbearing women and cry, "Christ is risen!" People, listen! Christ's resurrection exists! It's eternal joy for all of us. Come on, convince yourselves. Let's go to the place of execution and see. All those who have been executed will rise up before God alive.

---

[6]Mt. 5:15; Mk. 4:21; Lk. 8:16, 11:33.
[7]Mt. 6:6.

Can there be any joy greater than the paschal joy?! Let's now sing the paschal stichera:[8]

Let God arise; let his enemies be scattered.

Today a sacred Pascha is revealed to us, a new and holy Pascha, a mystical Pascha, a Pascha worthy of veneration, a Pascha which is Christ, the Redeemer. A blameless Pascha, a great Pascha, a Pascha of the faithful, a Pascha which opens to us the gates of paradise, a Pascha which sanctifies all the faithful.

As smoke vanishes, so let them vanish.

Come from that scene, O women bearers of glad tidings, and say to Zion; "Receive from us the glad tidings of joy, of Christ's resurrection. Exult and be glad, and rejoice, O Jerusalem, seeing Christ the King come forth from the tomb like a Bridegroom in procession!"

So shall the sinners perish before the face of God, but let the righteous be glad.

The myrrhbearing women at the break of dawn drew near to the tomb of the Lifegiver. There they found an angel sitting upon the stone. He greeted them with these words: "Why do you seek the Living among the dead? Why mourn the Incorrupt amid corruption? Go and proclaim the glad tidings to His disciples."

This is the day which the Lord has made; let us rejoice and be glad in it.

Pascha of beauty, Pascha, the Pascha of the Lord! A Pascha worthy of all honor has dawned for us! Pascha!

---

[8]A series of Psalm verses and hymns sung during the Easter midnight Matins service and throughout the paschal season. Here the stichera are followed by "The Angel Cried," a paschal hymn to the Virgin Mary.

Let us embrace each other joyously! O Pascha, ransom from affliction: for today as from a bridal chamber Christ has shown forth from the tomb and filled the women with joy saying: "Go and proclaim the glad tidings to the apostles."

Glory to the Father, and to the Son and to the Holy Spirit, now and ever and unto ages of ages. Amen.

This is the day of Resurrection. Let us be illumined by the feast. Let us embrace each other joyously. Let us call "brothers" even those that hate us, and forgive all by the resurrection. And so, let us cry: Christ is risen from the dead, trampling down death by death, and upon those in the tombs bestowing life!

The angel cried to the Lady full of grace: Rejoice, O pure Virgin! Again I say: Rejoice! Your Son is risen from His three days in the tomb. With Himself He has raised all the dead. Rejoice, all ye people!

Before going on to the next part of our discussion I must make some observations. As I've found out, some people take our discussions too enthusiastically and some, too critically. Some agree with me, others condemn me. But judging from the fact that attendance is growing time after time, I see that interest isn't declining. Quite to the contrary.

To my well-wishers I can only say, thank you for your dear kindness which emboldens me. To my critics I can only answer a few of their questions briefly.

"First of all," they tell me, "what you've undertaken requires a special blessing, the advice of your elders. But *you* do it by your own will."

My answer: I haven't "undertaken" anything special. I only do what *every* priest ought to do. I have seen how atheism undermines the health of man's religious organism and I've begun to do what's needed to awaken the vital forces of that organism and to help it resist this disease. Should I be doing this? I *must*! Woe to me if I *don't* proclaim the good news.[9] I am a *priest,* you know. I've got to proclaim the good news. And no special blessing is required for that. I was blessed to do so when I was ordained. Once and for all.

So I'm doing what I have to do. Furthermore, I'd just mention that when I do so I don't go outside the walls of my church. That's the minimum we can accept. The atheists have their literature and art and movies and clubs, and all I have is my little pulpit. If I had to go and do missionary work among the atheists on the public square, for example, or in the atheists' club—yes, I would need a special blessing for that.

As a priest I believe that anyone who believes and is baptized (as it says in the Gospel) will be saved.[10] But if I see that people *don't* believe and *aren't* being baptised, I know they're perishing. Don't I have the right to offer a helping hand to those who are perishing? I *must*! If I don't, I'm not a priest. So there's nothing special in my activities. It's absolutely normal Christian work.

Some say, "Your discussions have become a sensation." I reply: There's no sensation here. We're doing what should be done everywhere, in every church. But if they choose to regard this as sensational, then I can only sigh sadly . . . .

I look at the notes I get which say that anyone who attends my discussions will be transfered, and I'll be thrown in jail or in a mental hospital. I view this as simple alarmism. We're just too scared. We're getting to the point that we're afraid of everything. But it is precisely atheism that we ought to fear. It's more horrible than war or the plague, because with those only your body is destroyed, but atheism destroys *everything,* including your soul.

Furthermore, let *me* ask: why *should* they jail us? For doing good to each other? For being concerned about human morals? I don't see any crime in this for which you'd need to persecute us. People don't come here to get drunk or to cause trouble. They just come to listen to discussions. Who does any harm? In my opinion, what we're doing here is not only reli-

---

[9]1 Cor. 9:16.
[10]Mk. 16:16.

gious, but also simply patriotic. We're concerned with the moral condition of our compatriots. We want to reduce the number of drunks, hooligans, seducers and blasphemers.

In addition, I'd just also mention that these discussions began not on my personal initiative but at the request of my parishioners. They ask me questions and I have to answer them. So there's nothing sensational here, there's nothing terrible. Everything's absolutely natural. No one for whom this *is* terrible is being forced to come to our discussions. But I can reassure those listeners who are so frightened that their anxiety is in vain. As you see, neither the ecclesiastical nor the civil authorities are stopping me. That means they don't find anything illicit or harmful in these discussions.

But now let's get right to the questions that we must resolve today.

QUESTION: Dear Father Dmitrii, please explain the origin and meaning of the feast of Pascha. Why do the various peoples of the world celebrate it in different ways? And why isn't Christ's resurrection observed on a set date?

ANSWER: Here's what we read on this subject in the *Church Slavonic Dictionary*:

"Pascha" is a Hebrew word altered by the Greeks which, in this form, came into our own language. The Hebrew word *"pesach"* literally means "passage," "change of place." The Jews use this word in a special sense to designate their feast, established in commemoration of the passage from slavery in the land of Egypt to freedom in the promised land of Canaan. By this same term they also designate the actual lamb which, according to the Law of Moses, they eat at this feast together with unleavened bread and bitter herbs. In addition to this meaning of "pascha," as a commemoration of the exodus from Egypt, the word had another, more important significance. This was the commemoration of Israel's election as the people of God ... The paschal lamb is the prefiguration of Jesus Christ and of His death on the Cross. The Lord is the true

Lamb. "Behold, the Lamb of God," it says in the Gospel according to John. For Christ our Pascha has been slain for us. As a prefiguration, the paschal lamb was to be without blemish and its bones were not to be broken. The paschal lamb was a true sacrifice, both purifying and reconciling. Precisely in this way did Jesus Christ offer Himself upon the Cross as a sacrifice for our sins, and, on the eve of His death, He established a true sacrifice of peace and thanksgiving, the Holy Eucharist. The Christian Church, seeing in the Hebrew pascha a prefiguration of her own Christian Pascha (i.e., the passage from death to life and from earth to heaven) accepted even the very name of the feast from the Jews. One must note that just as the Jews understood by the name "pascha" not only the feast but also the actual paschal lamb as well, so "even Christ our passover is sacrificed for us" (1 Cor. 5:7).

In the *Ecclesiastical Encyclopedia* we read as follows:

The feast of Christ's Resurrection (or Pascha) is the most ancient of all Christian feasts. It began at the very moment of Christ's resurrection. The holy apostles celebrated it solemnly and commanded that all believers celebrate it. In the *Apostolic Constitutions* it says: "During the great week of the Holy Pascha let no one work. It is the week of the Lord's resurrection, and during it one must become acquainted with the One who suffered and was resurrected." Furthermore, the holy fathers of the Church testify to the apostolic origin of the feast of Pascha. The apostles even indicated the actual time at which the Christian Pascha is to be celebrated, namely *after* the first full moon of spring, and not with the Jews. Because the Jews celebrate their pascha at the first full moon of spring, it was established that the Christian Pascha be celebrated not on the actual day of the full moon but on the first Sunday after the full moon. Furthermore, in order that the Christian Pascha not precede the Jewish one, it was

established that the full moons in March which precede
the vernal equinox *not* be considered paschal; in such
cases the celebration of Pascha is postponed to the Sunday following the (first) full moon in April. But inasmuch as it is necessary to know the date of the equinox
and the date and day of the full moon, the connection
between the calendar question and the paschalia is
clear. It is likewise clear that a change in the calendar
could make it impossible accurately to observe the
"catholic" determination of the day for celebrating
Pascha, a determination adjusted to the Julian calendar.
The use of the Gregorian calendar of the Western
Church for the calculation of the paschalia is inade-
quate (as many theologians admit) for fully satisfying
the demands of a strict observance of ecclesiastical
rules. Therefore, we Orthodox do not celebrate Pascha
on the same date as the Catholics.

All nations celebrate Pascha because all people are called to
salvation, and not just one particular nation. Furthermore,
I'd add that the failure to celebrate Pascha on a single date all
the world over is the fruit of our ecclesiastical disagreement.
But let's view this as an external side of the matter. The
essence of the feast is the same for us all—Christ's resurrection.

QUESTION: Why does Orthodoxy put such stress on the
resurrection of the flesh? Could this be some sort of astral
body? The resurrection of the flesh is somehow hard to grasp.
Isn't it like idolizing matter?

ANSWER: Orthodoxy speaks precisely of the resurrection
of the soul *and* the body—not of some astral body, but of *our*
body, because God came to save the *whole* man. In general
Christianity doesn't neglect the flesh. Rather, it *transforms* it.
Philosophers such as Vladimir Solov'ev and Evgenii Trubetskoi[11] (not to speak of the holy fathers) understood this beau-
tifully. Trubetskoi says in his book *The Meaning of Life*: "It
is not just some *part* of the human being which must come to

---

[11]See above, nn. 1 and 2 to the Seventh Discussion.

this fulness of life, but the whole man, both spirit and body."
Solov'ev writes:

> The spiritual power which in Christ is internally free
> from all limitations and morally infinite is in this resur-
> rection naturally set free from all external limitations,
> and preeminently from the one-sidedness of an exist-
> ence which would be wholly spiritual as opposed to the
> physical. The resurrected Christ is more than spirit.
> Spirit has no flesh or bones; spirit does not partake of
> food. As spirit eternally incarnate, Christ with all the
> fulness of His inner psychological being also unites all
> the positive possibilities of physical existence, but with
> none of its external limitations.

All of Solov'ev's arguments on the resurrection are very
interesting. He says, for example, that the miracle of Christ's
resurrection "is a miracle only in the sense that when something
new, something unusual and unprecedented, appears for the
first time, we are amazed by it or made to marvel." For example, "the appearance of the first living organism in the
midst of inorganic nature," or "the appearance of the first intelligent being above the kingdom of dumb creatures," likewise, "the appearance of the first wholly spiritual Man who,
therefore, is not subject to death—the first-born of the dead.
But that which would appear to be a miracle, we understand to
be an event which is wholly natural, necessary, and judicious.
The truth of Christ's resurrection is an all-encompassing, full
truth, not just the truth of faith, but the truth of reason as well."

That's what a great philosopher writes. But that which our
reason at times finds hard to grasp (and so we seek some sort
of "astral body") originates, in the first place, in our misunderstanding of Christianity and, in the second place, under the
influence of the occult sciences. It's no secret that a lot of
people who've been wandering about lost in the desert of materialism for a long time, are now throwing themselves greedi-
ly upon anything spiritual that falls within their grasp.

QUESTION: Father Dmitrii, you probably aren't aware of

the fact that people of non-Christian faiths are also coming to your discussions. It was precisely your directness and sincerity which attracted us. But we get a little offended when you make Christians out to be the only ones who believe. We too are believers—and perhaps we are no less so than your people. Why Christ all the time—and not Moses, for instance, or Mohammed or Buddha? We respect your Christ, so why don't you accept our religious figures?

ANSWER: For me it's an unexpected pleasure to have non-Christians come to us. Thank you for such attention!

You are wrong in concluding that I consider only Christians to be believers. I even believe that there are Christian non-believers, for in the words of the apostle, "faith without works is dead," and dead faith might even be worse than non-belief. I deeply respect each person's faith, regardless of what religion he may confess. Furthermore, I'd say that there is one God of us all. But I can't set Christ and Buddha, for example, on the same level. Why? Because Buddha was a prophet. Mohammed was a prophet. Moses was a prophet. But Christ is God Himself Who accepted our human form. Furthermore, I'd say that every prophet in some measure sensed Christ's coming to earth. Even the pagan ones did—that's why they have their risen gods. The atheists reproach us, saying that we've replaced pagan beliefs with our own. But *we* say that the pagans just anticipated Christ. Christ is a single, unique phenomenon. God himself appeared to men in the likeness of man. God came to us. He was with us. "God is with us!" as we sing.

Don't reproach us because Christians can be less perfect morally than other people—here you're talking about individual *Christians*, not about *Christ*. Christ is the fulness of divine revelation. If you can't accept this, if you want to argue and refute, then I'll give immediate notice that I *won't* do so. The truth of Christianity is so great that it isn't proven—it's revealed. When Christianity is revealed to you, when Christ begins to speak in your heart, then you won't need any proof of the fact that there is no substitute for the Christian revelation. It's got *everything*—God, man's salvation, the path of salvation, the resurrection from the dead. Christianity has absorbed everything that's somehow scattered about in all the other religions, but it also gives something that they don't have: the Christian Pascha. Today you heard our hymn: " . . . let us embrace each other joyously, and forgive all by the resurrection. And so, let us cry: Christ is risen from the dead . . . " Does this say anything to your heart?

QUESTION: Father Dmitrii, why are you so sharp with atheists? Don't you see that in accusing them, you are making use of their own methods?

ANSWER: The question makes it sound as though I've offended the sacred feelings of the atheists. Forgive me, good atheists, if that's the case. I'd like to express how I *personally* feel about you. If your atheism is sincere, and if, with your atheistic convictions, you do good, I not only revere you but I'm even prepared to set you up as an example to believers. Look— no faith in God yet they do good. That means they're greater than we believers are. In order to justify ourselves before them we've got to do a lot *more* good than they do, but if we can't even do as much as they do, we have no right even to call ourselves believers. That's how highly I think of atheists. I'm not sharp with *them* but with the works done in their name. But I won't speak about this. I've already done so in previous discussions.

Now, concerning method—I just don't think you're right. The Gospel contains even sharper words: "Generation of vipers, where will you run from the anger of God?" . . . We've become too spineless, too liberal, but often this is only the result of our "lukewarmness." But remember the Apocalypse: "Oh, if only you were cold or hot!"[12]

QUESTION: Father Dmitrii, don't you feel that in your sermons and discussions the element of propaganda and agitation is too prominent? Wouldn't it be better simply to reveal the truths of Christianity without any propaganda? That would be a sermon in and of itself. Is propaganda allowable in Christian work?

---

[12]Rev. 3:15.

ANSWER: Christian "truths," if they are "simply revealed" in isolation from our life, can sound abstract, dry and therefore false. And then, even the Gospel will appear to be propaganda and agitation to some. For example, Christ's words: "Go into all the world and preach ... He who believes and is baptised will be saved."[13]

QUESTION: How do you look upon people who are abnormal, those who are mentally ill? A lot of them believe in God, you know.

ANSWER: Here, for example, is how Vladimir Solov'ev looked at it: "I do not believe in purely physical reasons for spiritual diseases, and soon no one will believe in them. Psychic disorder ... is the ultimate means for man's self-realization of his inner being through the sacrifice of his visible cerebral 'I,' which is incapable of resolving the moral goal of our existence."

Personally, I've often encountered people with mental illnesses who were morally pure. They refused all earthly goods, explaining that they simply could not make use of them while a lot of other people were suffering. Who among us so-called "normal" people can rise to such heights? Often we label them "abnormal" but *we're* ready to bite each other's heads off over "good things" which really aren't worth a thing.

QUESTION: Father Dmitrii, you know, modern man just can't accept having to love his enemy. Couldn't this be put on some other plane? There are just too many enemies today. If you start loving everyone, there won't be enough of you to go around. Perhaps this could all be explained differently? Why do I speak this way? Because Christianity is near to me, but to love my enemies—I just can't accept that. Holy hatred, like the Moslems have—now that's closer to me. What do *you* say?

ANSWER: Yes, it *is* hard for modern man to love his enemies, since these days everyone has become an enemy. As Christ said: "In one house they will be divided in two."[14] But if you don't love your enemies, you can't speak seriously about

---

[13]Mk. 16:16.

Christianity. A Christian considers everyone to be his brother, no matter who he may be. A Christian has no enemies. Hence, the Christian's morality is to love all and to be concerned for all.

Literaturnaia Gazeta[15] often carries polemics about moral themes. Not long ago a former criminal wrote: "Crime begins when you divide people into 'your own' and 'strangers' " (*Literaturnaia Gazeta*, April 3, 1974, in an article by A. Firsov). Only criminals can love their own and hate the stranger. But if we divide the world into "our own" and "strangers," and then begin persecuting and badgering the "strangers," what do we get? All's fair in this war, as they say. You get brutality, and wars and lawlessness. But when there are no "strangers," no "enemies"—just the unfortunate, the sick, the criminals and the lost—then, rather than hostility reigning among people, you get an enormous love, a pure and unselfish love—and, therefore, that authentic morality for which this brutal world of hostility simply has no place.

QUESTION: Why do you think crime is increasing?

ANSWER: I think it's caused by social conditions. But that's not *the* major source. Not everyone who lives under difficult conditions will become a criminal. In our day more and more children of well-to-do parents are becoming criminals. Crime is growing today because people don't know how to satisfy the inquiries of their souls. They think that crime is heroic, that the criminal is some kind of a special person, someone who stands above all the rest. And indeed, criminals are very talented people, out of the ordinary. But, that's a *false* satisfaction of the soul's inquiries. Yes, for a moment crime *is* interesting, it tickles your vanity. But then it becomes empty again, boring. So there's more crime and more dissatisfaction. Death lies ahead for criminals just as it does for all, even the most

---

[14]Cf. Lk. 12:52.

[15]*Literaturnaia gazeta*: newspaper, organ of the "Ruling Union of Soviet Writers of the USSR." Published in various frequencies since 1929. Reorganized in 1947, it is now the "socio-political tribune of wide circles of the Soviet intelligentsia," dedicated to Soviet "literature, patriotism, international peace, and the destruction of bourgeois culture."

mediocre. You can't escape it anywhere. When a person who does good approaches death, he approaches the most mysterious and interesting of all things. That's where the ascetic feat of his whole life lies—the Kingdom of Heaven. But the criminal, dragging behind himself a trail of evil—and human blood at that—sees only that everything ends. There's *nothing* left— just horror. "Heroic" criminals almost always fear the approach of death and so often *seek* it. They often just kill themselves. But in order to meet death boldly, you have to live virtuously.

On Golgotha we see Christ crucified, with criminals on either side. The one reviles Christ, but the other restrains his fellow and asks Christ to remember him in the Kingdom of Heaven. Now, watch as Christ dies—aware of the duty which He has fulfilled, calmly, with no curses, but rather with a prayer for His enemies. That's not "spitting in the face of death," as they say. All of these "heroics" are but the beautiful words of those not yet near death. But if you love your enemy who is crucifying you—now that's *real* courage, authentic heroics and power. Who is capable of it? Not the criminal, to be sure— he can only curse.

Crime has taken on enormous proportions here—it's horrible even to mention the kinds there are. We *all* feel it, no matter what steps we take to fence ourselves off from the world. Even those who imagine they're completely immune feel it. Today crime surrounds every one of us. You know, it's not just the thieves and murderers sitting in prison who are criminals, not just those who pick people's pockets or commit murder. Rather, the real criminals are those who bear the guilt for the break-up of the family and morality in society, those who cause us to be afraid of each other, who cause us not to trust each other. Man has become his own worst enemy—and *that's* the worst crime of all. But we'll become friends only when we realize that all of us have one Father in heaven, and that we, His children, are brothers to each other. Without a religious Christian upbringing there can be no deliverance from crime.

I consider anyone who would tear people away from their faith in God to be a criminal. But once we understand this, we

have to *act*. It's hard—one against all. But to do anything useful, you've got to decide to do *everything,* otherwise you'll get
nowhere. At the same time, though, we've got to remember
that all these "enemies," this whole terrible world is nothing
but a bubble full of air. Of course, it can be popped—just
physically destroyed. But life is eternal, and destruction *here*
means gain *there.* In Christianity martyrdom is considered to
be a special feat. Our main support is God. One person with
God is more powerful than a multitude without Him. We
must remember this. Remember that faith moves mountains.
And here mountains of crime have risen up, and it seems as
though they have reached clear up to God's light. These mountains must be moved. But how? Only with faith do you dare
undertake such a feat.

Some people might find the things I say a bit incomprehensible. Many people would like to limit religion to a tiny narrow world, to allot it just a small, fixed portion of their lives.
But a Christian can not—a Christian must not—shut himself
off from the world when the world is perishing. These days,
all of our ascetical feats are done in the world. The era of
the monastery is past. "Whoever has ears to hear, let him
hear . . . "[16]

I've probably worn you out turning over all these heavy
questions. For a little breather I'll tell you how some children
once spoke about religion.

Three-year-old girl: "Mama, is it true that everything's got
a root? And is man's root his soul?

Seven-year-old boy: "In school the teacher was trying to
prove there ain't no God, 'cause the cosmonauts didn't see
Him,' she said. But some boy answered, 'They just flew too
low'."

A seven-year-old boy enters school, and his teacher asks:
"Have you seen God?" "God is invisible," answers the boy.
"You can't see Him. . . . "

"Papa, how come there ain't no cross on this church?"
"Evil people took it off," was his father's reply. So the boy

---

[16]Lk. 14:35.

took a piece of chalk and drew a cross on the wall of the church. . . .

Two men stand arguing about anti-religious topics. They look around and see next to them a little child building a church out of snow. . . .

Let's listen to these childish voices and contemplate them. They contain a certain spontaneous wisdom and an indictment of the brilliant, vain sophistication of adults. Indeed, by the mouths of children is truth spoken. A pure spiritual instinct draws children to God. And often in this way they expose our godless deeds.

But now—concerning adults. Here's what people sometimes say following life's bitter lessons:

Dear Father Dmitrii,

You asked your young parishioners to describe their path to faith. So I'm writing you about myself.

The people in my family are deeply atheistic by disposition. Even my grandmother and grandfather were nonbelievers. From childhood I learned my lesson well that God is just a fable invented by ignorant people. The very word "religion" evoked dark associations in me. I imagined emaciated faces with mindless eyes, dark, vaulted rooms, candles, tombs. . . . For me there was hardly any difference in meaning between "church" and "God." These were dark, mysterious words, foreign to me. But without realizing it, I was making my way towards God. Quite a switch—right?

The more I thought about what lay around me, the more clearly I saw—understood—that everything is gibberish, not worth a plugged nickel. So I came to the point of rejecting everything and everyone. Concepts such as conscience, truth and morality were empty for me.

Now I understand that without God things just could not be otherwise. Things either didn't matter to me at all or they irritated me—especially the audacious slogans . . . Nothing made me really happy. Nothing was pleasant. I started to drink. You get drunk and things get a little easier. The longer it went on, the longer it took me to get really smashed. And so it went . . . I had already become an alcoholic of sorts. On my days off I'd drink myself unconscious.

Then the gears began to grind. I got away with everything for a while, but—are they ever right in say-ing—you always reach the end of your rope. It all came very simply and very quickly. I got drunk, got into a fight, and found myself in jail on a Section 206.2 (for "hooliganism").

There was this guy in my cell, a Baptist who prayed a lot and would always cross himself before meals. Many people—including me—mocked him for this. Out of boredom I sort of dragged him into a dispute over religion. At first, for my part I just sort of ran off at the mouth, interspersing facetious comments about how old women just thought God up. He answered every one of my flippant arguments seriously. His un-shakable conviction that he was correct began to irri-tate me. Soon—just for the fun of it—I began defending atheism seriously, proving by whatever means necessary that God could not exist.

I really couldn't care less either about God or about atheism. I just wanted to break his confidence—that was the main thing. Arrogance pushed me on. And I achieved what I wanted. My partner fell silent. He fell silent and then began to cry. He began praying that his faith would be strengthened.

I felt no satisfaction in my victory. A horrible weight fell upon me. I felt sick, like I'd done something mean to someone. And he just kept on praying, but more calmly now. Suddenly he looked at me and smiled. I was amazed at his face—there was something joyous about it, pure, like it had been washed. The weight immediately fell from my soul. I understood that he had forgiven me. And then a light of some sort penetrated me, and I understood that God exists. It wasn't even so much that I *understood,* but that I *sensed* it with my whole being. He *exists*! He alone has always been and will always be. He is everywhere. He is our Father! We are His children, brothers one to another. I forgot that I was in prison and felt only one thing—a great joy and thankfulness to the Lord Who revealed Himself to me, who am unworthy.

After this a strange and radiant thing happened to me. As a non-believer, I had read the Holy Scriptures but had always hit upon the "dark" and "incomprehensible." For me, the Scriptures were "woven of contradictions." After I came to believe, each word of the Gospel was filled with meaning for me, close to my mind and heart.

Glory to the Father, and to the Son, and to the Holy Spirit, now and ever, and unto ages of ages. Amen.

P.S.—Re-reading what I wrote, I see that everything happened rather prosaically and simply, but that's not the case. You will, of course, understand that no words can communicate what I experienced at the moment when God revealed Himself to me.

Here's another letter:

Here are a few of the miracles which have happened in my life.

I was subject to repression even as a very young woman. Previously I hadn't been a full-fledged Christian. I didn't give much consideration to the canons of faith—more to novels and entertainment.

Difficult trials began for me in prison. I was accused of something of which I was not guilty. The realization that I was unable to justify myself and that without God I would perish shook my soul. I began praying earnestly and with cries for help to the Mother

---

[17]Certain icon-types of Christ or the Virgin Mary are known by the name of the attribute which they reveal—hence the Mother of God "Help of all who are perishing" (Bozhiia Mater' "Vsekh pogibaiushchikh") and "Tender mercy" ("Umilenia").

of God "Help of all who are perishing"[17] and immediately I was delivered from my feelings of fear and horror. I sensed that I had the strength to oppose them
and I answered their interrogations impulsively, and
what I said was a real miracle and acquittal for me.
Thus the truth of the Gospel was fulfilled in my life,
where it says that if they bring you before the judges,
don't think about what you should say, for the Lord
God will speak for you.

As a result they invited a hypnotist in to see me, and
in his trance I felt like I was falling into a pit, and a
horror and fear which cannot be put into words seized
my soul, and a sense that I was guilty of something. I
heard my own voice saying—as though I were an out-
sider: "I'm guilty. I'm guilty." I signed a confession
to everything that my family and I had "done" . . . The
next day they showed me what I had signed, and I understood that what I had done was base, and I refused
to sign again. I began praying fervently. I remember
how more than once my father had said that prayer
helps you against hypnosis. Right there in my cell I
memorized "He that dwells."[18] During the second session, when the hypnotist said "Look into my eyes," I
looked at him boldly and recited this wonderful prayer
to myself. The hypnotist became nervous and screamed,
"Stop that!" Then he broke out in a sweat all over and
said, "I'll have no more to do with her."

When they summoned me to be deported,[19] I was
first put into an isolation cell (a room just wide enough
to take one step) and I was seized with fear. Where
was I going? What was waiting for me? A feeling of
loneliness and helplessness seized my soul. I began
praying to the Mother of God, and said to myself,
"Lord, if only I knew that Thou art with me, I wouldn't
be afraid of anything . . ." And while I was praying
the door suddenly opened, and a hand covered with red

---

[18]Ps. 90.
[19]Na etap: literally "to the halting place" [for convicts] being transported.

hair and freckles reached in to me. And a voice said, "For you." I took something which turned out to be a tiny little icon. When I looked at it I fell down on my knees and in trembling began to thank the Mother of God that she would be traveling the road with me— because it turned out that on one side this little icon had Saint Seraphim of Sarov (whom, as a Russian, I had always venerated) and on the other, an image of the Mother of God "Tender mercy."

As I said good-bye to my mother she hung around my neck a cross made of cypress-wood, which had been brought long ago from Jerusalem. In Irkutsk, in the cell where they took me, some women who had been convicted of the same thing as I sat under their bunks. I crept to mine. The room was crowded and stuffy, filled with women. After a while a pleasant aroma began filling the room. All were amazed and began sniffing about trying to find out where this smell came from. I too began inhaling the scent when a woman sitting next to me said, "It's *you* that smell so good! It's your cross." They asked me to let them have my cross so they could make sure. The stream of scent flowing from the cross got even stronger, and many of the women began praying and crying. Finally, there was a Jewish woman sitting in the corner and saying over and over again, "I never saw or heard anything like this. Let me smell it." They gave her my cross, she smelled it, and the scent quit.

Indeed, the most powerful shocks and sufferings of the human soul draw man near to God, and to the realization that you, a person, are His child and His creation, and that He alone can help you. Sufferings accepted voluntarily according to the will of God develop a person's soul—precisely that "fourth dimension" which people can't conceive and yet so stubbornly seek.

My whole life has been full of miracles and the grace of God. But it's also been full of the excruciating sufferings, burns and spiritual shocks which—as a mani-

festation of demonic power—it is difficult for a person
to cope with without God.

I look upon these testimonies by adults to their faith as
testimonies to resurrection from the dead, and I feel that now
nothing can stop this progress.

At one of our discussions I was accused of undue optimism
—someone felt that the religious boom is making itself felt
only in Moscow and Leningrad. But now, this same person
recently spent some time in the provinces and writes from
there: "Attendance at services is greater here, and includes a
large proportion of young people. They stand more reverently here than in Moscow. Thus I'm convinced: the springtime
of religion is everywhere in Russia . . . " But he'll tell us about
it sometime in detail.

But now let's turn once again to a topic which is a bit less
pleasant. We can't even make it through this paschal season
without unpleasantness. But then—who knows—maybe as a
result of this unpleasantness we'll experience the paschal joy
more sharply.

QUESTION: Father Dmitrii, you probably read A. Chertkov's article entitled "A Paschal Fairy Tale" in the April 13,
1974, issue of *Moskovskaia Pravda*.[20] He signed his name, add-
ing the initials "M.Ph."—Master of Philosophy. But as we
know, this Chertkov graduated from the Moscow Theological
Academy—so he's a Master of Divinity. We also know that
you, too, graduated from the Moscow Theological Academy.
What do you have to say about this article and about Chertkov
himself? Perhaps you even knew him. If possible also tell us
how it happens that "masters of divinity" break with religion.
What's the reason? Chertkov's article seemed rather nasty,
especially since he hounds believers as though they were people
with a foreign ideology. It's as though he's saying: "Grab 'em!
Eat 'em up!" We saw for ourselves on the night of Pascha

---

[20]*Moskovskaia Pravda*: daily newspaper of the Moscow region, the organ of
the "Committees of the Communist Party of the Soviet Union for the Region and
City of Moscow." Founded in 1920.

how they'd come right up to you, take you by the sleeve and say: "Where are you going? Turn back!" And a police car was standing right there! I'm a member of the younger generation and I've been maimed by life. I've been everything—a drunkard, a hooligan. I've experienced in myself all of atheism's charms, and now I'm sensitive to untruth of any sort. So please be good enough to have your say.

ANSWER: My answer, it turns out, is rather long. Perhaps I'll divide it into three parts: (1) on the article in the newspaper and its author, (2) on reasons for breaking with religion, and (3) on hounding believers.

Let me begin by saying that Chertkov and I are indeed both Masters of Divinity. So we're on the same level. But first, one digression.

May, 1956. Exams were being given in the theological academy. It seems Chertkov was completing the academy that year. And I was returning from prison at the time. I was glad to be getting down to studying, but first I had to be reinstated in the academy, since I'd been taken to the camps during the first year of my studies. Some students meet me at the entrance. They interrogate me. "Who are you?" "Where are you from?" Chertkov, too, threw a question at me: "Why have you been wandering around for so long?" "I've got a reason," I said and shrugged my shoulders. I didn't want to give them the whole story. He cast a scornful glance over my sorry figure, and then (as I found out later) he told the students: "So that's the kind of troublemakers we get. They wander all over the place, and then we have to accept them."

I hear he was a successful student, in good standing with the Academy's administration—and especially in the good graces of the late Patriarch Alexis. Everything came easily for him. He was pampered by life, so how *could* he understand the grief of the former student whom he so lightly labeled a "troublemaker."

Why do I recall this now? Because just as in those days he had a superficial view of life and was unable to sympathize with another person's grief (sometimes it can be unpleasant to do so—and it can interfere with your success), so now he sees nothing in religion but "an alien ideology." He doesn't see people and their misfortunes, their worries and their tears. In the old days he was successful with Christian authorities. Now he's a success with the atheist authorities.

His article contains neither theology nor real-life experience. It's nothing but a play on words. So in my opinion, it's simply degrading for a believer even to argue with him. I won't even go over the article in detail, but just bring to your attention its final lines:

> People usually do not ponder very deeply the reasons why the church's preparation for Pascha makes such systematic use of theatrical performance. They do not think about the complex of ideas she instills in the people's minds on the day of Pascha and during the period of Lent which precedes it. These ideas—of sinfulness, and of love for your enemies, of peace among social classes and of war against social evils through self-perfection ... [*apparently "self-perfection" is an unpleasant word for the author*] ... the passing nature of everything earthly, the striving of all of man's thoughts towards heaven and life after death—are all alien to our ideology and morals.

Every word of this is a lie. I cite it not in order to argue but in order to demonstrate a typical cliché of typical atheistic propaganda.

No, citizen Chertkov, believers today *are* thinking deeply —and in part, they're thinking about why it's so common these days that their highest feelings are mocked, about why they are persecuted at work and in educational institutions, about why even in our churches we feel the atheists' cynical "work" —their "work" of demolishing or at least undermining everything from within one way or another; their "work" of fixing it so that the priest won't serve God but them, the atheists; their "work" of causing the priests to become careless in serving, of emasculating the services of any vital content so they in fact become blasphemous—much to the joy of the atheists' cause. Look, they've already partly succeeded, if only formally, in converting priests into hirelings. Priests are now just hired to work in church, you know. Could anything be a greater mockery of the priest's ministry? And what value is there in the way the atheists "keep order" on the night of Pascha? As soon as they spot some young people they rush over to them: "Where you going?" "You don't have any business here!" If they don't succeed in convincing the young people with their words, they use force to prevent them from entering. If you try offering resistance, they run for the militia and accuse you of being a hooligan. What right do they have to do this? There aren't any laws, you know—not even any written instructions—which prevent young people—or anyone else at all— from attending a worship service. Furthermore, Section 143 of the Universal Code of the Russian Soviet Federated Socialist Republic makes provisions for who is responsible when people are hindered from doing something—it's called "disturbing the peace." Thus according to the law, all these "guardians" should be tried as criminals.

I have personally appealed to these "guardians." I've told them that they're breaking the law, that they have no right to constrain believers, but without blinking an eye they lie to me: "We constrain only the children. After 10 P.M., children must sleep."

I say, "Why aren't you concerned about this on ordinary nights? I myself have watched scenes like this one at midnight. A mother and father, dead drunk, stagger down the street. With them is their child, half asleep." But the "guardians" won't listen to me. They race after the wife of one of our priests in order to restrain her, to keep her from entering the church for the paschal liturgy. I rush to her rescue. "What are you doing?" I ask. Now they're just plain rude to me: "Shove off! This is our business. Get into church—your business is in there." So the atheists have taken it upon themselves to decide who can enter the church and who can't. That's how they understand separation of Church and State. That's how they understand the laws that they themselves have written. There we have it—atheism in action, with all its "morality" and "legality." They want to make the priest into just a cultic figure who would be profitable for them, someone who'd notice nothing in real life—but just perform rituals. I asked for their names but not one of them would identify himself.

Finally, I just decided to speak openly with one of the men in charge of the militiamen. I called him aside and said, "Why do you sow enmity between believers and nonbelievers? Why do you break the law in this way? Why don't you allow people into church? So what if a child does enter? He'll experience the holy things and only become a better person. After all, if he doesn't have anything holy in his life what kind of a person will he be?

This guy who was in charge of the militiamen understood me. We spoke in private. He gave me one of those confused Russian smiles and said, "We've got to stop people. There are lots of hooligans around. They don't believe in anything, and they'll just wreck your whole service."

"Thanks," I said. "But just how are *you* people acting?

He said no more. He just stood there with that same confused smile. I felt sorry for him. Somehow, I got the feeling that these "guards" understand everything, but here they are fulfilling someone else's will. Someone is making them do something that they really don't want to do.

Then I watched to see who was more zealous, the uniformed militia or those who had just come, their faces hidden beneath hoods. As it turns out, it was the "hoods."

"They're workers," a militiaman told me. But I had a sinful thought: "Couldn't one of these be Chertkov?"

So you're forced to think about all these things, while all you really want to do is take a rest from all these thoughts, to escape entirely into the liturgy. But they just won't let you.

So, Citizen Chertkov, you are very much mistaken on this account. We think about many things. We even think about *your* destiny. Here's what I think, in part. You once called me a troublemaker, but I came to the Church honestly. But what have *you* become? A "Master of Philosophy" ought to think philosophically. You aren't able to distinguish humility from servility. The ideas of sinfulness and the depravity of man are foreign to your ideology. Self-perfection, too, is foreign to you. You think that you have nothing to repent of. Perhaps you secretly consider yourself a saint. In your opinion, believers don't resist evil. When we love our enemies (in your opinion) we hate mankind. We shouldn't yearn for heaven; there's no life after death; only this earth exists—a civilized paradise for criminals and troublemakers.

I'd recommend that *you* begin doing some real thinking, Mr. Chertkov—it wouldn't hurt much. You don't know life. For you, life is just a game. But the game—your premature success—will end. The *only* truth—Christ's resurrection—is beyond you for now. If you won't understand this, then . . .

I'll stop here. I just want to say in conclusion: May the Lord forgive you! You know not what you are doing. These days even the atheists need to seek a common language with the Church. The Church is *the* best helper in the matter of educating society. Can prisons correct anyone? People come out of prison confirmed criminals. Prisons just deepen criminality. But, then, believers aren't corrupted by being sent to prison, with its corrupting atmosphere. Even if they go off to prison not yet fully firm in their faith, when they come out they're deeply believing people. This is especially observable lately. Not long ago I heard about how a former Komsomol organizer sent a letter to his grandmother asking her to pray to God for him. He said he'd been stupid, not believing in God while he was free.

So it wouldn't hurt you to think about this, Mr. Chertkov.

This has been part one of the question. Now for part two: the reasons for breaking with religion. This is a difficult question. There can be many, different reasons. It wouldn't hurt for us to analyse them carefully. Perhaps then one of the tragedies of our time will become understandable. I personally look at every case of someone breaking with religion as a tragedy. I don't judge them. I mourn deeply for them.

I'll now recall several of those who have broken with religion. You've probably read Doluman's works. I studied with him in the Academy. He wasn't a bad person, he was interested in lots of things. Unfortunately I don't know why he broke with religion. I heard that he had a disagreement over something with the teachers in the theological seminary. (He also taught, I believe it was in Odessa.)

When I was freed from prison I wrote asking him to explain why he had written about the psychology of (so-called)
unbelief. He said he'd do so on one condition—that I first
write to him about the psychology of faith. I replied that he
himself knew the psychology of faith because he himself had
been a believer, whereas I didn't know the psychology of the
unbeliever because I hadn't been one. He got irritated, abused
me, and then said, "O.K., I'll write! Forty pages I'll write!
Just remember, atheists keep their word."

Unfortunately, he still hasn't written. And I still don't
know his reasons for breaking with religion.

A second case: Father John Kubin. I studied with him in
the Academy after my imprisonment. He was from the working class. He told me how he came to faith, how the faith of
the children of some strangers (perhaps even unbelievers) had
once moved him. I found all of this was very touching. He
did well in his studies. He wasn't a bad fellow. He treated me
with respect. In moments of annoyance he'd tell about his en-
counters with the bishops. They'd literally mock him. They
were despots. They'd make him do things that were repulsive
to his conscience.

"You shouldn't submit," I'd tell him. "You should submit
in *all* things to God alone. A bishop is a person, capable of
giving orders which are repulsive to God."

"Just try *not* submitting," he said. "They'll give you the
kind of parish where you'll die of hunger. And I've got kids to
feed."

He wouldn't be able to sleep nights, thinking things over.
Then suddenly, I heard that he'd broken with religion. I don't
know what he wrote in his article of renunciation. Probably
the usual clichés—you know, they just repeat each other, almost
word-for-word. I think it was probably just that he wasn't a
militant person—he was weak . . . May God help him and forgive his weakness.

A third case: Vladimir Shnurovtsev. He was a deacon. He
wasn't very diligent in his studies. Mostly he read the works of
Lenin during lectures. They say that before I came he used to
pray a lot, but I never observed him to be especially religious.
But he was a good person. He'd seek out poor old ladies and

help them. He helped me, too, right after I got out of prison. Now, whereas Chertkov called me a troublemaker to my face, Shnurovtsev took a stroll with me, talked sympathetically, and later said humbly: "You're probably in need. Here, take ten rubles. I can't give any more. I just receive a stipend myself."

Judging by his studies (at that time they gave out stipends according to how you ranked academically in your class) he must not have gotten very much—so the ten rubles he gave me were probably half his stipend, maybe more. I'll never forget those ten rubles from him, and when the Dread Judgment comes, I'll say to God, "No matter what kind of person this Shnurovtsev was, Lord, forgive him, for the sake of these ten rubles, for they were the widow's mite which you praised, Lord."[21]

After his denial he wrote me: "I'll tell you frankly, Mitia,[22] I don't know whether I ever really believed in God or not, but I'll get my revenge on those lousy priests!" Thus, I conclude that somebody got his goat and that's why he broke with religion.

I also heard about such a denial. A priest lost his faith, went to the Patriarchate and said, "I have no faith. You can keep yours, but I don't believe." He didn't start writing articles all over the place. He didn't begin building for himself a career based on his unbelief. I've also heard about one archimandrite.[23] What caused him to leave the Church God only knows. But soon the atheists rejected him, too, over something, so he went to a church and the nice old ladies fed him.

As you see, there are all sorts of reasons why people break with religion. It wouldn't hurt if a psychology of atheism were to be written, somewhat like Dostoevskii did in describing Ivan Karamazov's psychology. One person told me that he was awakened to faith precisely through the barrenness of the psychology of unbelief. He was scared of the world of Ivan Karamazov. There's nothing there to live for, he thought. Ivan

---

[21]Lk. 21:2-3.

[22]Diminutive for Dmitrii.

[23]Monastic superior, analogous to a prior in the West. The title is now often bestowed honorifically upon monastic clergy.

Karamazov isn't the same as the modern atheist. Ivan had iron logic. He'd no sooner hurl an accusation at you than your skin would begin to crawl. "I return my ticket to the Kingdom of Heaven over one little tear of a tormented child." I think that if a psychology of today's atheist were to be written, it would spur a massive number of people to come to faith.

Finally, the third question, about how the atheists hound believers—but I think we've already talked about that enough when we recalled the night of Pascha.

Now to conclude our discussion, let's sing "The Angel Cried":

The angel cried to the Lady full of Grace:
Rejoice, O Pure Virgin! Again I say: Rejoice!
Your son is risen from His three days in the tomb.
With Himself He has raised all the dead.
Rejoice, all ye people!

The "Last" Discussion

Father Dmitrii stood in the altar during this vigil service but did not serve, since the warden refused to give him any vestments. The Dean of Clergy, Father Anatolii, as well as the rector, Father Vadim, expended much energy in seeking to prevent Father Dmitrii from speaking to the people. However, they were unsuccessful...

When people part they say good-bye. The condemned man is allowed a last word. The law allows this right even to a criminal. So I too will make use of this right.

As you recall, on Saturday, May 4, I announced that the Patriarch had prohibited me from conducting discussions until I had spoken with him. However no matter how hard I tried to arrange such a discussion, the Patriarch would not receive me. Through his secretary he simply demanded that I write an explanation. I did so. I will now take the liberty of reading it:

TO: His Holiness, The Most Holy Patriarch of
      Moscow and All Russia, PIMEN
FROM: Priest Dmitrii Dudko (St. Nicholas Church,
       Preobrazhenskii val, 25)

AN EXPLANATION

Your Holiness, Most Holy Master:
    Your secretary, Father Matfei, asked me to write you an explanation for the discussions which I have been

conducting in church following Saturday evening vigil services. In Father Matfei's words these discussions are for some reason termed lectures. I was asked to give an account in this explanation of in what way I mentioned your name, of what sorts of questions were asked, and of why I did not obey the Dean of Clergy and the Rector of this church, who asked me to discontinue these discussions.

Bless me, Your Holiness!

The discussions took the form of sermons but with consideration being given to the desires of the parishioners. The discussions arose spontaneously, one could say, according to the desires of the believers. At first I did not think that they would become interesting and popular, nor that they would attract such a multitude of people. (People even came from other parishes in order to listen.)

The flow of people from other parishes gave rise to a variety of questions, certain of which became rather sharp, particularly the question in answer to which I mentioned your name. I tried to defend the Church and and your name. How successful I was is not mine to judge.

Scandal began to grow surrounding the discussions, as I was told by both the Dean of Clergy and the Rector of our church. I paid no attention to the attempts which the Dean and the Rector made at prohibiting me from conducting discussions, since I considered their counsels to be not prohibition but advice and since I realized that no one can prohibit a sermon. Had these discussions continued further (unfortunately, they conveyed to me that you had prohibited me from conducting them until I had spoken with you), I should have appeared at an audience before your Holiness in order to receive your blessing and advice as to how I should proceed, since such a large number of people were now gathering that the church could no longer accommodate them, and I was unable alone to satisfy all the inquiries of those who asked.

Your Holiness, Most Holy Master:

I dare to make a request of you. The discussions and the character of the questions asked have demonstrated that interest in Christianity among the population is very great. But at times (and perhaps, even frequently) the form of sermons in contemporary church practice is so abstract that they are inaccessible to modern man. The form of discussion which I have chosen has apparently proved to be closer to people and clearer, and this is probably why such an interest in them has appeared.

I would ask you, Your Holiness, in the future to bless not only me but other priests to find a living form of communication between the pastor and his parish.

Of course, anything new carries within itself certain elements of failure, and there have probably been such elements of failure in my discussions as well. In the future this failure can be corrected by our common efforts.

Your Holiness' humble servant,
Priest D. DUDKO.

In answer to this explanation I received an edict directing me to place myself at the disposal of Metropolitan Seraphim, that is, the regional church authority. Unsure as to the reasons behind this decision I addressed a petition to the Patriarch. Here is that petition:

I received through your secretary, Father Matfei, your edict directing me to place myself at the disposal of Metropolitan Seraphim.

Several times I have requested that you receive me. As your secretary, Father Matfei, conveyed to me, Your Holiness has declined to do so. Therefore, not knowing what has been reported to you concerning myself, nor for what reason or by what right I have been placed at Metropolitan Seraphim's disposal, I must interpret all of this to be measures aimed at paralyzing my priestly activity, for canonically I have not transgressed. In order, therefore, not to confuse matters further, I consider it necessary to go into retirement.

I went into retirement not because I didn't want to appear before the regional church authority, but because this directive is a measure of reprisal. And what guarantee would I have that tomorrow Metropolitan Seraphim wouldn't publish an even stricter and equally unjustified edict? It is obvious that they are demanding of me that I cease my active priestly ministry of preaching. As the parishioners of our parish remember, this isn't the first attempt at reprisal against me. Two years ago it was undertaken by the Procurator's office, but thanks alone to the believers' interference I have remained in my place. Now it's the Patriarch who is doing the job. But the source is one and the same: Certain people are obviously interfering in the internal affairs of the Church, and that's forbidden by Soviet law.

Today as before, I appeal to public opinion. I have no other way out. Once again they are interfering with my carrying out of my ministry in accordance with the laws of both the Gospel and the Church and with my serving according to the commands of my priestly conscience. Again they are throwing me and my young children out onto the street. And *why?* Because I try to be of benefit to people.

I ask for your prayers.

In conclusion, a small explanation. Some say to me: "But then, they aren't prohibiting you from serving. They are just sending you to the regional authorities, and you simply won't obey your bishop." I explain that I went into retirement in order to deprive the atheists of the possibility of punishing and removing—at the hands of the bishops—anyone they don't like. My retirement is a protest against atheistic interference in the Church's affairs.

I can't be sure that tomorrow, as a result of the things that I as a priest am obliged to do, they won't apply to me an even greater measure of punishment: for example, prohibiting me from serving altogether, or even defrocking me. They don't even have to dig up a reason for doing so. After all, they aren't transferring me now because I've transgressed the canons in some way or because I am guilty of something. As everyone knows, in such cases you're often not punished at all, and at other times someone just "admonishes" you. No, they're tearing me away from you for some other, unknown reason. But then, it's not too hard to guess why: I haven't pleased the atheists.

I'm ready to submit to any bishop, but only when he speaks in the name of the Church and not in the name of the atheists. The atheists are using the bishops' power to smother the Church, to dispose of those who don't please them. . . .

"Christ is risen!" was said in conclusion.
"Indeed He is risen!" roared all those who were present.

The next day a rumor spread abroad in Moscow concerning the arrest of Fr. Dmitrii as he left the church. This was based upon a misunderstanding. The fact is that a number of militiamen and guardsmen had gathered next to the church, and in order to deliver the priest from their provocations some young believers accompanied him home, forming a tight ring around him. However, the very fact that this rumor ever began is significant in and of itself.

The
Tenth
Discussion

This discussion, set for May 4, 1974, did not take place in church. After vigil Father Dmitrii announced to those who were present that the Patriarch had prohibited him from conducting discussions until such time as he had spoken with him. Not withstanding, a group of parishioners asked Father Dmitrii to conduct this discussion, privately, at home, in order that they might receive answers to some questions that were bothering them. Father Dmitrii heeded his parishioners' request. The discussion is published from the notes of those who listened.

PARISHIONER: Father Dmitrii, we'd really like to ask you to speak with us anyway and to answer our questions. We're very much interested in how you'll answer them. In addition, there are all sorts of rumors going around that claim that the discussions you planned for the future would have nothing to do with the Church and would even have an anti-Soviet character. We don't believe these rumors because we've been present at your previous discussions and we know how far removed you are from such sentiments. But the rumors are going around, and we'd . . .

PRIEST: I understand. And I'm ready to satisfy your request and to have a discussion with you in private, so to speak. It seems as though no one has prohibited me from doing *that* yet. As far as the anti-Soviet character of our discussions is concerned, let me say that such an opinion can only be held by those who would like to accuse *any* Christian sermon of being anti-Soviet. This, of course, is simply crazy. But then, everyone knows that if you really want to, you can uncover anti-Soviet activities even in agriculture or in construction—if you want to.

So, let's start our "living-room" discussion. I'm very happy to meet with you, even in such a small group. For me your coming is a witness to the friendship which has arisen among us as a result of our discussions, and this is a great joy—friendship between a priest and his parish.

Before moving on to our main topic of discussion for today, I'd like to answer a question which someone asked about delusion.[1] They ask: "What is delusion in general, and what is spiritual delusion in particular?" It's apparent that this question wasn't just asked out of the blue. Certain people in the Church obviously think I've fallen into delusion, since I've undertaken discussions and gathered people around me.

Delusion is a very dangerous condition in which everything presents itself to a person in a distorted light. Either the person is enticed by a false idea or he's seduced by his own qualities and virtues. It's difficult for a person to judge about himself, especially if he's fallen into delusion. And it's difficult for me to judge about *myself*. So let's all of us here determine what delusion is. Among you there are some who aren't yet fully church people, so I'll try to speak in a language understandable to all. Delusion is self-deception by those things which do not exist in fact, but only in your imagination. This is what I'd like to ask those who accuse me of delusion: That which I speak of and which I preach here: is it the truth or my own inventions? They could ask me a counter-question, saying, "No one else does this (i.e., holds discussions). Do you really think you'll change everything?" As a matter of fact that's what the whole accusation of delusion rests upon. "You're trying to become famous," they say. How can I answer that? I'll just say one thing: When ruin threatens, you forget about everything extraneous and begin to act. Let those in whom a feeling of

---

[1] *Prelest'*: see above, n. 2 to the Third Discussion.

Christian truth is alive help me. I'll accept help with thanks. I harbor no personal motives of vainglory.

Now, concerning the main theme of our discussion for today. Nine discussions have passed. But that was just preparation. The main task lies ahead. The past discussions have outlined some things, the basic lines have been sketched in: resurrection from the dead—*Christ is risen!*—and the Kingdom of Heaven. These are our basic themes. Unless these are understood, nothing in Christianity can be.

For the most part it's Christians who come to our discussions, but there are also people of other faiths here as well —and some atheists, too. I've already said that in addition to everything else, my goal is to gather people—so that God's house might be filled. My goal is to summon vital forces into the Church. After all, it's no secret that many so-called churchly people turn into mere ritualists, that they lose the vitality of their faith and its spirit. But now so many people have begun to come that the church can't hold them all. And we can't move the walls, after all. I say this in order to summon you to keep order in church during the discussions. But so far everything has gone well, thanks to God.

I rejoice over each person who comes into church, and I want to find a common language with all. The forces which oppose us are great, while we are weak—but only in human terms. In actual fact our power is greater than meets the eye. God and Christ and the heavenly powers and all the saints (especially the Russian martyrs)—these are our power. This power is invisible, concealed. It acts only through our faith. According to our faith will it be done to us.[2] It's very important, therefore, that we strengthen our faith, that we muster it together, that we temper it and that we be daring.

Today let's just try to be daring!

There have been nine discussions—three times three—an image, as it were, of the Holy Trinity. Let's say a few words about the Holy Trinity. The image of the Holy Trinity was already perceptible in the Old Testament, but—to be sure— un-

---

[2]Mt. 9:29.

clearly, through a veil. When God said, "Let us create," He said it in the plural. The holy fathers saw in this an indication of the Trinity, but the image of the Trinity was revealed *openly* only in the New Testament. Christ revealed the Trinity to us. He Himself is the second person of the Holy Trinity. He brought to us the fulness of revelation concerning God. Now we look at everything through the eyes of Christ. He is our Way and the Truth.

This probably isn't clear to everyone present—not even to those who are Christians. These days, as many people are beginning to get interested in religious questions after many years of wandering about in atheism, some of them have begun to resolve these questions in their own ways—even the idea of creating a universal religion has arisen. At this point I'd like to answer two questions.

QUESTION: Father Dmitrii, have you given much thought to the idea that all religions contain an element of truth and that—at the same time—they all lay claim to an absolute universal significance, thereby fanning the flames of mutual enmity? How do you look upon the idea of a universal religion?

ANSWER: In my view there are three parts to this question. I'll answer them in order.

1) All religions do, indeed, contain some truth in themselves—some more, others less. Therefore I welcome all religions and would like to find a common language with them all. This, however, does not in any way exclude the fact that I myself consider Christianity to be the *only* religion which satisfies all the needs of the human spirit—and, moreover, Christianity in the Orthodox understanding.

2) Claims to universality and absoluteness that foster enmity among religions—this comes from introducing human passions into religion. True religion is a stranger to hostility. People might be hostile, but religions aren't.

3) The creation of a universal religion, which would unite within itself the qualities of all the various religions, is nothing but human impudence, impossible pretention. True religion can only be revealed by God. Religion that is not revealed is only religious philosophy, not religion in the true sense of the

word. The creation of a universal religion is human fantasy. I haven't given much thought to it, nor do I want to. For me, Christianity is *complete* religion. It gives everything to man and satisfies all of his needs. Now if Christianity fails to satisfy someone—that's a matter for his own conscience. Let God judge him—I won't. But my opinion about such people is this: God hasn't yet revealed Himself to them from the Christian point of view. Seek and you will find—just don't try to create your own religion. By the way, let me note that in such questions one must be utterly sincere and a stranger to pride and self-importance.

QUESTION: Tell us about God's incarnation and about reincarnation.

ANSWER: God became man. That's the incarnation. He didn't become an imaginary, illusory man, but a very real one, with flesh, bones and infirmities. He took upon Himself everything human—except sin. The union of God and man, in which the one does not destroy the other, is what is of the greatest significance here. Only the God-man could save man and conquer sin and death. Man was simply unable to do this. The union of God and man arouses the activity of both sides.

Reincarnation, though, eliminates man as a person. It eliminates all human activity. The idea of reincarnation leads man to passivity, it turns him into a toy of the elements. It's a non-Christian idea.

I must say that these questions are rather hard to understand, and I'm afraid that you haven't all caught the meaning of my answers. But the main thing to remember is that the incarnation of God—Christ's incarnation—arouses human activity. Those of us who believe in Christ must be active. The atheists would portray us as passive people, reconciled with evil, submitting to our fate. But that's just the way *they* understand things. On the contrary—we're active. Often this Christian activity leads to sufferings and death. From this the atheists conclude that pessimism and defeatism are the characteristics of Christianity. But this is a false understanding. After all, suffering and death aren't necessarily a defeat. After Christ's crucifixion on the Cross came the resurrection.

Through His sufferings and death Christ conquered all tortures and death. Eternity exists, the Kingdom of Heaven exists. The atheists smirk at these words. "Oh, well, eternity and the Kingdom of Heaven—these are abstract concepts," they say, "but in fact people want to live today, in the *real* day." But eternity and the Kingdom of Heaven aren't just abstract concepts. They're reality and they exist, whereas if we consider it seriously, "today" is an abstract concept. It's water flowing through our fingers, a shadow which appears for a moment and then vanishes.

And that's what I'd like to take note of here. Aiming at today—or, more precisely, at earthly goods—has corrupted us. If we look about impartially and with our eyes open, we'll see that striving for earthly goods has made us into egotists. Everything is for me. Nothing is for anyone else. And if at times it would seem as though I am fighting on behalf of others, in fact, it's only for the sake of my own benefit. It's not even worth speaking about morality *per se* in its true sense. Let's just consider the language we use in communicating with each other. A lot of the time it's just jargon interspersed with obscenities. And it seems that even highly cultured people have begun to speak this language. There's even literature written in it. An unsophisticated person or someone from the eighteenth century would be embarrassed to read the stuff we write. We boast of realism, forgetting that our attention is fixated on pathology, on human abnormality. We exalt this. We call it aesthetical. Just look at how we dress. The pursuit of fashion is an index to the spiritual bankruptcy of our souls.

But language and clothing form only the external side of man. It's even sadder that *internally* people have become cynical, depraved, mistrustful. They've begun to fear each other. We shout about collectivism, but we're more alone than ever before. It's called "being alone in a crowd." You begin to trust someone and confide in him—and all you get is a plague of denunciation. This is a horrible evil, but we've gotten so used to it that it doesn't even seem so horrible to us any more. Some people even build a career for themselves out of it and set themselves up in life. Such people are truly unfortunate, the most unfortunate people of all—more unfortunate than those whom they cause to suffer—even if they don't understand their misfortune. Morality is being destroyed by this evil. Of course, this is an ancient evil. But whereas previously there were only isolated instances—Judas was just one among the twelve apostles—these days one in three is a Judas, as we've come to say.

Perhaps this is why our faith is burdened by doubts. Everything is under suspicion, so no one trusts anyone. Nor is there any love. Frequently this evil is encouraged by our leaders. (They're even paid for this.) This evil which keeps us apart must be condemned from the pulpit. But frequently priests are afraid of exposing it, because they think it can't be defeated. . . . Tomorrow Judas will steal in secretly with a denunciation, and the next regularly-scheduled sacrifice will be hung on the Cross.

Perhaps I sound like a naïve child talking about this in the open. But I can't help but speak.

The *evil* of eavesdropping, the *evil* of denunciation, the *evil* of informing—that's putting it mildly. If we put it more crudely, it's just *finking*.[3] As long as we have this with us, we'll never learn to understand each other. Perhaps I won't be understood—that in exposing this evil I don't wish evil on anyone. There are probably already whole piles of paper somewhere describing me as a wicked man, an evil-wisher. Lord, save us from this evil! How can we but feel horror as we gaze upon the Innocent One crucified on Golgotha, and upon the sorry figure of the guy who hated and betrayed everyone—including himself—and who is now dangling from the limb of a tree, having hanged himself. Let's look more closely. Let's not be afraid of Golgotha, for from it will shine forth the light of the resurrection. Only by passing through Golgotha can we crush the head of Leviathan and with pity and love take down that corpse and lament over it. How horrible is the traitor's lot!

I've concentrated so much upon this evil because in it, as in a prism, are concentrated many of the evil traits of modern man. And this isn't happening in Russia alone, but all over the world.

---

[3]*Stukachestvo*: from *stukach* (slang): an informer; hence *stukachestvo*, the state or activity of an informer.

We've achieved great progress. We're waging a titanic battle to save the world and to ward off destruction. But progress has cost us quite a bit. The family has gone to pieces. Lewdness, drunkenness and crime are flourishing. Often criminals dress in the finest of clothes and occupy executive armchairs. And what catastrophe progress has brought to nature! Nature will yet have vengeance for the barbaric way we've treated her. And cancer—why, it's become as common these days as the 'flu! Understand all of this and you'll be horrified: destruction, chaos!

Some might say that I'm exaggerating, that some good still exists. May God grant that this be so!

"The earth was without form and void, and darkness was upon the face of the deep; and the Spirit of God was moving over the face of the waters. And God said, 'Let there be light,'" we read in the Bible.[4] The earth is without form and void. Darkness is upon the face of the deep. But the Spirit of God exists, and a voice is heard: "Let there be light!"

I'd like each of you to feel as though you are there, at the beginning of the creation of the world. We're all called upon to create. But where shall we start? What shall we do?

The earth is without form. Darkness is upon the face of the deep. Disorder in the family, in society, in the world. We must realize clearly that we're called by God to create—with Him—a new world.

"Let there be light!" Oh, if only it were so! In order to do something serious, it's necessary that light—real light—enlighten us. When God created the world, the first thing He did was say, "Let there be light." If there's no light in our soul, if we don't set before ourselves the goal towards which we're working, then nothing will come of our work. We'll just wander about in darkness, and no one who walks in darkness knows where he is going, as it says in the Gospel.[5]

Often human labor is like wandering in darkness. Without some lofty goal, human labor requires constant prodding and encouragement, and even so things often end up being done

[4]Gen. 1:2-3.
[5]Jn. 12:35.

in a slipshod way. When the guy who's supposed to urge us on is actually watching, we work, but when he isn't watching, it's O.K. to kill time. When you do things that way, what can you hope to accomplish? Every bit of energy is spent in arranging your own affairs. Some grow fat while others are in need. But then some catastrophe occurs and suddenly everyone sees —there's nothing left, and everything you've done to establish yourself has gone to dust. How are you to live? What are you to do? Keep your spirits up—and in good spirits sink to the bottom? Put on a forced smile on command? But then, neither labor considered in and of itself nor earthly goods in and of themselves give man anything. Not long ago there was an article in *Literaturnaia Gazeta* describing how people are swallowed up by *things,* how some people don't see anything beyond material goods. The article told in particular about how one man who'd gotten rich off other people's grief during the blockade of Leningrad came home only to find that he no longer had a house. A bomb had demolished it along will all the riches he'd gathered. He sank down to the ground and never rose again.

There's no meaning in labor in and of itself nor in earthly goods in and of themselves. The slave's work is a curse. Earthly goods can make a person repulsive to those around him. We need light in all we do. We must know for what purpose we are laboring.

I don't want to criticize anyone right now—please understand me correctly. I welcome people who set lofty, sincere goals before themselves. I myself, as a Christian and as a priest, set a goal before myself. My goal is to bring to people the light of Christ and to call them into the Kingdom of Heaven. I see that without this goal everything we have will come crashing down, everything will perish, and that all of our achievements will be empty. This doesn't mean that in general terms I'm against the achievements of progress, but these achievements must be filled with the true light.

"Let there be light!" "Thy Kingdom come!"—*that* should be our motto today. Let there be light in all of our deeds and actions, the Light of Christ. Let Thy Kingdom come, O Lord, on earth as it is in heaven. The Kingdom of God doesn't come visibly. It's within us, as the Gospel says.[6] Oh, if it were only so! How happy we'd be. Happy in all the vicissitudes of life, even when death approaches. Then we'd pass not into non-being but from temporal life into life eternal. Life is everywhere, both there and here.

QUESTION: It would seem that, from your point of view, the believer does good because of his hope for a reward after death. Don't you find something repulsive, mercenary, and ultimately anti-Christian in this? Isn't it like bargaining over good—a disguised egotism? Didn't Christ command us to do good in such a way that our right hand wouldn't know what our left hand is doing, i.e., unselfishly? True good is its own reward and goal. It doesn't need the carrot and the stick. And if you understand good in such a vulgar, common manner, don't you introduce a certain degradation into Christian morality? Doesn't it lead to widespread hypocrisy?

ANSWER: The question is posed seriously, although judging from it, the person who asked it lacks a clear-cut Christian understanding of good, and he has misunderstood my words on this topic. I can understand his indignation against "self-interest," "disguised egotism," "moral degradation" and "hypocrisy." I also understand his honest striving to understand these things. I see his sincerity, his nobility, but at the same time I'd like to note that in the question many things have been invented and are stated too sharply, with no condescension to the weaknesses of others.

Do things in such a way that your left hand doesn't know what your right hand is doing. It's true, that's what Christ said.[7] But he also said: "Rejoice and be glad, for great is your reward in heaven."[8] Let's cool off a little and think. What difference is there between getting your reward here and getting it there? Misunderstanding often results from vagueness on this question. It's true that getting your reward *here* causes self-interest, greediness, egotism and hypocrisy to develop.

---

[6]Lk. 17:21.
[7]Mt. 6:3.
[8]Mt. 5:12.

When we get it *there,* such evil feelings can't develop—because we neither see nor sense our reward. Can the idea that in the Kingdom of Heaven greediness will not be rewarded cause anyone to become self-interested? Will one become an egotist if he believes that egotism won't be rewarded in the Kingdom of Heaven? Disinterest, selflessness, humility—these will be rewarded there. Reward in the Kingdom of Heaven is entirely different from reward here. Reward *there* means developing your good qualities. To do something in hope of reward in the Kingdom of Heaven means to do so disinterestedly, unselfishly, humbly—to do so without regard for reward. According to the Christian understanding, if you consider yourself to be good that's already a sign that you're *not* good. When we Christians do something, we know that what we've done won't die, but that it will live on eternally in a most real way—and not just in the memory of our descendants—because the Kingdom of Heaven itself exists. Is that a reward? Yes, it is, because good doesn't disappear. And the person who asked the question was right—real good *is* its own reward. But the Kingdom of God isn't retribution understood in a vulgar sort of way, but precisely eternity, the impossibility that good will be annihilated.

Let me offer an example from life. Not long ago I was told about a woman who worked as a nurse in a hospital. In it, there was an eight-year-old boy whom everyone had abandoned. His parents had rejected him entirely. He lived in a shelter of some sort. Unlike most children, he was bitter towards everything. His disease was hopeless. He received routine care, but they knew he'd die anyway. And he understood this too. Everyone was an annoyance to him. He believed no one. But this nurse, because of her faith, was filled with pity for him. At first he wouldn't believe her any more than he would anyone else, and got irritated at her. But later he somehow saw that her pity for him was sincere and selfless, and then became at ease with her. She was his only joy, and he would accept things from no one else but her. He began to calm down and his temper became more even. This woman baptised him, and he died happy and at peace with everyone. She then made the rounds of all the churches requesting prayers for the repose of his soul. The boy became like her own child, very close. In everyday life some might think that this nurse was a hypocrite because she talks a lot about "rewards" in the Kingdom of Heaven. But consider what she really is.

Or, take the mother of seven children who goes to care for the sick and the aged. She thinks about rewards in the Kingdom of Heaven. Should we consider her a hypocrite?

One more example. A doctor heals sick people and at the same time reminds them that they should meditate upon God, that they should examine their consciences, since nothing in life happens by accident. "Perhaps," she says, "you have some unconfessed sins, so try to purify your soul." This doctor receives no rewards for these conversations. Obviously she isn't paid for them. On the contrary, many people probably consider her an egotist and a hypocrite. But she goes on with her task anyway—free of charge, subject to the hootings and mockery of some—because she knows that only those who use force, only those who are ridiculed and hated here will enter the Kingdom of God. "Rejoice and be exceedingly glad, for great is your reward in heaven." The people I have spoken of rejoice in the rewards which await them *there*. Is it possible that a certain corruption is thereby introduced into their Christian morality, making hypocrites of them? Or would it be better for morality if in these cases they were to receive wages for their deeds?

The Kingdom of Heaven and reward there isn't the same thing as earthly reward. There's only one thing it gives us: It develops in us kind, selfless feelings and then advances into kind, selfless action. And there's no bargaining involved in this. You can't strike a bargain with God. The fact that good isn't fiction, that good won't perish, that God sees every sigh and will forget *nothing*—now *that's* the Kingdom of Heaven. The Kingdom of God isn't a carrot and a stick but the certainty that good won't perish or be forgotten—even if the people around you don't notice it.

QUESTION: What do these words mean: "The earth was without form and void; darkness was upon the face of the deep, and the Spirit of God was above the waters"?

ANSWER: The formless, void earth is the primeval mass, darkness, chaos. It's the condition of complete disorder, in which, as the *Commentary on the Bible* says, neither the elements of the future world (fire, air, earth and water) nor the germ of plant and animal life, were as yet at all differentiated, but were still all mixed up together, as it were.

Scientists also talk of an uncooled mass out of which all things were later formed. As you see, this passage in the Bible doesn't disagree with scientific notions. Indeed, strictly speaking, the Bible doesn't disagree with science in general. It's just that sometimes people try to make science disagree with the Bible.

The darkness upon the face of the deep, as it says in the *Commentary*, is the natural result of the absence of light, which did not yet exist as a separate, independent element, but which only later was separated from the primeval chaos. The Spirit of God was above the waters. Here the commentators are at odds. Some—Tertullian, Ephraim the Syrian and Theodoret—see here merely the indication of an ordinary wind sent down by God to dry the earth. Others—Chrysostom—speak of an angel, a special intelligent power. Some—Basil the Great, Athanasius and Jerome—think that it speaks of the hypostatic Spirit of God, i.e., of the third Person of the Holy Trinity. I find this last interpretation to be the most convincing. It indicates the part played by the Spirit of God in the work of creation. The action of the Holy Spirit upon chaos, as is shown in this interpretation, is like that of a bird when she hatches her eggs, warming them with her own body heat, awakening life in them. "In this way," it says in the *Commentary*, "on the one hand, one might see in chaos a certain action of natural forces, analogous to the process whereby the embryo is gradually formed inside the egg. On the other hand, both these very forces and their results are placed in direct dependence upon God."

We're often too simplistic in the way we understand the Biblical narratives, and therefore we say that the Bible is just a collection of fables. But according to the interpretation I've just expounded, it turns out that in creating the world God allowed free development to everything which is going on.

And if we look at it like this, then the Biblical story doesn't contradict scientific notions.

QUESTION: Just why must one think that God created the world, rather than that the world created itself?

ANSWER: Because to admit the world's self-creation would mean to admit the omnipotence of chaos. It would be the same thing as admitting that the alphabet could of itself compose outstanding works of literature. Admitting God as Creator, we admit the participation of a higher Reason in everything. The world is excellent because God created it. A self-creating world would forever stew in its own juices. The atheists, in denying God, are forced to fabricate their own theories. How many of such theories have there been! But where are they all now?

QUESTION: What "light" is spoken of when God says: "Let there be light," since the lights in the firmament were created only on the fourth day.

ANSWER: This is what's said in the *Commentary*:"This first-created light was not our normal light in the full sense of the word. . . . It was the same phosphorescent ether which, being in a state of flux, dispelled the primieval darkness and thereby created the necessary conditions for the future appearance of all organic life on earth."

QUESTION: Is the creation of the world reflected in Orthodox worship?

ANSWER: Yes, it is. When at vespers we sing the psalm: "Bless the Lord, O my soul. O Lord, my God, Thou art very great," this expresses our joy at the world which God has created. When we sing "O Gladsome Light,"[9] we are singing about the light which illumines all men who come into the world, the Light of Christ. This is the Light which was already intended when the first light was created. Furthermore, we must pay attention to the fact that Orthodox worship begins

---

[9]"O Gladsome Light": ancient vesperal hymn still sung daily in the Orthodox Church.

in the evening, and the creation of the world also began in the evening. "And there was evening and there was morning, one day," says the Bible. If we think about it, the Bible and worship are somehow united. We note that creation is continuing even now: the creation of the new man. In this creation, all of us are taking an active part.

QUESTION: How could a person get the idea that there is no God?

ANSWER: The question is a serious one. Indeed, how *could* such an idea arise if everything that exists speaks of God and of His creation of the world, if all literature and art grew upon the soil of religion? After all, nothing of significance has been created in this area on an antireligious foundation. Atheism is just a leech which has no independent significance. If, for example, one were to stop talking about God, then atheism too would cease to exist. But let's philosophize a bit, especially since the question was posed philosophically.

We call God the Father of all. So let's draw a parallel between God and our father in the earthly sense. Let's imagine, for example, a person who says that he has no father—not that his father has died or that he has abandoned his family, as is often the case these days, but that he simply *never* had a father. He just appeared in the world, without a father. How would we look upon such a person? Well now, a two-year-old child might still be able to say that he was bought at the store, but a seven-year-old would already understand that that's just not how it happens—even if he doesn't knew exactly how it *does* happen, and even if perhaps he has never seen his own father. So, a child—one with little intelligence—might well say that he has no father. In the same way, a person who declares that there is no God still has the mind of a child. He's unreasonable, and his declaration is worthless save as a curiosity. Or else, someone who has lost his reason—someone who is insane —might say that he has no father. In such a state he might also say that there is no God. The Psalmist says in this regard: "The foolish man says in his heart, 'There is no God.' "[10] But there

---

[10]Ps. 53:1.

are no other cases imaginable in which a person would deny the existence of his own father—nor, likewise, the existence of God. To be sure, there are still situations in which a conflict exists. Someone might be holding a grudge against his father. He might not *want* to know him. Therefore, he says that he has no father. But this is a denial only in the figurative sense.

How, then, did the diabolical idea that there is no God arise? How did we Russians allow this idea to grow on our native soil? All of Russian history is built upon faith in God, upon Orthodoxy. Our entire literature is inwardly religious. But on an antireligious foundation the only thing to "arise" here has been the ruin of wonderful churches. It's not in vain that they say that atheism has torn across our land like a hurricane. You know, morality is from God, and life is from God. So why do we—out of fear—go on repeating this idea which is so utterly foreign to us: that there is no God? Someday we'll be ashamed of having said such things.

Philosophers say that the very existence of the idea that God does not exist is already a testimony to the fact that He *does* exist, and that He gave man the freedom even to deny His existence.

Man denies God because he himself wants to become a god. There's *no* other explanation for atheism. But it's time we understand that deifying ourselves leads to a dead end—one from which we cannot escape except by turning to God. Otherwise there's ruin.

We must begin our new creation with the words: "Let there be light!"—the Light of God, the Light of Christ!

QUESTION: Father Dmitrii, you attach great importance to the Church. But why then does the Church take such a small part in the life of society? What happens with all the money the believers bring? For example, there are known cases. One archimandrite was found to have 15,000 rubles in his possession, and a priest, whose name we won't mention, was found to have no less of a reserve. Is it possible that our money just profits the priests and, perhaps, the church-wardens?

ANSWER: If you look at this question only superficially it's devastating. The Church is completely finished off. She's not needed at all. And the antireligious propagandists often take advantage of this. But let's look at things a bit more closely.

The Church does indeed make a great deal of money. Contributions from believers are enormous. You probably read in the papers how Patriarch Pimen donated, if I'm not mistaken, about five million rubles to the peace fund. Frequent receptions for foreign delegations are also given with church money. All kinds of cheats and scoundrels pad their pockets with it—be they priests or wardens. But a lot does remain. Each parish puts considerable sums of money in the bank. And, it's asked, why not use these sincere donations from believers for good deeds? Why can't the Church create a temperance society, for example, which would do something useful, like curing drunks? Or organize a home for the aged or for children abandoned by their parents? Or, finally, she could simply help the sick and the needy, or set up a model school where children would receive a religiously-oriented education. We could use church money to heal the wounds which the atheists inflicted in their day upon our church buildings—after all, how many glorious, unique churches were damaged through the zeal of the atheists! There's no end of things that *could* be done . . .

But we can't. It's probably not common knowledge, but the atheists have forbidden the Church to carry on any charitable activity, and, as a result, she's unable to use her own resources for good deeds—because if she could, everyone would see that the Church is of some use after all, and *that* the atheists do not want.

Usually people avoid talking about this. It's considered seditious. Maybe tomorrow they'll take me out and crucify me for these words. But once you've *begun* to be daring, you've got to be sincere to the very end and tell all.

Once again I emphasize that I say this not for the sake of "politics," not to undermine anyone's authority. I say it as a warning. I see the danger and disease which confront us all. Therefore I speak the truth. That's not politics. How can speaking from the pulpit about peace and disarmament *not* be politics, while pointing out our internal diseases and exposing the falsehood and enmity which spoil life in Russia, the home we all share, *is* politics?

I know that some people charge me with being arbitrary.
"He didn't get permission for these discussions," they say.
But do you really have to get someone's permission in order
to pull a child out of a fire? Suppose there's a fire, but the
authorities are just standing off to one side enjoying the sight
while there is a child in mortal danger. What do *you* think
should be done? Run off to get permission?

They'll say that I'm exaggerating. Would to God that it
were so! But it seems to me that rather than exaggerating
things, I'm smoothing a lot of things over. I'm shouting about
what I've noticed, but I haven't really noticed all that much.
But in my opinion, it's better to see a little clearly than to close
your eyes to everything and limit yourself to your own narrow
interests.

QUESTION: On what basis or by what canonical rules can
a rector prohibit the giving of sermons or lessons at baptisms
or funerals? Does he have such a right? If he doesn't, but he
prohibits them anyway, how should a priest proceed in such a
case?

ANSWER: Let me note one thing right away. It was a
priest who asked me this question. Up until now, no priests
have asked me any questions, perhaps because while we're
having our discussions in church they're busy conducting a
service. This is a vital question, an urgent one. It may not be
a subject of interest to everyone, but nevertheless it does
touch upon more than just our priestly practice. Be patient.
Perhaps our troubles as priests wil become clearer to you.
After all, in the final analysis, all of us in the Church share
these problems. All of us—priests and laymen alike—bear responsibility for the Church. After all, in Orthodoxy all the
people are the preservers of the truth, and the hierarchy is
bound to the people not by a bond of authority, but of love.

So, on what basis can the rector prohibit a priest from
giving a sermon? To make the answer short: There's *no* basis
for this. If he does prohibit it, he does so not on the basis of
canon law but at his own whim. That's all. He has *no* canonical right in this.

But you might ask: How can you fail to obey the rector?

Let's think about it. What does obedience mean, both in general terms and in this particular case? Obedience in the Christian understanding is the active realization of the will of God. Christ said, "Go and preach!" That's the will of God. The apostle Paul says, "Be urgent in season and out of season."[11] This too is the will of God, even if it's expressed through an apostolic admonition. According to canonical rules, the priest's first duty is to preach, even if he doesn't serve—to preach everywhere: in conversations, in discussions ... "Woe to me if I *don't* preach."[12] But suddenly the rector prohibits it. Whose will is he doing in such a case? Certainly not God's will. In this case, if someone must be accused of disobedience, it's the rector. In this case the rector is insisting upon the infallibility of human authority *per se* and trying to build the Church on it. In this case one may fail to listen to the rector without thereby violating the commandment of obedience. In this case *not* listening to the rector means listening to God rather than to man. When the apostles were told: "We charged you not to teach in His Name ...," how did they answer? "We must obey God rather than men."[13] All of us—priests and bishops alike—must obey God first of all. But in our day-to-day life we often substitute obedience to man's whim for obedience to the will of God. This should not be so. The atheists often play upon this misconstrued obedience, forcing Christians to do things which aren't at all from God but rather—to be blunt—from the devil. A diabolical policy is often pursued in church matters, one result of the atheists' efforts to override the Church. It is said: "Test the spirits, whether they are from God or someone else."[14] We should test any given order before obeying it. But in practice it often happens that if you obey the orders of the rector or the bishop you must disobey God. How can this be so? It's something to think over. How often the church authorities who give the orders aren't being guided by God's

---

[11] 2 Tim. 4:2.
[12] 1 Cor. 9:16.
[13] Acts 5:27-29.
[14] 1 Jn. 4:1.

precepts but by cowardly worldly considerations! They don't want to disturb the powers of this world. God, they say, isn't visible but the atheists are, and what's more, they're threatening us. So it often turns out that in these commands it's not God's will which is heard but that of the atheists. This is the result of confusion in our church consciousness. Often we just serve—formally—in church, but in essence we are pursuing an anti-church policy. As a result we become bad Christians, we lose our moral and spiritual aspect, we tear down the Church. We suppose that we're doing the will of God, but in fact we serve as a weapon of the devil's destructive power. The Church's goal is to make people perfect, to bring them into the Kingdom of Heaven. But the atheists want to turn the Church into some kind of a museum where people go just to listen to the singing or to feast their eyes upon the icons. They treat believers like some kind of museum exhibits and not like living, modern people. But the Church must save people and not just entertain them. To save from godlessness and moral decomposition, to extend a helping hand to all those who labor and are burdened—that's the Church's high calling, and she has no other. If a rector forbids a priest to preach, that is the result of a non-churchly understanding of the nature of the Church's affairs.

Sometimes it's said that we should just somehow endure and that things will work out by themselves. But the proverb is right that says: "Water doesn't flow under a rolling stone." In the second place, we're not stupid blockheads but living people called by Christ to ascetic feats. Church affairs can only be corrected by our own hands. God helps those who try to act and don't wait for everything to be done by itself. Nothing gets done by itself, but things can be destroyed by themselves.

I'd like to say this to my dear brother who sent me this note: May God help you, Father. Speak up. Don't be silent. This is why God sent you into the world and blessed you. But those who would try to lead you astray, who would bind you to something else—they must be accused of their untruth, no matter what position of authority they might hold.

QUESTION: Father Dmitrii, here in Russia the Church officially is separated from the State. But sometimes one reads in the newspapers that this definition means state regulation of religion ... [*Let me just interrupt the question immediately. It makes you just want to scream: What's this "state regulation of religion"? How's it possible? That's the kind of question you should ask Mr. Kuroedov, the Minister of Religion! The question continues:*] ... In *The Journal of the Moscow Patriarchate* Professor Zabolotskii writes that the Orthodox Church strives for a "symphony" between the Church and the State like that in antiquity in Byzantium. How should this all be understood?

ANSWER: Byzantium was a religious country, and under such conditions "symphony" had soil to support it. In our country atheism is the reigning ideology. So what "symphony" can there be? It's just plain rhetoric. You can't unite belief and unbelief, especially not by suppressing faith by unbelief. No symphony results from this but rather the cacophony that we observe around us. I'd recommend that you turn to Prof. Zabolotskii with your question. Perhaps he has indeed made some kind of unprecedented discovery.

QUESTION: What's the difference between catholicity[15] and universality? Do the Pope of Rome in the West and the Councils in the East decide this question of catholicity?

ANSWER: This question is very urgent, very complex, and very disturbing. We often confuse catholicity with universality or with the councils. More often still, it's just a meaningless word for us. But in fact, catholicity is the basic principle of our church structure. Through the principle of catholicity the Church is built upon a rock—that is, upon Christ. And we are all bricks. Or, to put it yet another way: Christ is the vine and we're the branches. The Church could be universal and yet not catholic. It could have a pope and councils and yet at the same time not be catholic. *Why?* Because if it absolutizes just one element—the pope or the councils—rather than developing *all* its branches simultaneously, if there isn't

---

[15]Russian: *sobornost'*.

participation in the Church by each and every individual
through personal responsibility for the truth, then the Church
is not catholic. Each member of the Church—and not just the
councils or the Pope or the Patriarch—must join himself to
the Holy Spirit and live by Christ's precepts. Anyone who
fails to live in this way is a member of the Church only in a
formal way. Anyone can be in error—including councils.
Only the Holy Spirit working through righteous people can
be without error. We know of examples of this from history.
Let's recall if nothing else how Athanasius the Great when
only a deacon defended the truth while all others, including
the bishops, went astray.

Catholicity isn't a juridical concept, and only the person
who is living a full Christian life is capable of understanding
its meaning. Without this, all appeals to the decisions of the
councils are simply hollow. The canons of the Church do not
exist for their own sake but in order that by following them
we might live a Christian life. Without this, observing the
letter of the canons at times can kill. As the Apostle Paul
said: "The letter kills, but the spirit gives life."[16] The atheists
often play upon the letter of the canons, thereby killing our
natural church life. They strangle us with our own hands.
It's time for us to come to our senses. In our church politics
it's often the case that a run-of-the-mill bishop, or even a
rector, sets himself up higher than the Pope of Rome. In his
encyclicals, the Pope at least appeals to *Christ*, but with us,
when internal church decisions are made, the appeal is sometimes to ... Ah— ... I don't even want to talk about it. We
must all remember that all of us are Christians, members of
the catholic Church, and each of us must in his own way do
God's work. In this is the essence of catholicity.

QUESTION: What is the role of humility in the Christian
life, and in the Orthodox life in particular? We all know
that Christ was humble, and He called people to humility.
But He also called the pharisees "snakes, a generation of
vipers," and He plaited a whip out of cords and drove the

---

[16]2 Cor. 3:6.

sellers from the Temple and overturned their tables.[17] Don't we sometimes confuse humility, like Christ's in the Garden of Gethsemane, with slavelike submissiveness to the mighty ones of this world? Don't we try to look the other way so that they won't touch us, to the detriment of our higher spiritual interests? Some Orthodox have a tendency to think that you've got to ask for a blessing every time you have to sneeze, and that in general you should just sit there quietly and not pay a bit of attention to anything. In the West, in the Roman Church, such a tendency was condemned in the seventeenth century under the name of "quietism." Where do we stand on this?

ANSWER: And just where do we stand on anything in general? That's what I'd like to ask in return. It's true, we often do understand humility as submission to those who are over us rather than to God who stands over all. Everything that's outside the boundaries of our human understanding we are inclined to consider as non-churchly. And the bartering which sometimes goes on in church is worse now than it was in the Temple of Jerusalem—but this doesn't bother us. We don't dare even *think* about making a whip to drive out all those who are leeching off the church, who have no need of God but only of something else—their own profit. Perhaps many people would even think that this episode from the Gospel must be understood as some kind of allegory, since —they'd say—that meek, humble Christ couldn't really have driven anyone out of the Temple with a whip. They consider anyone who lifts up his voice against the disorder we're in as proud, a troublemaker, and they try to get rid of such a person as quickly as possible.

Humility is submission to the truth of God. It's righteous anger against all untruth. Humility is love of good and hatred of evil. But when humility makes peace with evil, it becomes an affected, pharisaic humility, indifferent to everything—except, of course, to its own personal interests.

I'm very glad that such sharp, profound questions have begun to come in. Thanks to whoever asked it.

---

[17]Mt. 23:30, 21:12.

QUESTION: Father Dmitrii, I know that in other Ortho-dox countries—Romania and Serbia—new churches are being built, ten to fifteen per year, and in Romania eight mona-steries have even been founded. Tell me, in your opinion is anything like that possible here? At least couldn't the churches which aren't being used for worship be opened? After all, the population is growing, and there are more and more believers, and already the churches are incapable of accommodating all who wish to be in them.

ANSWER: It's true, churches are being built in other coun-tries, including the socialist ones, while here they are being closed. Why, right before our eyes the Church of the Trans-figuration on Transfiguration Square was blown up. Right before our eyes they've closed the seminaries. Only two re-main, plus two academies—for a country of this size! And this happened recently—long after the revolutions and wars had passed. The atheists have begun to destroy and bomb all popular holy things—literally. But it's not just the atheists who must answer for this. We too are guilty for tolerating such tyranny. (This includes some hierarchs as well.) Some cynically declare that the churches are being closed and de-stroyed at the people's request. I'd recommend, if this bothers any of you, that you send a protest to our hierarchs and to the atheists. Let them get used to hearing the voice of the people. But you know, it turns out that *in fact* we do go along with them. If we were to demand the opening of some churches that are not functioning at present—now *that* would be real Christian daring. After all, no one has deprived us of the right to express our will. Here in Russia we believers are citi-zens with full rights under the law. So why is it possible to open churches in Romania and Serbia, but not here?

Many of you probably have heard about Bishop Hermo-genes, who is now cloistered in the Zhirovits monastery.[18]

---

[18]Bishop Hermogenes (Golubev): Archbishop of Kaluga and Borovsk. Con-secrated in 1953 for the see of Tashkent and Central Asia, he was one of eight Russian bishops who in 1965 submitted to Patriarch Alexis a declaration criti-cizing the decision of the Council of Bishops in 1961. They demanded true separation of Church and State as required by the Soviet Constitution, and ad-

One of the reasons for his dismissal from his diocese was that he dared to build a church in Tashkent. Can you imagine that? But anyone who would say a single word about this would be stoned by the atheists and by certain hierarchs who are obedient to them. These hierarchs think they'll propitiate the atheists by acting this way, but they are forgetting that their lives will come to such an end that... Well, it's horrible even to think about it... Somehow they just don't realize that as a result of all these atheistic efforts we are threatened with moral destruction, and all our colossal technical, scientific and social progress will turn into an empty shell. We often close our eyes to this. "It'll last as long as we do," they say. But later on they'll change their minds and begin storming into our churches by force—if it's not too late already.

QUESTION: What is spiritual direction? How does it differ from the Sacrament of Confession? Is it absolutely necessary for a Christian?

ANSWER: Spiritual direction. The Sacrament of Confession. What grand words! And how important these are for a person! But to direct someone spiritually, you've got to *live* spiritually. Maybe there are some great ascetics around somewhere, but who is aware of them? And those of us who live with a troubled conscience, with worries about this or that—how dare *we* direct anyone spiritually? Even for the Sacrament of Confession we must be sufficiently prepared. But we are tossed about. Often we don't trust the priests. But then, there are reasons for this. A whole lot of people need spiritual direction, and many desire it. They discover that an honest man has appeared somewhere and they are drawn to him. But the majority have to save themselves by their own spiritual strength. It's good if they really are on the way to salvation. The ancient ascetics foretold that in the latter times spiritual direction would dry up and people would

---

ministrative decentralization of the Church. For exercising his pastoral conscience in this way Abp. Hermogenes was "retired" to a monastery.

be saved through sufferings, that they'd be convinced by visions and by calling upon the Name of God.

You have to be sincere and strive towards the good. Stop looking around—especially at the atheists—and then the Lord God will direct us. But if you go to confession as you should and if you find a spiritual director, be aware that you are very fortunate. Such a person can be envied.

QUESTION: Father Dmitrii, I don't know if you've heard, but there's a church in Moscow—I won't name it—in which the rector—he's the dean of clergy as well—does everything possible to turn believers away from the church. During the censing, for example, he ventures to tell obscene jokes. He's despotic in his treatment of his fellow priests, and he laughs at their zeal in serving. He has driven the singers away, and in general everyone is running away from his parish. What's going to happen there? The people aren't stopping him. He's in full control of the situation. What should we do, because that parish is being destroyed. All of this is just playing into the hands of the atheists.

ANSWER: What'll happen? I'd compare this kind of rector with the Russian policemen who were in Nazi captivity. They too leaned over backwards to please their new masters, to gain favor with them at the expense of their own people. Such rectors are making illegal profits off of the fact that the Church is powerless in the face of arbitrary rule. They are useful to the atheists. Not long ago one atheist told me directly, "Real priests are no good to us." By the way, it's not just certain rectors. Some bishops also are "fakes" like that. Perhaps some of you read Bishop Hermogenes' *Open Letter* in which he named a certain metropolitan who'd been married three times and ordained three times. Still, he was retained in his diocese. But how many years now have they been tormenting this Bishop Hermogenes in the Zhirovits monastery, not allowing him to direct a diocese? There's only one way out. Our much-suffering Church is *occupied* by the atheists. They've muzzled her, and they're doing everything possible to discredit her. All who understand this and mourn over it must not keep silent. Believers could do an awful lot.

We've got to demand that such clerics finally be called to order. We're all responsible for what's done in the Church.

QUESTION: Father Dmitrii, you are citing scandalous facts of perversions—even crimes—within the Church. But you don't name names, and this can create the impression that you are just inventing all of this.

ANSWER: You forget, my fellow questioners, that our discussions aren't a judicial process. Our goal is to appeal to each person's conscience. My words contain no fabrications. Anyone who wishes can convince himself of their truth. And a lot of what I'm talking about here is common knowledge. Just look around with open, honest eyes, with a mind not darkened by demagogy, and you'll see. And then, obey your conscience, as though you were standing before God.

In general we need to spend more time imagining that we stand before the face of God. Vladimir Solov'ev wrote that in order to test whether you're doing right, you must picture Christ for yourself and then ask yourself, "How would *He* act?" Christ is our way and our Truth. We must imitate *Him*. Then all that has entangled us will fall away and He will uphold us Himself.

Well, we've held another discussion, even if our circle was pretty narrow. Of course, I haven't answered all the questions. A lot remain. There are letters I wanted to read in church. What I'd like *all* of us to retain from today's conversation is the realization that we believers are all called by God to co-creation with Him. Around us lie chaos and disintegration.

"Let there be light!" That's our main motto. If the light of Christ is in us, we'll know what we should do and how we should live. We must live in the name of the Kingdom of God. Then everything will be good here on earth.

In conclusion, one piece of advice. Many people ask "How should we pray when there's just no time?" Saint Seraphim of Sarov[19] advised every Christian to fulfill this rule of prayer: recite "Our Father" three times, the Creed once, and

---

[19]Saint Seraphim of Sarov (1759-1833): renowned Russian monk and mystic.

"Rejoice O Virgin Theotokos" three times. The Saint said that through these prayers a person is raised to the heights of Christian understanding. They contain everything—how to pray, what to believe in, who it was that ministered to the mystery of our salvation and about whom we must never forget in our earthly life.

PARISHIONER: Tell me Father Dmitrii, will we really never be able to hold our discussions in church again? Who didn't like what in them? Where do all these bans come from?

ANSWER: The question's a bit naive, but sincere. "Who didn't like what?" Who?... the atheists. What?... Christian preaching. But, of course, they'll heap up all sorts of demagogy to accuse me personally. In order to avoid any false rumors among you believers, I want to tell you what I myself conceive to be the meaning of our discussion.

I haven't engaged in any politics during our discussions, contrary to what some people would like to think. And if I've spoken about certain perversions in our life it's only from a strong desire to correct them. My discussions were aimed at strengthening morality in society, at strengthening the family and awakening faith in people. I didn't disturb authority and the government. I approach them in a Christian way: All authority is from God. But with this I never forget that you must render to God that which is God's, and to Caesar only that which is Caesar's. By no means should everything—both God's and Caesar's—go to Caesar. I haven't criticised the Patriarch at all, as some accuse me of doing. On the contrary, I've tried to defend him from attacks. No, I wasn't authorized to defend the Patriarch, but then such defense isn't something that one is authorized to do. It's simply a matter of conscience and good will.

The misunderstandings which have arisen between the Church and the State I consider to be fruits of atheism, which in its zeal has overstepped all bounds of legality. Yes, I've been irreconcilable towards atheism in the discussions, but not so much for ideological reasons—I respect all convictions, including atheistic ones—as because in Russia atheism has ceased to be just an ideology. It's begun to spread itself by force, to suppress all other opinion, and in practice it has overflowed into crime.

As concerns my future destiny: it's as yet undetermined. Apparently they'll either forbid me to serve or transfer me to the kind of parish where no activity at all is possible. It will be done—ostensibly—in the name of the Patriarch, but in reality it'll originate not with the Patriarch but with the atheists. Most likely the reason given will be that I didn't obtain permission for the discussions. But that's just the formal occasion. It was utterly unnecessary for me to get such permission because the discussion is just a form of preaching, and I was blessed to preach when I was ordained. Preaching is the priest's first obligation, and without it I can't conceive what my ministry would be like. Furthermore, I didn't obtain permission for the discussions because I didn't want to involve anyone else in this matter, since, after all, the outcome could be predicted from the very beginning.

The discussions arose because believers desired them. They asked me questions and I answered them. That's the priest's obligation. But questions came up again and again, and I decided that I'd hold collective discussions rather than individual ones. I had no right to leave people without an answer. In the Gospel it says: "Be prepared to give anyone an answer."[20] So there's nothing illegal here. Everything was done according to the Gospel commandments. I'll remind you that we're all responsible for Christian truth, and we must all defend it not upon instructions from our superiors but upon command of the heart and the conscience—which I have done. There's been nothing secret or hidden in our discussions. Everything was above board. The doors of the church were open.

But in order that no doubt remain as to the source of all this calumny and suspicion, I'll tell you about one conversation I had.

July 27, 1972. The phone rang in our church. I was serving at the time, and so the church sexton and server, Nikolai

---

[20] 1 Pet. 3:15.

Petrovich, answered the phone. A syrupy sweet voice asked:
"Is this Dmitrii Sergeevich?"[21]

"Dmitrii Sergeevich is busy. May I take a message?"

"When he's free, have him call the Procurator at 233-
3928."

It took me a while to get free. But soon after the phone
call a telegram arrived: REPORT 3 P.M. TO PROCURATOR.
STOP. NOVOKUZNETSKII STREET, 28-A, APT. 40 TO INVESTI-
GATORY DIVISION CHIEF SOLOV'EV. STOP.

As soon as I got free I called the number specified and
arranged for a convenient time to meet. I arrived there at
1 P.M. With me were my wife and this same Nikolai Petrovich, my good friend. The office was full of all sorts of
people. We took a seat in the waiting room. A woman came
out of the office. A while later a tall man appeared.

"Are you Dmitrii Sergeevich?" he asked. "Wait a moment, I'l call you."

We waited. After a while this same tall fellow came out.
"Come in."

I entered the office. There I found several men, all in
civilian clothing. I asked which of them was Solov'ev.

"Wait," they said.

I sat. I waited. Finally in came Solov'ev, a bit upset. He
greeted me and sat down at his desk opposite me.

To my left sat two men. One was a bit bald with a rather
angry expression on his face, or so it seemed to me. Next to
him sat another man—sluggish, as I mentally characterized
him at the time. Behind me was the tall man who had come
into the waiting room. (I've had to characterize them in this
way because none of them would give his name.)

"Who's the person that came with you?" asked Solov'ev.

"He's my friend. He works with me."

"What's his name?"

"I don't remember," I said.

"What do you mean, you don't remember? You work
with him but don't remember? What's his first name?"

---

[21] I.e., Father Dudko. The name-and-patronymic is the standard civil form of
address in the Soviet Union.

"Go ahead and ask him yourself. He's right here," I smiled.

"We've um ... already come to an agreement," said the bald man.

It seems that before entering the office Solov'ev had held the following conversation in the waiting room with Nikolai Petrovich:

"What's your name?" Solov'ev had asked him.

"Why d'you want to know? I didn't come to see you. I came with Dmitrii Sergeevich," answered Nikolai Petrovich.

"I must know all who come to see me."

"But I *didn't* come to see you."

"Then I'll summon you."

"O.K., and when you do, you'll find out what my name is. But any citizen can sit in your waiting room."

Solov'ev just looked at my wife, but didn't say a thing. . . .

And so, the conversation with me began in the office.

Solov'ev pointed to a pile of my books and papers lying on the desk.

"Would you like them?" he asked.

"Of course," I answered.

"They're all of a pretty slanderous nature," said the bald man, his face all flushed.

"They're all of a religious nature," I objected. "Perhaps some are written in a rather sharp tone, but they're all of a religious nature."

"But this," said the bald man, taking a piece of paper from the desk. "This is a record of Paustovskii's words as he was discussing Dudintsev's novel."[22]

He read the page aloud.

"But you wouldn't call Paustovskii an anti-Soviet slanderer, would you? He is a Soviet author," I objected.

"Nevertheless, it's slander," said the bald man. (He turned out to be the most zealous of them all.)

---

[22]Vladimir Dudintsev (b. 1918): his novel *Ne khlebom edinym* (1956), first published in *Novyi mir* No. 10 (1956), stirred controversy because of its portrayal of the hero as an individualist, in opposition to the traditional heroes in Soviet literature.

"Well then, let's start by deciding just what slander is," I suggested. "If we consider as slander any reference to our deficiencies or any reminder of the camps under Stalin, then a great number of people could be accused of slander. Take any magazine. Look over all the discussions of the Twenty-second Party Congress . . ."[23] Is all of that slander?"

"And here's Dr. Sakharov's letter."[24] The bald man grabbed a new sheet of paper from the desk.

"What? You want my opinion of it?"

"We want to know why you have such literature in your possession. Where did you get it? Give us a name," the bald man pressed on.

"Just—a coincidence. I can't remember who brought it."

"But it's in your possession, so you're responsible."

"I have lots of different kinds of literature—*A History of the Communist Party of the Soviet Union*, for example, or *Dialectical and Historical Materialism*. I have literature on atheism. I have fiction. I subscribe to a number of journals and newspapers. But you judge my loyalty on the basis of literature selectively confiscated. Why didn't you confiscate my *History of the CPSU*.[25] I have a library, and quite a variety of literature can be collected in a library . . ."

"But here's something you've written yourself," the bald man interrupted me, and read an excerpt from one of my stories. "Here you write that we have many prisoners serving ten- to fifteen-year sentences, that it is necessary to organize, that antisemitism is widespread in our country . . ."

"*I* don't say that. The hero in my story does, and that's not the same thing. An author describes life and depicts various people with various views which don't always correspond with his own. It's artistic license."

"Well, what d'ya know!" said the bald man in amazement.

"But what other things do you write?" the sluggish man interjected: " 'They killed a girl in the flower of her years.' Who do you make into the hero?"

---

[23]At which a policy of de-Stalinization was initiated.

[24]Soviet physicist and outspoken proponent of human rights in the Soviet Union.

[25]CPSU: Communist Party of the Soviet Union.

"I wrote that while I was in prison. That's why the colors are so gloomy. But, then, isn't that natural for a prisoner who's surrounded by violence?"

"You look younger than we do ... " Solov'ev cut into the conversation.

"You live better than we do," the bald man interrupted him. "You have a three-room apartment. Do you think you should pay only what you're paying for it? It's worth a lot more than that. Our government is humane. Why do you oppose it?"

"I don't oppose the government. Nor do I oppose the powers that be. I'm a priest, and opposition to the government isn't my theme. But I *do* oppose the defects in our life ... "

"But these little stories of yours ... "

"So what? In them I've described only what I've observed in real life."

"It's described all right," said the bald man, clenching his teeth. "It's all *slander.*"

"Pardon me," I disagreed. "But in this way you can accuse anyone you wish of slander. Have you read the novel *Whatever You Want?* Hm, now what's the author's name?"

"Kochetov," said the sluggish man.

"Kochetov. Right. Now *he* portrays people who have antisoviet attitudes," I said. "If we were to apply your reasoning, Kochetov would turn out to be anti-soviet. But you probably wouldn't say that, would you?"

Silence reigned.

"Why don't you recall another image from one of my other stories," I continued, "from my story 'The Voice of a Dying Birch'? There I depict a man who spent twenty-five years in the camps and yet didn't become embittered. By the way, this particular hero is very close to me. I was imprisoned for eight and a half years, but I wish evil on no one. I consider it unnecessary to oppose the powers that be. We must love our country."

"We aren't accusing you of anti-soviet speeches, were accusing you of slander," said the bald man.

"I don't slander anyone."

"Tell us, why do so many young people come to you?" asked the sluggish man, changing the subject.

"I love young people," I answered.

"Now that's frank," the sluggish man rejoiced.

"Being around young people, you get younger yourself," I said.

"And with what do you fill the young people?" continued the sluggish man. "You're filling them with slanderous ideas."

"I speak with them concerning religious topics."

"Ninety-nine per cent of the people in the churches are old," said the sluggish man, "yet you attract young people there."

"You've fallen behind the times a bit. A lot of young people now go to church. And I think you should be thankful to me for attracting the youth there, for distracting them from excesses, from hooliganism and criminality. It's very good that thirst for religion is growing in people. I'll tell you about one incident. The son of one highly-placed person (a chekist,[26] incidentally, and a Party member since 1917) comes to me to confession. He's a profoundly believing young person. His father intended to tell me off. But when he came and talked with me, he understood that I was having a good influence on his son, who used to be carried away with drunkenness. I also helped his son smooth out his family life. The father invited me to his home, and after his son had left the room he bent over to me and said softly: 'Thanks, you're having a good influence on my son.'"

"What's this man's name?" asked the bald man.

"I won't say right now. When the need arises I'll tell."

"You're slandering this father." The bald man became upset. "One might think that he was unable to bring his son up in an antireligious spirit.

"*Everything's* slanderous to you—everything that doesn't conform to your opinions," I sighed. "Nevertheless, young people *are* interested in religious questions."

"Because you're filling them up with it."

"You can't fill them with religion. I'm sceptical of proofs

---

[26]Chekist: member of the secret police. From *Cheka: Chrezvychainye komissii* ("Extraordinary Commissions")—the first political police agency of the Soviet State, founded in 1918 to aid in the "battle against counter-revolution, speculation, and labor crimes."

of religion. Not that I reject them, I just don't consider them to be too important for believers. Religion must be felt. And young people are beginning to feel it. In twelve years I've baptised about a thousand adults. I don't know how they come to God. But anti-religious propaganda tries to *prove* everything. It imposes its own ideas. And the reaction is the exact opposite of what the atheists want. No one's interested in atheism any more, no one reads atheistic literature . . . "

I paused a moment and then asked, "O.K., to put it briefly then, just what do you want from me?"

"That you not slander," said the bald man.

"I repeat: I do not slander anyone," I sighed. "I do not engage in slander. I am not at all anti-soviet. I do not yearn for the West. I consider our life here to be meaningful—in spite of all our deficiencies."

"We're not accusing you of anti-soviet agitation," said the sluggish man. "That's Article 70. We're accusing you under Article 190—slander."

"That's your business. But I don't agree with the accusation."

"Do you understand what slander is?" screamed the bald man. "Slander's when you focus attention just on defects," the bald man explained.

"Correct," I agreed. "And here you are, slandering me. And why? Because you see in me only the dark side. To be sure, I'm a human being and I can be wrong occasionally, but . . . "

"You look younger than we do," Solov'ev interrupted me, repeating that same strange phrase.

"So how old are you?" I asked.

"Forty," said Solov'ev.

"I'm fifty," I said. "I've got a grey beard and I'm bald over most of my head, and yet you say that I look younger than you."

"Younger," said Solov'ev.

"They say that I have young eyes," I smiled. "But I'm already getting old, and I've already endured so much . . . "

"And you live more elegantly than we do," the bald man interjected.

"What do you mean—more elegantly? You know that I

only just found a cooperative apartment not long ago—which I still haven't paid off. Before that I wandered from barrack to barrack. At the age of twelve hunger was eating me up. I survived the war and the camps. And even now my life isn't very easy."

"How much do you earn?" the bald man inquired.

"No matter how much I earn, I give more than half my salary away in taxes."

"But how much is left?"

"Two hundred rubles a month. That's not very much for supporting five people. And my wife doesn't work because our children are still too small."

"What! Two hundred?" The bald man was doubtful. "It's got to be more. What's your salary?"

"I'm sort of embarrassed even to say," I stopped short. "Six hundred rubles."

"So why do you only get two hundred?" the bald man was amazed.

"Taxes eat up the rest," I said. "So don't be too envious."

"You don't do physical work," said the bald man.

"Neither do you, right?"

"Yes, but I'm in socially useful work," the bald man was outraged.

"Me too," I said somewhat defiantly, and the bald man fell silent.

"So, why then do you engage in slander?" Solov'ev continued the conversation. "The State protects you. We're concerned about you."

"Thanks for the concern."

"There's no need for engaging in slander," Solov'ev said didactically.

"You meet with foreigners." The bald man found a new accusation.

"I don't meet with foreigners on purpose."

"Which foreigners have you met with?" asked the sluggish man.

"Well, I happened to be in church once, and there I saw

Metropolitan Bloom,[27] and I went up to him to get his blessing. There have been foreigners in our church. You can't drive them out if they want to come in."

"And Lawrence?"[28] said the bald man. "He was in your church and in your home. What did you talk to him about?"

"He *wasn't* in my home."

"We know he was. First he was in the sanctuary of your church, and then you locked yourself up with him in your office. What did you talk to him about?"

"I don't remember. Probably about religion. Even though he's a Protestant, he prayed with me warmly and piously."

"Why don't you want to tell us what you spoke about with him?" Solov'ev asked reproachfully. "We know there was nothing wrong there. As you see, we're well disposed towards you. Why are you afraid to say anything?"

"You know," I said, after thinking a bit, "if some spy comes to me, I'll certainly make a point of coming right to you myself to tell you about it. But I won't work for you."

"You think a spy would just *inform* you that he's a spy?" said Solov'ev, without taking a bit of offense. "They're clever."

"O.K., so I'll try not to meet with foreigners."

"Sticking together, huh?" smiled the bald man.

"You've got to understand I'm a priest, and I can't engage in denunciations."

"A priest," the bald man smiled again. "*We* know you. Tell us, do you know Solzhenitsyn personally?"

"No."

"So why did he write to you?"

"Because I sent him congratulations on his fiftieth birthday."

"We've got to finish up," said the sluggish man.

"You know we can do anything we want with you," the bald man informed me.

---

[27]Metropolitan Antony (Bloom): preacher, author of books in English on spirituality, and recently retired as Patriarchal Exarch to Western Europe of the Moscow Patriarchate.

[28]Sir John Lawrence: editor of *Frontier*, chairman of the Council of Management of the Center for the Study of Religion and Communism (Keston College, England).

"I'm ready for anything, so don't bother threatening me. I'm prepared for the cross, for any suffering, to be shot . . . "

"Why do you talk of being shot?" yelled Solov'ev.

"You say you can do anything with me, but all of us—*you* and I—are in the hand of God. *God* can do anything, but we can't."

"I'd be happy to talk with you about the Bible," the sluggish man said unexpectedly. "I'd rather not have to talk about what we've been talking about. There are a few places which aren't clear to me . . . "

"So let's talk," I rejoiced. "Let's forget our unpleasant conversation. You know what? Why don't you come over to my house. After all, lots of people visit me, including atheists. Some begin the conversation saying that religion is obscurantism, but they leave in an entirely different mood."

"A little less lyrical—O.K.?" the sluggish man cut me short. "Let's finish up. We can conclude this conversation if you'll repent."

"But I don't know what to repent of. Let's be concrete: I shouldn't have this literature?"

"No, that's not it at all," said the sluggish man. "There just shouldn't be anything slanderous."

"I don't have anything slanderous."

"And *this?*" he pointed to a pile of books on the desk.

"That's not slanderous literature."

"And Vysheslavtsev's book?" said the sluggish man. "Let's see, now . . . it's called *The Poverty of Marxism.*"

"That's no slanderous book. It's *critical,* but not slanderous."

"You distribute monarchistic literature," the bald man entered the conversation. "For example, Gilliard's *The Final Days of Nicholas II.*"

"You gather young people around yourself," added the sluggish man.

"What should I do, drive people away?"

"No, but you shouldn't fill them with slanderous ideas."

"I don't fill people with anything."

"You know very well yourself what we want from you,"

said the bald man. "You must explain to us where you get this sort of literature. Name those who gave them to you."

"I've already explained."

"We've got to finish up. Our conversation has dragged on," the sluggish man frowned. "You understand, Dmitrii Sergeevich, that we, too, are under orders. What'll we tell the general? Keep in mind—we can arrest you."

"Here's the decision of the Procurator in Tashkent in connection with the case of the Priest Adelheim, who's now in jail," said the sluggish man: " 'Literature confiscated from Citizen Dudko is of a slanderous character. The local procurator must decide what to do with him.' "

"We don't want to take strict measures against you," said the sluggish man. "We'd like to be humane with you."

"A lot of complaints have come in about you," the bald man interjected. "Here one citizen writes: 'Protect my daughter from the priest Dudko.' "

"If that's the mother I think it is," I answered, "I'd say you ought to protect the daughter from *her*. She's poisoning her daughter, driving her out of the house, making her ill. For two years now the daughter has been unable to sleep. Now, if you want to find real antireligious obscurantism, the mother is the one you ought to look at. Why don't you pay any attention to that?"

"We can't keep an eye on everyone," said the bald man, making a helpless gesture. "But we've been observing *you* since 1959."

"No. Since 1956, from the moment I was set free."

"And now we've decided to put an end to your activities."

"Here's the kind of material we've gathered against you," Solov'ev pointed to a thick folder.

"Oh, quite a bit more than that, I'd say," I smiled.

"Don't think your conviction has been lifted," the sluggish man nodded.

"What do you mean—not been lifted? I have a document stating that I'm free and that my conviction and all disenfranchisement are lifted."

"It's not lifted," the bald man repeated.

"We can conclude our conversation," the sluggish man said once again.

"What then? You want me to give you a note of explanation?"

"You'll have to give us one, one way or another."

"With a detailed list of the surnames of those from whom you have received the literature," said a high voice, coming at long last from the man sitting behind us.

"Pay attention to the fact that we can deprive you of your registration," the sluggish man threatened. "We just inform the Representative for Cultic Affairs, and he'll lift your registration. What'll you do then? At age 50 it's a little late to change professions. Your wife has no profession. You have two kids . . . "

"As God gives. We all walk under God."

They demanded that I write an explanation within a week. I said I'd need a minimum of a month. They said they could demand the one-week limit.

"What good will haste do anyone?" I asked. "One must ponder every word—I can see that you find fault with everything."

"Go on—and think everything over really well," said the sluggish man.

From all indications the conversation was coming to an end.

"Is your son a Pioneer?"[29] Solov'ev asked as if in passing.

"No," I said. "I consider it criminal to train children to be two-faced. My son's a believer. He can't be both a believer and a Pioneer. I wouldn't be against the Pioneer organization if it didn't meddle with its members' religious convictions.

"You want him to become a priest?" asked Solov'ev.

"I want to give him an education. When he grows up he can decide for himself what he wants to be. The priest's task is very difficult. It's easy just to serve rites on demand, but to be a real priest is very difficult, especially in our times. But I'd be glad if he wanted to be a priest."

We fell silent.

---

[29]Pioneers: see above, n. 2 to the Sixth Discussion.

"Are you returning my typewriter to me?" I asked. "Of course," said the sluggish man, "but we have to check to be sure it hasn't been used to print anything . . . "

"In two and a half years you haven't been able to check that yet? You have no right to hold my typewriter that long."

"If anything illegal was printed on it, then it has to be confiscated."

"It seems to me that it can only be confiscated on a warrant."

"Your typewriter is here. Do you want me to show it to you?"

"No. I'll give it to you as a present."

Another long silence.

"Quite a cowardly search they made of me," I said. "Nine men—all afraid to give me their names."

"Why should *we* be afraid of *you*?" Solov'ev was amazed. "*You* should be afraid of *us*."

"It's amazing. *I'm* not afraid, but *you* are. Your job isn't an enviable one. If I had to make a choice between doing what you do and going to prison, I'd prefer prison."

"Why?" Solov'ev was again amazed.

"Just because. Look, you can't even settle matters with *me*. And others, you know, don't talk to you so politely. They swear and scream."

I looked at their faces and indeed felt sorry for them. It's as though they're at bay, all crumpled up, sullen.

"I may have to summon you here again," said Solov'ev as he was saying good-bye. "So don't bring anyone else with you."

"And I'll ask you not to call me at work. You scared everyone there. Procurator or not, if you don't want to send a summons, just send a car for me and I'll pay for it."

"We did send you a summons."

"I haven't gotten it yet."

"Impossible," said Solov'ev.

"What? You think I'd lie?"

"Well, maybe it just hasn't come yet," said the sluggish man.

As we parted I asked, "May I shake hands with you?"

Solov'ev extended his hand to me.

"I wish you all the best," I said. "I wish you no evil. I'm not vindictive."

The bald man and the sluggish man also gave me their hands. The man who was sitting in back also got up. I turned to him.

"And may I give you my hand? You look too gloomy."

He gave me his hand silently, frowning the whole time. I left.

"Three hours exactly they kept you," said Nikolai Petrovich, standing up to meet me.

"Well?" asked my wife.

"Let's go. We'll talk out on the street," I said.

To this day they have returned neither typewriter nor the confiscated literature.

Three months after this conversation the warden of our church announced that she had been *ordered* to terminate my contract. That's what she said, "They ordered it." So after the early liturgy on Sunday I addressed the faithful from the pulpit. I informed them that I was being thrown out on the street, and I asked for their prayerful support that I might bear this new cross.

Three days passed and the Assistant Representative for Matters of the Russian Orthodox Church, Mr. Ivanov, summoned me to his office. He warned me over the phone:

"Just don't announce it to the people."

"No," I answered, "I won't announce it."

And I *didn't* announce anything. But rumor somehow spread, and when I arrived at the Representative's place on Furmanovskii Lane, his private residence was already "surrounded" by believers. It turned out that a letter in my defense had already been submitted.

The Representative met me on the steps.

"Dmitrii Sergeevich, didn't I summon you alone?" he asked in an aggitated voice.

Three others came up on the stairway with me.

"But they won't let me go anywhere alone any more," I said. "The people have taken me under their protection."

"Who are they?" asked the Representative.

"Believers . . . "

"No. No. Who *are* they?"

"Just look at them. They've got eyes and noses and ears and hands and feet—just like everybody . . . "

"They might be fanatics," the Representative said fearfully, looking over my companions. "They might even murder me."

No. I'll vouch for them," I replied, now in serious tone. "They're absolutely peaceful people. No one will touch you."

My companions remained below (I asked them not to come up) while the Representative and I went indoors. We passed through an enormous corridor and entered an enormous office with a large desk and many chairs.

"What right did you have to use the church pulpit for personal goals?" asked the Representative after sitting down at his desk.

"I have no personal goal," I answered. "If a bell-tower falls, we ask the faithful for help. When the war[30] came we also turned to the faithful. Persecution of priests isn't uncommon here, unfortunately, and this isn't just the personal matter of the individual priests. It's the whole church's misfortune. Why shouldn't we turn to the faithful in this case also?"

"You should have written us . . . "

"I know what it means to write to you. In searching my place they confiscated some books and even my typewriter. I've written three complaints but nothing's been returned, not even the typewriter."

"Dmitrii Sergeevich, a typewriter is such a little thing . . . "

"Yeh, maybe so, but when you put it together with everything else, it's no little thing."

"If you'd like, I'll call them and have them return your typewriter."

"Don't bother. Let them return it by law, not by phone call."

"O.K. . . . what right did you have to use the church pulpit

---

[30]World War II. Patriarch Sergius summoned the Orthodox faithful wholeheartedly to support the beleaguered war effort, and thereby gained badly-needed toleration for the Church from the Soviet government.

for personal goals?" the Representative returned to his first question, but his tone, I thought, contained an unnatural pathos.

"I repeat: It's *not* a personal goal. When I spoke at the Procurator's office I said: If I'm guilty, judge me according to the law. But they have decided to do everything on the sly, to use other people's hands to cast me and my young children to the mercy of fate in such a way that no one will know what happened. I'm used to difficulties myself, but just let the people know what's going on here. If something happens to me, maybe they'll at least give a piece of bread to my children. So I spoke in order that everyone would know our situation."

"No one is going to imprison you."

"Prohibit me from serving in church—that's no better."

"No one will prohibit you from serving. We only suggested this to the warden for her consideration."

"What . . . 'consideration'? The warden said clearly that the Representative *ordered* her to terminate my contract, since —she says—the case has been brought from the Procurator's office."

"Yes, the case has been brought. I have no right to show you, but I will. 'Priest Dmitrii Dudko,' he read, 'undertakes anti-social activities. Books confiscated from him have a slanderous character. A number of complaints have come in against him . . . ' But we only suggested to the warden that she consider it," the Representative added, closing the folder.

"What . . . 'consider'? The warden definitely said that they had *ordered* her."

"We have no right to order this."

"I know you don't. But you did."

"We only suggested it."

"O.K. We've got to express ourselves more precisely then. . . . 'Nikolai Semenovich'—your name is as Russian as can be. You and I speak Russian, but somehow we just aren't understanding each other."

"I'll admit you're a brilliant orator, but I still maintain that you cannot use the church pulpit for personal goals."

"Now, what kind of a personal goal is this . . . to defend the internal life of the Church from outside interference? And what good will it do if my children are forced to take to the streets? And why? For what offenses? Because I do my best for people, for my compatriots? Because I worry about the people's moral condition? But all I get is threats ..."

Our conversation began going around in an endless circle. The questions were repeated. And the answers were repeated. Finally, the Representative began trying to persuade me to go to the Patriarchate and request a transfer to another parish.

"Why?" I asked. "I'm happy with the one I have."

"But I thought your contract was already terminated," the Representative admitted.

"No. I demanded that they give me a written explanation of the bases upon which my contract was being terminated, and I declared that without it I wouldn't leave. Let them use the militia to take me out. Then at least everyone will see who's interfering in the internal affairs of the Church."

We began to say good-bye. The Representative shook my hand three times absent-mindedly.

"Go on," he said. "You know yourself what you must do." A little old man came out of the adjoining room, quietly, ghost-like. He didn't look at me.

When I stepped outside, my parishioners were there to meet me at the doorway. They threw worried questions at me.

Why have I told you about these two meetings? So that it will become clear to you where everything originates in Russia and who in fact is in command of the destinies and reputations of the clergy.

Well, perhaps that's enough for today. Good-bye. May God preserve you all!

PARISHIONER: Father, thanks for everything. You're opening our eyes to a lot of things. Will you let us come again?

PRIEST: Of course, come. I'm happy to have you.

The
Eleventh
Discussion

This discussion was also conducted at home, when a group of parishioners again visited Father Dmitrii. It is presented here on the basis of notes by eyewitnesses.

QUESTION: Father Dmitrii, first of all we'd all like to know what position we, your spiritual children, are in now that you're going into retirement? What can you do now as a priest?

ANSWER: I petitioned to go into retirement, but so far I haven't received an answer. If it's approved, I'll do what any retired priest can do. That is, I'll direct you spiritually: hear confessions, admonish, and preach. I don't think that the bond between us will be broken if we really have a need for each other.

Well, on with our discussion. Today we'll be talking about the Gospel. Judging from the slips of paper with your questions, lots of people are interested in this theme. But I've decided to structure this discussion a little differently. For some reason, the question-and-answer form has upset the staff in the Patriarchate. They've told me that. O.K. We'll do things differently. Today I won't read each question individually. But I think that in the course of the discussion everyone will see that we're talking about the problems that bother them.

First, concerning the resurrectional Gospels.

There are eleven resurrectional Gospels.[1] Today the eighth

---

[1] In the Orthodox Church, Sunday always celebrates the Resurrection. The

one was read. Many people who come to church complain about how incomprehensible the readings in Slavonic are. They fight for services in modern Russian. But in the first place, it's not so easy to make such reforms. Furthermore, there's a danger that we'll squander the riches which we now have in our order of services. In the second place, people are becoming better educated, and anyone who wants to can master the Slavonic language well enough to understand the services. It's not *that* difficult. It's not a foreign language after all, but our native tongue, just half-forgotten today.

Be that as it may, let's read today's Gospel in Russian.[2] Please listen closely.

> Mary stood crying outside the tomb. Still crying, she bent over and looked into the tomb, and saw two angels there, dressed in white, sitting where the body of Jesus had been, one at the head, the other at the feet. "Women, why are you crying?" they asked her. She answered. "They have taken my Lord away, and I do not know where they have taken Him!" When she had said this, she turned around and saw Jesus standing there: but she did not know that it was Jesus. "Woman, why are you crying?" Jesus asked her. "Who is it that you are looking for?" She thought He was the gardener, so she said to Him, "If you took Him away, sir, tell me where you have put Him, and I will go and get Him." Jesus said to her, "Mary!" She turned toward Him and said in Hebrew, "Rabboni!" (This means "Teacher.") "Do not hold on to Me," Jesus told her, "because I have not yet gone back to the Father. But go to My brothers and tell them for Me, 'I go back up to Him who is My Father and your Father, My God and your God.' So Mary Magdalene went and told the dis-

---

account of the post-resurrectional events in the four Gospels is divided into eleven portions, one of which is read at Matins each week in succession throughout the year.

[2]The text is rendered in English according to the *Today's English Version*, in order to reflect the simplicity of the Russian compared to the Slavonic.

ciples that she had seen the Lord, and that He had told her this (Jn. 20:11-18).

There's the Gospel, put plainly.[3] Let's try to imagine what is being spoken of here.

Mary Magdalene comes to Christ's tomb. We know from the Gospel that she had been possessed by seven demons and that Christ drove them out of her. Now she comes to Christ's tomb because she loved Him, and this love draws her there naturally. It was already discovered that the body had disappeared from the tomb, and Mary is crying about it. She cries bitterly, painfully, in tremendous sorrow. Suddenly she sees angels dressed in white, one at the head, the other at the foot. They ask her why she's crying. She complains to them that someone has taken away the body of her Lord and she doesn't know where they took Him. As soon as she had spoken, she sees Jesus next to her, but she doesn't recognize Him. She thinks He is the gardener. But since the gardener might have seen where the body had been taken, she asks him where she might find it. Suddenly she hears a familiar voice say her name. She recognizes Jesus. Probably at that very moment she threw herself upon Him. But He warned her not to do so. He didn't allow her to touch Him, but commanded her to go to His brothers and tell them about her meeting with Him. And she went to tell Jesus' disciples about all of this.

Today many people are inclined to deny the existence of angels. So I'll say right off that the Orthodox Church recognizes the existence of good spirits, the angels. There's a whole world of angels. There are nine ranks of them. Each person is given an angel at Baptism. The Archpriest Sergius Bulgakov[4] said that angels are heavenly persons, the mirror image, as it were, of a human being. Angels are sent to serve man-

---

[3]Lit.: "in Russian."

[4]Father Sergei Nikolaevich Bulgakov (1871-1944): Russian theologian, economist and philosopher. Born in a clerical family, he became a Marxist in the university. Converted from Marxism to Christianity, he was ordained an Orthodox priest in 1918, and was forced to resign his professional chair by the Bolsheviks. He emigrated in 1922, and from 1925-1944 he was dean of St. Sergius Theological Institute in Paris.

kind, to worry about mankind, and, according to Church doctrine, when we leave this world the angels are the first ones to
meet us in order to escort us into the next world. In the present
instance the appearance of angels at the Lord's tomb isn't some
kind of figurative expression, but the reality which the evan-
gelist witnessed.

To what should we pay special attention in this narrative?

Did Mary Magdalene understand that she had seen angels?
This is what the *Commentary* says concerning this point:

> The heavenly emissaries ask her the reason for her
> tears, and Mary answers them as though they were ordi-
> nary people, not even imagining that those who stood
> before her were angels, for she would hardly have
> counted it necessary to inform of the loss of Christ's
> body those who, of course, themselves knew what had
> in fact occurred.

But here a second question arises. As is clear from another
gospel account, Peter and John were at the tomb but saw no
angels. Why? In the *Commentary* it says this, conjecturally,
on this question: "Probably from them, as apostles, faith was
required; they had no need of extraordinary angelic appear-
ances of the sort of which Mary and the other women were
deemed worthy."

That's how it happens in life. For some people faith comes
from some extraordinary appearance, while for others belief
comes because their soul desires it. We won't discuss which of
these ways is better or which is worse. Only God knows, and
He knows *what* to send to *whom*.

Now, let's turn our attention to the fact that, although
Mary spoke to angels as though they were people, she didn't
recognize Jesus when she looked at Him. Why not?—that's
the question. She'd seen Christ more than once, so why didn't
she recognize Him now? In the *Commentary* it says that her
eyes were closed, just like those of the two men on the road to
Emmaus. Apparently the risen Christ was so transformed in
appearance that it was hard to recognize Him with one's phys-

ical eyes. Faith is necessary. Anyone who tries to recognize
Christ in His physical substance alone will run into obstacles.
Let's pay attention here to the fact that Christ risen from the
dead is no longer an object of physical sensation, but an object
of faith. Faith, as we know, requires effort and cleansing from
sin. The holy fathers frequently warned people against the
temptation of seeing Christ with their physical eyes. This
temptation is often utilized by the spirit of evil, who shows us
not Christ, but whomever he wants. The risen Christ is an object of faith. It's no accident that when Mary wanted to touch
Christ He told her: "Don't hold me." Mary recognized Christ
by His voice, His tone. "Mary!" He said. And she said: "Rabboni!"

"Rabboni" (from the word "rabbi") means "teacher."
From Mary's lips this word acquires a special meaning and
significance. This is what the *Commentary* says on this point:
"The fact is that in ancient Hebrew the word 'rabban' signified
not a teacher or scribe, but was equivalent to the expression
'adon' ('master'). By using this term to address the living
Christ Who appeared to her, Mary apparently recognized in
Him the Master of life."

Now, concerning the prohibition from touching Christ.
This is what is said in the *Commentary*:

Probably in unexpected joy, Mary threw herself at
Christ in order to seize His feet. This alone can explain
Christ's words: "Do not touch me" (more accurately:
"Do not seize Me," or "Do not hold Me"). Christ forbids Mary to hug His feet because He had not yet
ascended to His father. By this He gives Mary to understand that the time has not yet come for believers to renew their personal contact with Him. That contact will
become necessary only once He has again entered the
condition in which He existed before coming into the
world.

But Christ's coming was the necessary condition for the fulfilling of God's will that all mankind be saved. By restricting

Christ to the circle of His former disciples, as it were, Mary was interfering with the task of expanding the boundaries of Christ's contact with mankind outwards to the limits which He Himself had set when He said that He would draw all men to Himself.

"Don't touch!" "Don't hold!" This must remind us all that it is impossible to have only a strictly personal contact with Christ, with no concern for the fact that Christ has become the inheritance of all people. Often we, like Mary Magdalene, wish that just we alone might contemplate Christ, whereas Christ came to save the whole world. When a person just believes in Christ but pays no attention to what goes on in the world—to how people are perishing without Christ—then his faith becomes egotistical. In warning Mary against this, Christ warns all of us as well. He sends Mary to tell about everything she's seen. "Go . . . and tell," He says. What does He command her to tell about? That "I go back up to Him Who is my Father and your Father, my God and your God." The *Commentary* teaches that Christ speaks here not about the ascension which was to be accomplished after forty days, but has in mind the fact that with Christ's resurrection all people are glorified with the Father in Heaven. Hence the words: "my God and your God."

According to our faith, Christ is God. He has no need of the resurrection because He always lives and triumphs. We men, subject to sin through which came death, need the resurrection.

Today, when much of life has become senseless, without any way of justifying itself, the question of immortality arises with special sharpness before the religious mind. Why was man born? Why does he live? Is it possible that—at best—you set for yourself some noble goal, you struggle to attain it, and after failing to do so you pass into nothingness? Or—at worst ——you are ordered about with no goals for yourself, you suffer in this life and then vanish forever. Think about it—it's horrible! That's why the atheists are trying to resolve the question of immortality. But the solutions they propose are really humorous. For instance, I'm supposed to live on in a flower, upon which someone else will feast his eyes. This is just poetic imagery, pretty words. Or the idea of immortality in the memory of posterity: Our descendents, they say, will remember us. But in the first place, not everyone is remembered, and in the second place, everyone is forgotten in the end. Furthermore, they say that man's immortality lies in his deeds. But that's highly conditional. The deeds of but a few are remembered, and how many are the deeds which are forgotten! So this "immortality" is also invented, unreal.

Why do so many people drink nowadays? Why is there so much lewdness? Why do all sorts of diseases and catastrophes frighten us so? The reason lies in our having misunderstood our place in the world. We've lost the meaning of our life. Why should we live? The ideals of our fathers are subject to re-evaluation. That's why the religious question is now of the greatest importance.

Not long ago in *Literaturnaia Gazeta* there was a discussion of the topic "To live eternally: Is it possible? Is it expedient?" (May 8, 1974). Georgii Gurevich, the fantasy writer, and Igor' Bestuzhev-Lada, a doctor of history, held a debate. Obviously they are non-believers, but the way the question was formulated was somehow close to the religious problem. I'll remind you of the content of the discussion in this debate.

GUREVICH: Well, Igor' Vasil'evich, my point of view is extremely simple: Without a doubt dying is bad for your health.

BESTUZHEV-LADA: For your *personal* health. But that's only while you still have your health. But is personal immortality good for the health of humanity?

GUREVICH: Perhaps we should first specify what we mean by the vague word "immortality." We do not, of course, mean creative immortality, not the immortality of human creations in the memory of one's descendants. We are speaking of biological immortality.

Bestuzhev-Lada goes on to specify that "we are speaking about *practical* immortality, about the prolongation of life for an indefinitely long period of time, after which an inevitable end will follow anyway." The conversation continues with a discussion of what interferes with this "immortality": diseases, old age, catastrophes. Bestuzhev-Lada says that one could divide society into immortal castes: children, young people, and old people. But then everything is dehumanized. Children remain eternal little brats, teenagers never become adults, and old people are doomed to eternal oldness. The psychological mechanism which provides for the normal vital activity of the human organism is broken. These immortal quasi-people wouldn't differ from dolls or robots. They'd become somewhat like actors playing a single role. Gurevich objects that the cemetery is no way out. People die. People are lost. They must be saved. In order to ensure progress, nature has invented nothing better than the annihilation—to the very last member—of each generation. He hopes that wise scientists are capable of proposing something more humane.

BESTUZHEV-LADA: We must have hope. . . . But fortunately each of us even now can lengthen his short life considerably. And that, perhaps, is the most humane thing that we can practically propose for now. When a person has God-only-knows how much time ahead of him, he can spend a hundred years living like Oblomov,[5] or in violence for a hundred years like Nozdrev,[6] etc. But when you know you've only got seventy years to live, you begin to value time. I remember being struck by the calculations which one French sociologist made of what man does with his life. Of our seventy years we spend about 20-25 years in sleeping, 2-3 years in chewing, 2-3 years in washing, combing, fixing ourselves up, dressing and undressing. We spend 2-3 years just jabbering.

GUREVICH: Judging by today, it's more than that!

The discussion continued as to how we can be freed from all of this. Gurevich proposed: "Even if one institute should

---

[5]Protagonist in Goncharov's (1812-1891) novel *Oblomov*. In Russian literature Oblomov became the symbol of the lazy, pampered, superfluous gentry of the nineteenth century.

[6]The landlord in Gogol's *Dead Souls*.

succeed in holding the bird of hygiene in hand, someone else will still have to shoot the two birds of immortality in the bush."

BESTUZHEV-LADA: "Shoot? Perhaps we ought to examine the target better first?"

Yes, that's well put. Examine the target better.

Often just formulating the question of immortality in a religious context evokes ironical smiles: "Oh, those are just fairy tales. It's impossible for a person to die and afterwards be alive. It's improbable." In such cases I immediately have to ask: "But what *is* probable?" You know, if we really look at the visible world and if we think about it seriously, we'll realize that what we see is absurdity. And for some reason, people prefer to believe in *this* absurdity rather than to resolve the question of immortality with the help of Christianity. But now, let's just discard all the fruitless scepticism of the atheists, and together with Mary Magdalene let us approach the Lord's tomb.

"Mary stood crying outside the tomb."

Who is this Mary? Outside whose tomb is she standing and why is she crying?

In fact, we're all there—all people are there. We're crying outside the tomb if Christ isn't there, if He isn't risen. Why search for truth, why sacrifice if Christ isn't risen? Everything's empty if there is no Christ with His universal resurrection. Is it possible that some bones in a grave could contain the whole meaning of life? Bestuzhev-Lada recommends that we examine the target. Let's try to examine it.

Here I am, walking past a bar. There's an enormous line. People are drinking and swearing—among them engineers, writers, artists. At other times such people speak of things like beauty. They debate and defend their opinions. But when they're in line for beer, all of this is just rhetoric. For them life is but an empty tomb. And the tears they cry aren't Mary's radiant ones, but drunken ones, empty, touching no one.

And their wives and children—what do *they* cry about? About their father being a drunkard? About life being disorganized? At first glance—yes. But—no, not really. They cry because Christ has been stolen from their hearts. Christ has been stolen from human hearts, and life has become an empty tomb. Lots of people, though, don't understand this.

People seduce themselves too early with success and glory and achievements of all sorts. But ruin strikes. People are after their heads, and suddenly they begin to see and understand things they've neither seen nor understood before. Most of all, they realize that before they were blind.

Let's recall the title of this debate in *Literaturnaia Gazeta*: "To live eternally: Is it possible? Is it expedient?" Let's think it over. Let's ask ourselves: Is it possible that there is anyone who doesn't want to live, who wants to die? I heard about one old woman who had lived her life in relative comfort and free from pain. Then suddenly death approached. Apparently, she'd thought that she would live forever, and so she screamed in horror: "I want to live! I don't want to die!" Those around her closed their ears to her cry and ran from the house. What is this? Where does such fear come from? The truth is that this woman's perfectly happy life proved to have been an empty grave. No matter how long life manages to be prolonged, no matter how much a person is rejuvenated, if there's nothing beyond this life, if Christ isn't risen, bringing resurrection to us all, then life is just an empty, joyless tomb, over which all we can do is cry. And all of our earthly joys, all our dreams, the moments which seem to shine, turn into passing smoke when confronted with the empty tomb of Christ.

"Mary stood crying outside the tomb."

To live eternally. Is it possible? It's rather horrible for a non-believer even to *think* about immortality.

Is it expedient? The desire exists, of course, but if life is nothing but a pigsty, a whore house—if hooliganism and crime are rampant—then it's just *not* expedient to live eternally. But then, when *is* it expedient? When *does* life make sense?

Well, let's not fantasize. Otherwise we might be accused of being carried away by fairy tales. Let's take a very simple example from life. There's an old lady that everyone has forgotten. How should we comfort her? By giving her a ticket to the club or the theater? That won't do her any good. But if she comes to church and prays and thinks about the eternity which awaits her, she's no longer rejected or forgotten or unnecessary. She lives eternally. Compare these two old people: the one, screaming away on her death bed, wanting to live, and the other, who's praying. What a striking difference! And which of them is happier? The one who was filled with earthly good things, or the one who partakes of eternity?

In the countryside where I was born, I happened to hear the story of a girl, "the bride of Christ," as they called her. She had a dream. "Get ready," she was told, "soon you will have to leave." "But I haven't done anything yet," she said. "It is already time," was the reply. And so she told everyone that she was dying. All were startled. They sent for a doctor. But she waited calmly for her hour. They never diagnosed her disease, for they had no chance. She asked for a candle, lit it, and immediately passed away, a smile upon her lips.

I didn't make this up. It happened. For this girl, life wasn't a barren tomb. Life isn't a barren tomb for anyone who knows Christ.

In order to do something serious in our life, the Light of Christ must illumine us, the light of the resurrection. It's not by accident that at the creation of the world, the words "Let there be light!" were pronounced. If there's no light in our soul, if we don't know how and why we are doing things, then we'll get lost in the darkness and gloom. And no one who walks in darkness knows where he's going.

Often human effort is the same thing as working in the dark. Success seduces us, but at the very first catastrophe the empty tomb is revealed.

Resurrection from the dead isn't given for free. We must work and work for this resurrection—disinterestedly and unselfishly. Nothing makes a person such an unselfish worker as faith in Christ's resurrection and the Kingdom of Heaven. There can be many different goals of human activity, but the Christian goal shines the brightest, and nothing so trains a person to be an honest and joyful worker as does striving towards this goal.

They've stolen this goal from us, and we stand and cry outside the empty tomb. True, some people look upon our

Christian goal incorrectly. They distort it. They say, for example, that hope in reward after death destroys the unselfishness of one's deed and leads to bartering in good. This is an incorrect view, and I already spoke about it in some detail at our last discussion.

"Mary stood crying outside the tomb." The angels asked her why she was crying. And Mary told them.

We have to know why we're crying. Without the concept of Christ's resurrection, people don't know why they're crying. They don't understand, for example, how one could cry over his own sins. Without Christ's resurrection we lose the distinction between sin and virtue. We sin and then cry, without knowing why.

Why are we crying? That's the question the angels are asking us.

Nowadays they'd like to make a museum out of Christianity. But they won't succeed. Christianity must illumine all aspects of life. It must—and can—take an active part in life. Then *why* we should live eternally, and whether or not it's expedient to do so, will not be misunderstood. Eternity is expedient only for good. But if good is a relative concept and dies, then everything is inexpedient and senseless.

"Mary!" Christ called out to Mary Magdalene, the myrrh-bearing woman. "Rabboni!" she said, glancing at Him.

"Rabboni." That means Teacher and Master of life. Christ is the Master of life. When Christ becomes the Master of *our* lives then everything in our lives will become normal.

These days we're used to finding proofs for everything, seeking confirmations for everything. There once was a mother who tried to prove to her son that "verily Christ is risen." All of her proofs went in one ear and out the other. The only thing he really assimilated was that Christ was risen *"warringly."*[7] It's very interesting what the boy understood: not *"verily,"* but *"warringly."* How true that is! If Christ's resurrec-

---

[7]The Russian is based upon a subtle play on words which cannot be duplicated in English. The greeting "Christ is risen!" is answered in Slavonic by *"Voistinu voskrese!"* ("Indeed—or: Verily—He is risen!"). The boy in this incident understood the answer to be *"Voinstinu voskrese!"* ("Militantly—He is risen!").

tion were a fairytale, no matter how beautiful it might be, it wouldn't have much meaning for us. But Christ's "warring" resurrection shakes our entire existence.

In general, I must say that children are somehow able to grasp the meaning of Christ's resurrection immediately. Just a few words suffice for understanding and faith to sprout in them. Once a mother told her child that the words "Christ is risen" mean that no one will die, that everyone—and he too—will live forever. "It's clear, mama," said the child. "I believe."

Everything's clear. We believe. If only everyone could say that! To believe means to find the meaning of life. To believe means to find rest. To believe means to forget our fears and anxieties.

While she was crying Mary saw two angels. Who were they?

Anyone who has contemplated life seriously at any time, who has endured things for someone else's sake, who though innocent has suffered or has been tormented by slander—he has seen angels. And doubtless he has heard their voice: "Why are you crying?"

The voice of the angels can be most clearly heard when you're not indifferent to the destinies of other people. Mary came to the tomb because she was upset over the Innocent One Who had been crucified. And she cried because they had taken away the Lord and she didn't know where they had put Him. Oh, what an earnest cry this is! They took the Lord away! Here's the tomb, but the Lord's not there. Can one possibly die in vain for truth's sake? Is it possible that the Lord is not on earth? Perhaps He's just present in our dreams, or in the clouds somewhere—but not on earth? Can there be engineers and builders and even gardeners on earth, but no Lord? The planets whirl around, airplanes and satellites fly, but there's no Lord? Maybe some people are able to resign themselves to this and even be satisfied. Maybe some can be indifferent to this. But not someone from whom the Lord has driven out demons and given healing. In our day it's not just Mary who has felt the healing hand of the Lord. Mary won't agree that there is no Lord. She'll just stand there outside the empty tomb and cry that they have taken the Lord away. She'll seek Him, she'll ask questions. Without the Lord, many people are crying these days. They are grieving and dreaming, but they find no rest. People *need* the Lord.

"Mary!" someone said. Who is that "someone"? A familiar voice. Mary listened. She turned and saw that it was the One for whom her heart was seeking, the One about whom she was worried.

Seeking the Lord has even come into fashion today. People seek Him in various ways—this is natural after wandering through the dense forest of atheism. Some even try to create their own religion. They criticize all existing religions. They don't feel satisfied by any of them. They criticise the Church with special zeal. "God's O.K.," they say, "but why the Church?" Especially once they learn about certain aspects of "behind-the-scenes" church life. "Why all the rituals and incomprehensible services?" they ask.

Mary wanted to seize Jesus' feet. "Do not hold Me," said Christ.

So many of those who search for religion immediately seize at Christ. They admit no intermediaries and forget that the Church possesses the experience of centuries, that she has had within herself the greatest ascetics of the spirit. They see only her present spokesmen, some of whom at times do a better job of alienating people than could any blasphemer.

There were the apostles, the holy fathers, the teachers of the Church. For many modern seekers after God, all of this is incomprehensible. But there are also those who are interested in the Church's spiritual treasury. There are some who pay large amounts of money to buy the writings of the holy fathers—the *Philocalia*, for example[8]—and who, once they have plunged into the depths of this wisdom, are convinced of just how shallow the new-fangled theories of the God-seekers are.

"Don't hold Me!" says Christ. This applies to all of us.

---

[8]*Philocalia*: lit.: "Love of Goodness"—Slavonic: *Dobrotoliubie.* An eighteenth-century compilation by Macarius of Corinth and Nicodemus of the Holy Mountain of a large selection of spiritual texts from the fathers throughout the centuries. Paissii Velichkovskii published a Slavonic abridgement, and Theophan the Recluse an enlarged Russian translation (five volumes) in the late nineteenth century.

We mustn't come to Christ with our proud daydreams. "I can do anything I wish! Let me through to Christ!" Christ accepts anyone who suffers, but we shouldn't forget that God opposes the proud, but gives grace to the humble.[9]

"I will ascend to My God and your God." This doesn't mean that Christ has a god in the same way that we do. It means that for Christ incarnate—i.e., for humanity, and for each person in particular—there is one God. There is only one God of us all. There is no other god. But for each person God reveals Himself in His own way. And we Orthodox Christians must treasure our faith, being respectful at the same time of the beliefs of others. The pure in heart recognize and see God. Therefore we must work on ourselves in order to see the risen Lord.

Sometimes it happens that our entire religiosity takes the form of mere ritualism. Come to church. Light a candle. Request a prayer service. And sometimes it's limited to just discussing God very esoterically. We dispute, but we go on living the same life that the pagans and unbelievers do.

"If your righteousness doesn't exceed the righteousness of the scribes and pharisees, you will not enter the Kingdom of Heaven."[10] That's what Christ said. To paraphrase it, we could say that no one who just talks about his faith but doesn't try to live by it—even if the way he lives is no worse than the way good non-believers do—will enter the Kingdom of Heaven. He'll understand neither the meaning of Christ's resurrection nor how Christ appeared to people—whether in the past or now.

Let's try to imagine that we've arrived at Christ's tomb. Everyone has been led here for his own reasons. We stand outside the empty tomb and cry. One person is in despair. Another experiences radiant moments as angels appear. Someone takes Christ for the gardener. But then, deep in the soul, a voice is heard, familiar yet at the same time not of this world. It calls us by name. Will we answer?

Finally, let's recall the words with which Christ parted from

---

[9]Jas. 4:6.
[10]Mt. 5:20.

Mary once she'd recognized Him: "Go to My brothers and tell them what you've seen and heard."

What does this mean? Simply, that having recognized the risen Christ you can't lock yourself up in your own private world. No one who tries to protect his faith by running away from all trials and tribulations knows Christ yet. Christ is the Savior of the world. He came to save each person. Knowing this, how can we not proclaim the risen Christ to the world? Can we look on calmly as people perish, not knowing Christ —some of these, moreover, being very gifted people who could do quite a bit? We see how people stumble about with no support, enduring their earthly trials. Why—out of personal fear —are we unable to *give* them support? Often we're afraid to reach out a hand to those who don't know God, thinking that in this way we are defending, protecting our faith, though in reality we are losing it. Could Mary have left the tomb without saying a thing to anyone? Could threats have made her be afraid? After all, threats are just amusing if you know that Christ is risen. What can our personal earthly well-being mean in the face of this fact?

Anyone who knows the risen Christ has a heavy responsibility placed upon himself. He must bring to people the news of Christ's resurrection, in whatever way he can and wherever destiny leads him. If you've been with Mary to Christ's tomb, if you've been convinced that it's empty because Christ is risen, then go and tell everyone about it. Christ is risen! May God bless you and help you! Amen.